M000036117

PUBLISHED BY

Copyright © 2013

Published in the United States by
Insight Publishing Company
707 West Main Street, Suite 5 • Sevierville, Tennessee • 37862

Disclaimer: This book is a compilation of ideas from numerous experts who have each contributed a chapter. As such, the views expressed in each chapter are of those who were interviewed and not necessarily of the interviewer or Insight Publishing.

10 9 8 7 6 5 4 3 2 1

The interviews in this book were conducted by David E. Wright, the President and founder of Insight Publishing and ISN Works.

Wouldn't it be great to have words of wisdom tucked away, ready to pull out when you are preparing to meet a challenge? Between the covers of this book you will find many words—and phrases—of wisdom that can give you a boost just when you need it.

The authors in *Words of Wisdom* have gathered their expertise from the "school of hard knocks"—daily life. They have each learned the artistry of turning a challenge into an opportunity to learn and grow.

This is your opportunity to learn from them. You will have a unique learning experience when you sit down and have a session with these insightful authors.

You'll find that *Words of Wisdom* is a valuable tool for you to use whether you consider yourself successful or if you're seeking success. Find the words of wisdom awaiting you from these esteemed authors. I know that I did!

Chapter One

It's All About Relationships 1

By Katherin Scott

Chapter Two

Rescuing Your Retirement in a
"New Normal" Economy 17

By Steve Watts

Chapter Three

Advice on Building Healthy Relationships 35

By John Gray

Chapter Four

Open-Minded Relationships 53

By Ann Van Eron PhD

Chapter Five

Living Your Dream..75

By Jennifer Powell

Chapter Six

Working with Family? 89
By Rhonda R. Savage, DDS

Chapter Seven

Making Meaning on Multiple Levels 115
By Irena Yashin-Shaw, PhD

Chapter Eight

Secrets for Successful Networking.................. 133
By Sima Dahl

Chapter Nine

Perform Like a Top-Notch Fire Crew 149
By Bernie Fitterer

Chapter Ten

Take Off the Mask and Create the Character that is YOU 169
By Rachel Bellack

Chapter Eleven

Sustaining Meaningful Relationships
A Pathway to Harmony.....................................187
By Mary Beth Carlson

Chapter Twelve

The Interview..219
By Brian Tracy

Chapter Thirteen

Wisdom and Wooden: Lessons For Life.........233
By Lynn Guerin

Chapter Fourteen

Show Me The Way...255
By Chris Jennings

Chapter Fifteen

Work Life Wisdom..271
By Helen Harkness

Chapter Sixteen

Wisdom Through The Ages............................291

By Trinidad Hunt

Chapter Seventeen

Real Life Relationship Strategies 311

By Janice Bastani

CHAPTER ONE

It's All About Relationships

By Katherin Scott

DAVID WRIGHT (WRIGHT)

Today I'm talking with Katherin Scott. *Cosmopolitan* magazine, the *Wall Street Journal,* Match.com, *Discovery Channel,* and *Precious* magazine of Japan are among the prestigious media outlets that routinely seek out the sassy, studied, and provocative commentary of America's Premier Date2Mate™ Coach Katherin Scott.

The author of *ABC's of Dating: Simple Strategies for Dating Success* and *First Glance: 7 Steps to a Memorable First Impression,* Katherin is affectionately named "Coach Cupid" by the media and many of her now happily married clients.

Katherin coaches singles worldwide to tap into the power of the subconscious mind coupled with the Law of Attraction, and navigate the dating scene to romantic and lasting outcomes.

Katherin, as a dating and relationship coach, I imagine you've studied and thought a lot about relationships between men and women. Before we get into the dynamics of dating, let's start with a question about relationships in general. What are the keys to a healthy relationship in business, in love, in life?

KATHERIN SCOTT (SCOTT)

That's a great question, David, and I believe the keys to a healthy relationship are the same for business, love, and life, with just a slight twist.

The first key is Mutual Respect. Regardless of what type of relationship you may be in, Mutual Respect is a must. Without it the relationship is doomed to fail at best, or destructive at its worst.

Ask yourself: "Do I feel respect from this person?" And be honest. If you find yourself making excuses for the person, don't. Just sit with the question, then give an honest answer.

If you don't think you are respected by this person, go a bit deeper. Can you name a particular behavior this person does that makes you feel disrespected or are you dumping on the label of disrespect from another time or person? In other words, your past experience may be clouding your judgment of your relationship with this person.

Also, be willing to look at how this person treats you on a regular basis and think about your interactions with him or her since "we teach others how to treat us."

So, do you feel respect? That's the first question to ask yourself and the easiest.

The second question is: "Do I treat this person with respect?" This question isn't always as easy for people to look at, especially if they've felt disrespect from someone. The bottom line is that we need to feel secure and open to treat others with respect *first*, even if we haven't necessarily felt respected by them. Take the high road. You don't have to be in relationship with them, just be *your* best self in how you treat others.

The second key is to Value the Differences. Remember when you first met someone and the cute things he or she did? Then, as the relationship progresses those are the things that make you crazy!

We choose our friends because they're like us and have similar qualities. Mostly we choose our mates because they have *complementary* qualities, helping us to grow and reach our greatest potential. Sometimes, however, those differences begin to feel constricting and frustrating instead of like gentle hands supporting us forward. So understand that it is *because* of our differences that we grow and experience more from life and ourselves.

The third and final key is An Alignment of Purpose. Just like a mission statement for a company, having a purpose is vital for any relationship you're in. And notice I didn't say "Agreement of Purpose." Alignment implies a similar purpose moving in the same direction, not necessarily on the exact same path.

So figure out your purpose, your goals, and what has meaning for you. Then find someone (or a company) who independently came to a similar conclusion. Shared values and common goals are the glue that bring people together and keep them together.

Let's quickly circle back to these three keys for a healthy relationship as it relates to dating with three questions to ask when you meet a potential love interest.

1. For "Mutual Respect," ask yourself if you would like your children to be exactly like this person. If the answer is no, you probably don't have a deep respect for him or her.
2. For "Value the Differences," ask yourself if you would be happy if nothing about the person changed for the next twenty, thirty, or forty years. This question usually brings out those idiosyncrasies that are not so endearing over time.
3. For "Alignment of Purpose," first of all, do the work to understand your purpose in life, then ask yourself if this person has shared interests and common goals for his or her life.

WRIGHT

Katherin, how and when did you decide to become a Dating and Relationship Coach?

SCOTT

Great question, especially since I doubt not too many people decide to be a dating coach when they are thinking of what college to attend.

I had been a corporate manager for years in a Fortune 500 company and was regularly coaching my direct reports and others for performance improvement and goal attainment. I had completed my master's degree in Applied Behavioral Science as well as certification from Coach University so I was then a Life Coach. However, I knew Life coaching wasn't much of a niche.

I had an amazing woman I'll call Wendy working for me. She was smart and attractive and very professional. Unfortunately, Wendy found out that her husband, who was working in the same building one floor below us, was having an affair with her best friend who also worked at the company one floor above. Not an easy situation to deal with but Wendy managed her divorce and the awkward situation with poise and professionalism.

About a year later, Wendy came into my office all excited to tell me that she had a date scheduled for that upcoming Friday night. I was excited for her and asked where she had met him and if he was cute. Wendy said she had met him on an online dating site but she didn't know if he was cute or not as she hadn't seen a photo of him.

I thought that was weird but I didn't want to criticize her so I asked where she was going to meet him. Her response floored me, as she was going to meet him on Friday night at 9:00 PM at his house! All kinds of red flags went up in my head and I tried to talk with her about the dangers of what she was about to do. I had her log onto the dating site and told her I'd write him a nice note about asking for his photo before the date and to meet at a coffee shop around 7:00 PM on Friday, not 9:00.

Wendy looked panicked and said she was afraid he wouldn't like her if she was so "demanding" and direct. I convinced her to send the e-mail and within a short time she came back into my office. She told me he had sent a very nice response with a photo and yes, he was cute but that the reason he couldn't meet at 7:00 PM was that he

4

had six children who were all very ADHD and he couldn't ever find a babysitter who was willing to watch them! They would be in bed by 9:00 PM, so he thought it would be okay to meet at his house.

I decided to become a Dating Coach in that very moment for a number of reasons. First, because I knew it would be a rewarding niche and second, so much fun. Most importantly, I thought, if someone as amazing and smart as Wendy was thinking of doing something as unsafe as she had been considering, what were other women and men willing to do?

I went on to become Certified as a Master Dating and Relationship Coach through the Relationship Coaching Institute as well as other programs. It has been more than a decade now and I've enjoyed an amazing and rewarding career!

WRIGHT

Tell me about your "Date2Mate" program for singles.

SCOTT

For love relationships, the most important key is to *choose* a good partner in the first place. In my proprietary five-step Date2Mate process, the first two steps focus on how to specifically choose an ideal partner.

The first step is to clarify *who* you are. This includes your strengths and weaknesses, your relationship patterns and key lessons learned, your ability to communicate, how you behave in conflict, your beliefs, values, and world view, your problem solving and coping ability, your personality and social style. All of these make up *who* you are; most people are unaware of them. You are the *constant* in your relationships. It's important to understand *who* you are and what you bring to the table—both good and bad.

The next step is Characteristics—those characteristics and qualities of your ideal mate that you want. I teach singles how to create their Dream Mate List and how to organize it to reprogram the Reticular Activation System of their brain to attract their ideal mate. And I teach them to create five conversational questions (not interview or interrogation questions!) from their Dream Mate List so they can prequalify or disqualify a potential partner in five minutes or less! How's that for efficiency! No reason to waste months or years to decide if someone is a potential mate. The subconscious mind already knows these things. I help people tap into the brilliance of their subconscious mind.

WRIGHT

Okay, once singles have developed their five conversational questions, where can they go and meet other quality singles?

SCOTT

That's a great question, David, and for those who have worked with me and know my work, they've heard me say over and over "Love is geographical—wherever you go, you can find love *when* you know how!" And by that I mean, it doesn't matter where you are or where you go, you can meet quality singles anywhere—the post office, grocery store, at work, in a foreign country, and certainly through an online dating site, which I think is a great venue for meeting singles, as are speed dating events.

I think the first question single people need to ask themselves is: what am I looking for in a relationship? Is it friendship, or social connection, or sex, or a long-term partnership?

If your purpose for dating is for friendship or social connection and not to find the love of your life at the present time, no problem. Just be sure of your intention and be clear to those you're dating. Be up-front about your purpose and don't lead anyone into thinking you're looking for a life partner if you're not.

If you're dating just for sex, again, be very clear to those you're dating about your purpose. Go out and have sex—safe sex. However, don't fool yourself into thinking your sex partner will turn into your life partner. It rarely happens. On the other hand, if you're feeling drawn to have sex because you're "touch starved," I recommend you get regular massages rather than jumping into bed with the first person who shows interest in you. Get monthly massages at a minimum. A weekly massage is imperative if you haven't experienced healthy touch in a while.

If you *are* looking for a life partner, be sure you're ready and available. That sounds like common sense, doesn't it? But it's not. Too many people are looking for a life partner long before they're ready to even date. I've included a Dating Availability Assessment in the first chapter of my *ABC's of Dating* book. It's an important assessment to take before you rush out to date if you are looking for a quality life partner.

WRIGHT

Tell me more about your Dating Availability Assessment from your *ABC's of Dating* book. What are the questions in the assessment?

SCOTT

The assessment starts out with rating the statement: *I know who I am.* In other words: I have a clear understanding of my strengths and weaknesses and a defined plan for continual personal growth. This is the first step in my Date2Mate program I spoke with you about earlier.

The next three assessment questions originate from Step 2 of my Date2Mate program: *I know what I want,* which means I have a clear vision for my life and my relationship requirements, needs, and wants. And *I have narrowed the gaps* between *who I am* and *what I want* so I don't need to be "rescued" or "completed" by a partner.

Next is: I know my "Must-Have's." They have a *written list* of at least five non-negotiable requirements that must be present in their relationship with a partner, not just an imaginary list in their head that they can't clearly articulate and therefore their subconscious mind can't help them find.

Next is: I have clear conversational questions to quickly prequalify or disqualify a potential partner.

These are the questions I spoke about earlier. They allow a person to promptly screen a potential partner based on their "must-have's" or their non-negotiable requirements, as I call them.

Moving on to the next assessment statement to rate: *I am happy and successful being single.* The bottom line is that if a person thinks he or she is "broken" or needy or looking for a relationship to "complete the person," he or she is carrying some extra baggage that needs to be looked at and resolved before attracting a quality mate.

I am ready and available for commitment is the next assessment statement. Here we are looking for any legal, financial, or emotional issues that would negatively affect people's availability for a quality partner.

The next assessment statement is especially important for a single man. *My career is satisfying.* In other words, the work the person does is enjoyable, supports financial needs, and would not interfere with the person's relationship with a partner.

I have effective dating and relationship skills. Is this person comfortable initiating contact with potential partners and disengaging with others who are not a good match? Can the person maintain healthy boundaries, both physical and emotional, and can he or she allow himself or herself to be appropriately vulnerable with others?

And finally, they rate the statement: *I have effective communication skills.* How well do these singles clearly express their needs and wants and courageously communicate with others, even in times of stress/conflict?

This Dating Availability Assessment is a great place to jump-start a person's development in order to attract a quality relationship, and all of these key points are part of my Date2Mate program for singles.

WRIGHT

What do you think is the biggest obstacle singles face when dating today?

SCOTT

Regardless of what year or even what decade it is I believe the biggest obstacle is *inside* a person, namely their confidence level and how much the person loves and values himself or herself. The degree to which people love themselves will determine who they will ultimately attract. This is why I believe it is crucial for singles to build their confidence, and this is Step 3 in my Date2Mate program.

You can quote me on this: "Confidence looks sexy on *every* body!"

WRIGHT

How do you help singles build their confidence?

SCOTT

I have two fun yet very significant exercises, one for men and one for women, that will boost a person's confidence level in less than thirty days. These exercises take less than two minutes each day and *must* be done daily in order to create a new understanding in their subconscious mind. I recommend using something that can be purchased at a party store for less than $10 for these exercises.

WRIGHT

Now I'm intrigued! What are the party store items and how do they help build confidence?

SCOTT

Let's start with the women first:

I have women buy an inexpensive *crown* at a party store. They are to put on their crown first thing every morning (with no bobby pins allowed to hold it in place!), look directly into the mirror and say out loud, "I deserve love and I am loveable."

They are to notice their self-talk at that point and notice how it changes day by day. At first they may think this is silly. Some women cry because it brings up a deep desire to feel loved. Some women hear their subconscious mind repeat negative messages they are carrying around in their head like, "You don't deserve love," or something similar. No matter, I just ask them to do this exercise every day and wear their crown around the house until they can *own*

9

it and have the posture and "essence" of having the crown on when it isn't physically on their head to become the queen they truly are!

For men, I have them purchase a Viking helmet! First thing in the morning, they strip down to their naked chest, put on the Viking helmet, and do the body builder's pose in front of the mirror. Looking directly into their own eyes, I have them say out loud, "Damn, I'm hot!"

Again, I ask them to just listen to their self-talk and notice how it changes day by day.

I can always tell when a client is doing their exercise or not. When they do and they do it every day their whole persona changes! They start talking in a very different way about themselves and their dreams. They become the queens and strong kings they are meant to be!

WRIGHT

Let's be sure to finish talking about your Date2Mate program. What are the other steps in this successful program for singles?

SCOTT

Thanks for asking, David! The final two steps of the Date2Mate program are about Community and Celebration.

Community is about building a support community. Community can be a class you take, singles events you participate in, a coach you hire, same sex single friends you go out with, a dance class. Tell everyone you know that you're ready to date and are looking for a potential mate. Have them introduce you to other singles. Host a singles party with your friends. Their ticket in is to bring a potential match for you! Join a MeetUp group or create one for singles in your area. Join online dating sites—one large general site such as Match.com or POF.com and one boutique site (such as FitnessSingles or ChristianSingles or JDate). Don't be a lone ranger or hide the fact that you want to find a mate. Create a community of support while you're in the process of looking for a mate.

Celebration is about getting out there! Go out and date! Celebrate that you are here and now ready to find your mate and not ten years older than you are today. Become a successful single and then attract the mate of your dreams. Celebrate that you have the skills to attract a good partner. Celebrate with a new dating outfit or make-over. Have some fun with it. Dating is about meeting new people and having fun with them as you sort thorough potential matches. Celebrate and you will be successful!

WRIGHT

Once a person attracts and chooses a partner what are ways to keep the relationship healthy and solid?

SCOTT

Here are ten ways to keep your relationship with your partner solid and strong. A lot of these tips also apply to friendships and work relationships.

1. **Relationships are like plants—give your partner the attention he or she needs.** With live plants, we need to water them, put them in the proper sunlight, feed them, repot them, and so on. They are ever growing and changing and they need attention. So do relationships. Too many people act as if their relationship is a "silk plant" and doesn't need attention. Like a plant, the relationship will die without focused nurturing.

2. **Keep the "home fires burning."** In other words, take care of your mate. Do those romantic and sexy things you used to do while dating. Go on weekly dates, especially if you have kids. Make your mate feel special. Remember what endeared you to him or her in the beginning of the relationship and focus on what you love about your mate. Be intentional about spending quality time together. Take time to look directly into each other's eyes, lovingly, every day. Take time to touch each other every day.

11

Touch your mate's arm as you walk by. Massage your partner's shoulders after a long day at work. Hold each other closely in bed, breathing in unison together.

3. **Figure out what your partner needs to feel loved and give it to him or her.** In Gary Chapman's book, *The 5 Love Languages,* there are certain things everyone needs to feel loved. However, most people give others what they themselves need and not what their partner needs. Too many couples end up feeling depleted of love and resentful of their partners because their "love tank" is empty. Give your mate what he or she needs to feel loved and appreciated and do these tasks lovingly. Realize that the relationship will not last without it.

4. **Keep yourself in good shape.** Or get in shape if you're not at your best weight. Recent studies have shown that people put on weight after marriage due to being a couple, having babies or just letting themselves go. Keep your body attractive for your mate. Help your partner feel proud to be with you. Letting your body get out of shape sends a negative message to your partner that you no longer feel the need to be attractive to or for him or her.

5. **Keep yourself healthy.** Take vitamins, eat right, drink plenty of water, drink alcohol moderately, stay at your optimum weight, watch the prescriptions you may be taking, stay healthy, and disease free. All of this will keep up the libido. Find creative ways to keep the physical side of your relationship fulfilling for both of you.

6. **Get very good at communicating with your partner.** I created the "Courageous Communication Wheel" that helps people to speak from their heart in a non-defensive way. Good communication is essential to keeping a partnership healthy and going strong. Be courageous and bring up the little things as they occur. Have good communication skills and put exercises in place to check-in periodically with your partner and talk about what's

working well in the relationship, what's not, and ideas for making changes to improve the relationship. And understand that *listening* is a key part of communication. Listen to what your partner is communicating to you without judgment. Put yourself in your partner's "moccasins" and truly "feel" what is being expressed to you. Use communication techniques such as paraphrasing so that you will both clearly understand each other. And take the *time* to truly communicate. It takes time to truly understand and continue to know what your partner is feeling and how the relationship is going.

7. **Maintain mutual respect with your partner.** I talked about Mutual Respect earlier but I want to mention it here again because it is so important. Check your behavior with your partner—is it respectful or is it condescending? Do you feel respected by your partner or are there things that make you feel less valued? Check in periodically with your mate to be sure you both feel respected. Be honest with each other and find ways to identify and remove disrespectful behavior immediately.

8. **Play together.** Couples who play together stay together. Couples need five times more fun than mundane activities to keep things strong as documented by Dr. John Gottman from the University of Washington. Make a point of exercising together or dancing or traveling or playing cards or going to concerts. Whatever you do to have fun together, do it. When the relationship gets a bit bogged-down, take an evening, a day, a weekend get-away and just have fun together—no conversations about bills or the kids or work. Just focus on fun and your relationship will be re-energized.

9. **Keep learning and growing.** Learn new things together. Learn Tantra and add spice to your love life. Tantra teaches couples to build intimacy in ways most Westerners were never taught and don't really

understand. I'm not talking of crazy, upside-down, twisted pretzel sex. Tantra is about breathing together, looking deeply into each other's eyes, caressing each other, and valuing your partner as the beautiful human being he or she is. Read books, go to seminars, travel to different cultures, attend university lectures. Expand your mind and share new ideas with your partner as you learn and grow.

10. **Remain trustworthy.** *The bottom line is: if you wouldn't feel comfortable having your partner watch you do something, you probably shouldn't be doing it.* This definitely includes contacting a previous lover via the Internet and sharing intimate conversations with them. Having lunch with a co-worker during the day is fine; however, it crosses the line when you share a meal at a romantic restaurant in a hidden booth, regardless of how "innocent" the meeting might be.

The bottom line is: commit to your partner. If this is indeed a good relationship, then personally commit to staying in the relationship—no matter what. When couples talk about divorce every time the sink overflows, they aren't really committed to one another. Just thinking of divorce begins to eat away at the intimacy of the relationship. As in the Law of Attraction "thoughts become things." When you truly commit to one another, you will find ways to work things out "for better, for worse, for rich or poorer, in sickness and in health, 'till death do us part."

WRIGHT

What is one final tip you would like to share about relationships?

SCOTT

I know we all lead very busy lives these days and I see most of us trying to juggle all of the different responsibilities we have in our life. I see relationships as one of the *glass objects* we are juggling along with our *health*. Most of the other things in our lives are unbreakable objects that we can afford to let drop once in a while. We can pick them up a bit later with little or no consequence for having dropped them. Not so with our key relationships. They are glass objects to be guarded and nurtured and appreciated every day. Do this and I guarantee you will have rewarding relationships and a rewarding life!

Guiding people beyond burnout to brilliance with every move they make is Katherin Scott's mission as a sought-after keynote speaker, workshop leader, and coach.

Author of *ABC's of Dating: Simple Steps for Dating Success* and *First Glance: 7 Steps to a Memorable First Impression*, Katherin shows people how to take specific, decisive steps forward to apply lessons that can have immediate and favorable impact on corporate culture, performance, and relationships. Her clients and seminar participants regularly report game-changing shifts in behavior that immediately translate to their balance sheets, their paychecks, their relationships, and their marriages.

Media outlets including the *Wall Street Journal, Cosmopolitan Magazine, Match.com, Precious Magazine* (Japan), and the Discovery Channel have interviewed Katherin for her insights on relationships, leadership, and the impact of body language on election results, business success, and dating.

Katherin guides without judgment and with a fierce and loving commitment to add value at every turn. Her direct and compassionately mischievous approach to working with clients is among her hallmark gifts.

Katherin Scott

Wake-Up Network, LLC
7829 Center Blvd SE, Ste. 216
Snoqualmie, WA 98065
CoachKatherin@yahoo.com
www.KatherinScott.com

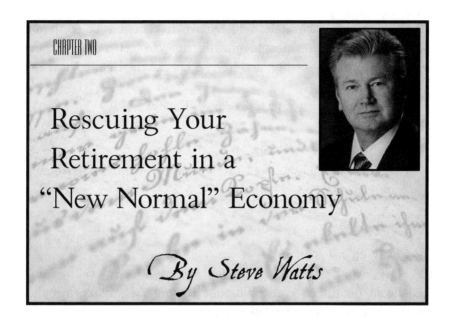

CHAPTER TWO

Rescuing Your Retirement in a "New Normal" Economy

By Steve Watts

DAVID WRIGHT (WRIGHT)

Today I am talking with Stephen Watts. Stephen has been a retirement phase financial specialist since 1997. Throughout his career he has been instrumental in developing retirement phase, educational business models for three large financial firms. He is currently the Co-Founder and Chief Executive Officer of Oak Harvest Financial Group, which is one of the fastest growing financial firms in Houston, Texas. They are successfully utilizing a unique educational system that is the evolution and culmination of his fifteen years as a top producer in the retirement income planning industry.

Mr. Watts is the co-host of a popular talk radio program called *The Retirement Rescue Show.* The show broadcasts the educational spirit of Oak Harvest to a host of retirees throughout the Houston area. He is also the author of *Retirement Rescue,* the book, subtitled *How to Protect Your Retirement in a New Normal Economy.* His book portrays the commonsense approach to retirement phase decision making such as how to remove risk from your portfolio without removing reasonable growth, how to get a substantial, guaranteed income for life, and how to choose the right advisor in your golden years.

Stephen Watts, welcome to *Words of Wisdom.*

STEVE WATTS (WATTS)

Hello David; I am honored to be a part of Words of Wisdom! How are you today?

WRIGHT

I'm doing just great.

Steve, you've been a financial expert who specializes in retirement for fifteen years. What are the biggest mistakes people make in regard to retirement planning?

WATTS

Well, David, the two things that come to mind instantly are not only the biggest mistakes but they're also the most common. In other words, they're the mistakes that have the most profound effect on your retirement and they're made most often.

First and foremost, people choose the wrong advisor, which I'll talk about later. The second most important and common mistake that people make is that they wait too long to start formulating a plan for retirement.

To illustrate this I'll tell you about a married couple for whom we designed and proposed a plan prior to the big stock market crash and banking system meltdown of 2008. They were planning to retire in 2011 and were delighted with the way we were able to meet all their retirement income needs and growth expectations without the worry of stock market risk. Then after implementing the proposal, they sat with their longtime friend and stockbroker to share the good news, to which he quipped, "You're not retiring for three years, you don't have to change everything now!"

When they shared his sentiments with me I asked them, "Have you ever gone on a long tropical vacation?" He said yes. Then I asked: "Did you wait to get there to start the planning?"

Well, against their better judgment, and against our recommendations, the couple took their stockbroker's advice to cancel the plan that we had prepared for them and kept their entire nest egg at risk. You can imagine the feeling they got when the market crashed shortly thereafter. They lost so much of their hard-earned nest egg in such a short period of time that they did not have time to react. Their stockbroker advised them to stay the course and wait for the market to come back.

Fast forward four years and they still have 25 percent less in their IRA due to market loss than they had before the crash, which they rode all the way down. Additionally, they missed out on four years of growth opportunity, which averaged about 6 percent for our clients during that same time frame. Since our strategies enjoy the benefit of tax deferral and compound interest the total amount of market and opportunity loss was well in excess of 50 percent. Now for the kicker. It takes a 100 percent total return gain in order to replenish that 50 percent loss.

To illustrate that, I will use an example of a $100,000 portfolio incurring a 50 percent loss below. It never ceases to amaze me how often people think it only takes 50 percent gain to recuperate from a 50 percent loss.

Example:

$100,000.00 − 50% = $50,000.00
$50,000.00 + 100% = $100,000.00

Obviously, their plans to retire in 2011 were shattered as a direct result of having fallen victim to the two most profound and common mistakes that people make with retirement planning—and unfortunately it's all too easy to make these mistakes at the same time with the same portfolio.

WRIGHT

I see and hear a lot of advertisements these days about retirement planning from various individuals and companies. How can we tell which ones are qualified to help us with our retirement needs?

WATTS

I think that question is more relevant today than ever before, David. The Baby Boomer generation has come of age and there are lots of financial firms jumping on the retirement bandwagon, so to speak. As a matter of fact there are 10,000 Baby Boomers retiring every day for the next eighteen years. This is causing every type of financial firm and advisor to jump on that bandwagon. You see advertisements from stockbrokers, brokerage firms, and even banks promoting their retirement plan.

Don't be fooled! Brokerage houses and banks are in full-fledged damage control mode because of the mass exodus from Wall Street and low paying CDs, so they now try to rope their clients back in and find new ones by using the new buzz word (retirement). Sadly, it is highly unlikely that you will find a truly qualified retirement specialist in either of those venues. Moreover, the conflicts of interest between a stockbroker or brokerage firm and an individual seeking safety are off the charts. Any securities licensed firm or individual primarily sells risk or risk management and are therefore allergic to safety.

Add to that the conflicts of interest inherent in a bank under current regulations that takes your deposits purported to be safe, and invests them in overseas derivatives or other highly speculative instruments. Yes your deposits are insured up to $250,000, but the strain of hundreds of bank failures over the past few years is beginning to take a toll on the FDIC, which is responsible for paying the shortfall when a bank becomes insolvent.

Taken together, it seems to us that banks and brokers might be the worst, most unsafe places in which to entrust your retirement nest egg.

If you agree, here are some of the qualifications to look for when you're deciding which advisor or firm is best to adeptly guide you through retirement. First of all, I recommend for you to seek out a firm as opposed to an individual or one man show. I applaud the folks out there being entrepreneurs and trying the one man show routine, but in most cases I feel there are just not enough hours in a day for one person to create business and provide customer service. Additionally, an advisor is not likely to pick up the phone while he or she is sitting with another client, which can pose a hardship in emergency or time restricted situations.

The firm you choose should specialize in and be experienced with the retirement and preretirement phase. If they also handle securities, such as stocks, bonds, and mutual funds, be careful! They may have a vested interest in keeping your portfolio at risk (mostly because of ongoing fees and/or the tendency to lean toward their expertise). Risk is retirement enemy number one and the ultimate goal is to greatly reduce or even eliminate market risk altogether as you enter the pre-retirement or retirement phases.

The right firm should be an agency that deals with the entire spectrum of retirement phase solutions, strategies, and insurance companies. This is the true form of an *independent* agency. An independent agency is the only type that has the wherewithal to properly fit you with the most consumer-friendly safe alternatives, due to their vast array of companies from which they can choose financial instruments.

The alternative to an independent agency is known as a *captive* agency, and it may have limited resources, limited options on their menu, and may rarely, if ever, have the most consumer-friendly solutions. If an agency has limited options with which to protect your assets, they must try to fit you into what they offer, as opposed to finding the right solutions to fit you. There is a huge difference between those two dynamics.

Last but not least, your retirement specialist, independent firm should have a simple, yet comprehensive, educational approach. This will help you arm yourself to make an informed decision when the time comes to sign the paperwork or walk away. It is also crucial that this process thoroughly cover the downside of their recommendations. Every financial strategy or vehicle has a design purpose and a downside. Knowing whether or not you can manage the downside is a key element in determining if you have the right plan. Generally speaking, the more a firm is willing to educate you on the downside, the more faith they have in their ability to solve your concerns in a consumer friendly fashion. In short, if the strategy or vehicle is consumer friendly then the downside can be easily managed, reduced, or altogether rendered moot.

This is your nest egg, the lion's share of your financial future, don't you want all the facts?

WRIGHT

So, Steve, when is the right time to start planning for retirement?

WATTS

Well that's the sixty-four-thousand-dollar question, isn't it? The planning starts from the time you're able to start putting away some of your income into savings accounts such as 401Ks, IRAs, or nonqualified savings vehicles. That should commence at the earliest possible age with as much discretionary money as you can afford. I recently made a live appearance on a local live television show here in Houston and fielded that very question from a twenty-three-year-old lady in the studio audience. I took one look at her expensive shoes and suggested she start saving right away! But this is generally my recommendation to everyone—it never hurts to start putting money away for retirement, no matter how young you are.

When one should save is also predicated on one's retirement lifestyle expectations. The right time to seek out a retirement phase professional, though, is at that time when you no longer want to take risks with at least part of your retirement nest egg and you want to ensure that you're on the right track to meet your retirement income goals. It would also be advisable to start planning when you have an insurable interest such as a spouse or child. It is of special importance when either spouse is dependent on the other's income.

When I first started my career, the median age for people to start planning was right around sixty-two, but due to increased uncertainty in the economic and financial forefronts, as well as increased awareness created by the Internet age, the median age for people starting is now about fifty-two. If Wall Street continues to be as unpredictable, volatile, and ineffective as it has been during the last twelve years, then the median age will continue to decline as well.

I think it shows great foresight to start at the earlier stage but it's important to note that's it's never too late to improve your situation or at least get a second opinion from a retirement specialist.

WRIGHT

On your radio show, *The Retirement Rescue Show*, and in your book, *Retirement Rescue,* you express reasons for the increased uncertainty in the economic forefront. Would you briefly tell our readers about that?

WATTS

Sure, David. The radio program is one of our favorite venues in which to educate our clients. One of the most frequent topics that we are asked to cover is something called the "New Normal Economy." There are several major contributing factors that have forever changed the economic landscape as we knew it. This turn of events is drastically changing the way we should approach our retirement phase decisions.

We believe the most drastic of these events happened in 1999 when Congress repealed the Glass Steagall Act of 1933, which removed the firewall between the banking industry and Wall Street. Commercial banks then began partnering with investment banks, investment banks began partnering with brokerage houses, and a glut of bank money began pouring into newly formed hedge funds. It became legal to short the market when in decline, which gives these investment banks and hedge funds the incentive to drive down the market.

In the stock market crash of 2008 there was a 77 percent decline before the recovery began. That is exactly the amount of control that the top ten investment banks have over the trading in Wall Street on any given day according to Bloomberg. This unprecedented amount of control was also acquired as a result of the aforementioned glut of money flowing from the local bank deposits into the investment banks in 1999. What a scary thought! Just this one event created an enormous conflict of interest between the stock market and you.

Let me see if I can illustrate that conflict. You take your money and open up an account at a brokerage house that, in turn, is partnered with an investment bank and they place you in stock market positions. Then they invest billions in hedge funds that bet against the very positions they sold you. They profit from your loss in this scenario and it is all quite legal! I call this a license to be legally unethical. As you might imagine, the end result of this legislative debacle is corruption and volatility run amok. In fact, the evidence would support that the housing bust and the near-fatal crisis visited upon the banking industry in 2008 can both be tied to this one issue.

Think about it: Because of the fall of Glass-Steagall, banks were then able to invest in the kind of incredibly profitable, and easily manipulable, custom-built securities such as credit-default swaps and mortgage-backed funds, many of them dreamed up by Lehman Brothers and Bear Sterns (both of which are now defunct). They put up huge sums of money—your deposits—then watched as they simply evaporated, dried up. For Lehman and Bear Sterns, it was too late. But Bank of America, Chase, and others benefited from the bank bailout and didn't have to close up shop—your tax dollars at work.

Meantime, those "mortgage-backed securities" were made up of actual mortgages, and as the value of those securities plummeted, the underlying assets became depressed. Hence, real estate values dropped catastrophically, and many homeowners found themselves under water—owing more money on their mortgages than their homes were now actually worth.

As if that weren't enough to plunge the economy into recession, in January 2001 our "Baby Boomer" generation, which comprises the vast majority of the nation's "Super Spenders," turned fifty-five and left the super spender demographic. In January 2011 they started to retire.

Now they are not only earning and spending less, but they are drawing out of the social system at a much larger clip than ever expected, while also contributing less to the institutional funds. Since spending is about 66 percent of our long-term stock market growth, the logical conclusion is that we'll experience long-term stock market decline since we're losing ten thousand Baby Boomers from the workforce a day for the next eighteen years.

Even further contributing to the decline, we have a $16 trillion (and rising) national debt that will invariably result in a tax tsunami and skyrocketing inflation. In fact, inflation is like a stallion in the gate chomping at the bit to get out, which will further erode your buying power when it hits. Arguably it already has.

Consider that most CDs these days are paying 2 percent or much less, treasury bills are paying in the neighborhood of 2 percent to 3 percent, and savings accounts are paying nothing at all. This is the very definition of erosion—as the prices of goods and services rise each year, your nest egg's purchasing power keeps slowly declining. And maybe not so slowly if inflation increases at a rate greater than 3 percent, which many experts agree is inevitable.

Now top all that off with the fact that we're living longer and the chances of outliving your nest egg increase exponentially. When social security was implemented the life expectancy for a male was sixty-five. It is now eighty-five for a male and eighty-nine for a female. Some say that these numbers are even conservative and will soon be outdated, which is substantiated by the declining cost of life insurance.

When you add all of this up, it isn't pretty. Volatility plus long-term market decline plus higher cost of living plus longevity equals *no way to spend retirement without proper guidance!*

The chances of outliving your nest egg increase substantially when you take any *one* of these factors into consideration, but retirees are now subject to *all* of them simultaneously.

WRIGHT

I can see there is great cause for concern with these matters. Why is it so common for people to ignore these reasons for getting a jumpstart on their planning?

WATTS

There are a host of factors involved with this dilemma, such as a lack of resources or the discipline that's required to really plan effectively. Some folks may not have the time to keep up with these changes because of their busy work load. But the most common reason is that many people rely on someone for financial advice who is either ill-equipped to give them that appropriate retirement phase direction or who is perhaps conflicted with that direction.

Understandably, many people make the mistake of seeking retirement-phase direction from the advisor who is managing their risk investments, such as stocks, bonds, and mutual funds. After all, those advisors may have served them well up to that point. But remember, accumulation-phase advisors deal in risk, and you should be looking for safety in retirement. So asking an accumulation-phase advisor for a safe retirement strategy is akin to asking, "Do you recommend that I leave you for another advisor?" Of course they will not answer your question in such a way that they might lose your business. Accumulation-phase advisors stand to lose their business if they give their retired clients commonsense insights into safe strategies.

WRIGHT

So what are some of these basic common sense insights?

WATTS

First and foremost you should never take risk with money you can't afford to lose. When is the last time you heard that from a stockbroker? The lion's share of today's retirees' money is in IRAs and 401Ks. Now think about that for a minute. This is money that should be earmarked to replace your wages in retirement; isn't that the very essence of money you can't afford to lose? I'm not saying you can't take *some* risk with this type of account in your younger years, but you wouldn't put *all* of your "milk money" on the craps table would you? You can see how deeply conflicted that an accumulation-phase advisor would be with this basic principle, considering that the person typically *only* has risk on his or her menu of options.

Along that same line of thought is the Rule of One Hundred. This comes from Economics 101 and states that if you subtract your age from the number one hundred the remainder is the highest percentage of your assets that you should have at risk. Of course, that doesn't mean that you can afford to risk anything at all, that means that's the *most* you should have at risk. In other words, if you're sixty-five years old, you subtract that from one hundred, which means 35 percent of your nest egg is the most you might afford to have at risk: and by risk we mean stocks, bonds, mutual funds, or any other securities investment.

Example: Your age, 65
100 – 65 = 35
35% is the *most* you can afford to risk

Once again, that conflict of interest between accumulation phase advisor and client comes into play in this scenario since the Boomers own most of the money in a typical stockbroker's book of business.

Another commonsense rule often ignored by accumulation-phase advisors is that diversification should not just mean diversity *among* risk but it should also include the integration of safe alternatives. I often see the portfolios of clients in their sixties, seventies, and even eighties, who have marked the box for conservative risk tolerance on their brokerage application, in 95 percent or more risk positions. This can spell total disaster!

WRIGHT

Tell us why in your book you refer to the three financial industries as the straw house, stick house, and brick house.

WATTS

The "straw house" refers to the securities industry, the "stick house" refers to the banking industry, and the "brick house" is the insurance industry. In the fable of the three pigs, the straw house and the stick house could not withstand the force of the wolf's huffing and puffing but the brick house was left standing due to its solid foundation. Let's relate this metaphor to the financial industries. In 1929, the stock market crashed and the banking industry melted down shortly thereafter, in large part because of the poisonous partnership between Wall Street and the banking industry during that era.

The insurance industry was not only unscathed, but was, in fact, instrumental in bailing out the banking system a few years later by loaning money to various institutions. In that economic storm, the straw house and the stick house blew over while the brick house was able to withstand the gale forces of an economy that essentially collapsed overnight.

In 2000, Wall Street suffered another catastrophic blow as it fell over 60 percent after the collapse of the "tech" bubble. In this instance the straw house blew over.

In 2008 the banking industry suffered a severe meltdown in what could have easily resulted in economic doomsday. Once again, the partnership between the banking industry and Wall Street in this era caused the ensuing meltdown of the stock market, which fell 77 percent before recovery finally began. Once again, the insurance industry withstood the greatest storm since 1929. In that economic storm, the straw house and stick house both were blown over while the brick house was left standing.

Can you see the pattern? There have been no less than eighteen stock market crashes since 1929, none of which were anything more than a brief nuisance for the insurance industry. Three of these crashes culminated in a decline of more than 50 percent and two of them were accompanied by total bank meltdowns. The FDIC is virtually insolvent and has been almost perpetually so since 1991. In this day and age it is a godsend to have a brick house that we can rely on to keep us protected from the economic storms.

WRIGHT

So what makes the insurance industry's foundation so solid?

WATTS

They're regulated by the most stringent regulations in the financial industry, called statutory accounting. The system does not allow for them to carry liabilities on their asset ledgers, which makes their financial health transparent.

Let me give you a contrast to that: In 2008 local banks, brokerage houses, and investment banks were all allowed to carry liabilities on their asset ledgers, which muddies the waters when trying to determine their solvency and financial strength ratings. Hence they were rated higher than their actual fiscal health, and that contributed to the largest bank meltdown we have had since 1929.

But the statutory accounting system is quite a bit different; there are multiple levels of consumer protection in this system. For instance, a dollar-for-dollar legal reserve mandate gives insurance companies ten times the solvency of a bank and allows them to use portfolio earnings for operating expenses when new insurance business is lean. They undergo frequent state audits—several times a year in most cases—and must open their books completely. Moreover, they're not allowed to commingle their assets with banks or brokerage houses like banks and brokerage houses do with one another. That is why they do not suffer simultaneous meltdowns with other financial industries such as the straw house and stick house do. In fact, they have rarely even been fazed to any significant degree by adverse economic climates. You could say that they live in their own self-created ecosystem that insulates them from the storm. I refer to them as the true form of a bank, or are what banks wish they could be.

WRIGHT

So how are insurance companies coping with the fact that people are living longer?

WATTS

This is the best part and I can think of two ways they're proactively solving this issue. First of all, the fact that we're living longer is causing the price of life insurance to decline. Now, what else can you think of that actually is in a price decline mode right now? Not much, right? But this has allowed them to take some of the cost of death benefit and shift it into living benefits with life insurance policies. They also have more innovative growth mechanisms such as Index Universal Life that greatly increase the likelihood of the policy's interest credits paying for all of the premiums without fear of premium nonpayment. In other words, we can now solve for retiree's income goals with life insurance much better than we were able to in the past.

We can also use life insurance to provide tax-free income much more effectively than in the past. Some of the life insurance companies have been turning the longevity challenge into a benefit for them by creating better financial vehicles that their clients would be crazy to replace. Since insurance companies have always relied on having your money for long periods of time, this is quite the win-win scenario for company and client. The theory, which is working like a charm, is that they know they're going to have your money for a long time if they build something special that entices you to stay in.

WRIGHT

Tell us more about some of these vehicles and strategies.

WATTS

We're now able to do some fantastic tax-free income planning with index universal life, for instance. We can also provide long-term care coverage with no annual premiums through the proper usage of several types of life insurance vehicles such as single premium whole life.

With single premium life insurance, the underwriting is quite simplified so it is very easy to get approval. This type of strategy has several benefits over and above a traditional long-term care policy. For instance, you're actually investing in something that's completely liquid so you could take your money out of it if you have a change of circumstances or just change your mind. You can't do that with a traditional long-term care policy. It also has a small death benefit along with it. So you're never in that situation where you're investing money into something that you or your estate might not benefit from.

We've got financial instruments that can provide ridiculously good lifetime incomes without forcing clients to lose control of their principal. This type of instrument still confounds some CPAs who think you must annuitize to get a guaranteed life income. Annuitization quite frankly means locking up your money and losing access to your principal, but with these contracts you don't have to do that.

One of these types of vehicles allows a client to take his or her lifetime income out in the same tax efficient manner that was inherent only with annuitization until now. We have vehicles at our disposal that allow us to cover your long-term care costs, whether in-home or institutional, without underwriting.

WRIGHT

What are the most important lessons we can learn from our discussion today?

WATTS

The most important tidbits to take away from this discussion on retirement phase topics are pretty straightforward. First of all, we are in unchartered rough waters in our economic environment and we can no longer rely on conventional academia to solve our retirement goals.

The next thing is that there are extremely effective, safe, and viable alternatives to the old school of thought of buy and hold, or even worse, active trading. The most important of all is that you need to seek someone who understands how to help you navigate through those rough waters of retirement and who understands the paramount meaning of the words "safety first." After all, safety is where the *planning* begins. Without safety there is only income hoping or speculating! How ridiculous would that sound if your advisor called you up and said it was time to begin your retirement hoping? But you must first get an education so you can be an informed consumer and learn how to purchase some sleep insurance. After all, that's what everyone wants, correct? Peace of mind and a good night's sleep.

WRIGHT

How can we get more information about you and Oak Harvest Financial Group?

WATTS

For more information about how to get *Retirement Rescue: The Book,* or to get more information about *The Retirement Rescue Radio Show,* you can go to our Web site at www.OakHarvestFG.com, you can email us at info@OakHarvest.com, or you can call toll free to speak with us in person at 800-773-1768. If you live in the Greater Houston or even the Austin area you can call us locally at 281-822-1350, or you can tune in to *The Retirement Rescue Radio Show* every Saturday at 8:00 AM on 950AM radio.

WRIGHT

I appreciate all the time you've spent with me. This has been an interesting conversation for me and I've learned a lot. I've been thinking a lot about retirement lately; this is coming at the right time.

WATTS

Thank you, David, and I enjoyed it, too. When you're ready to start planning, call me first.

WRIGHT

Today I have been talking with Stephen Watts. Stephen is a retirement phase financial specialist, he is also the Co-Founder and Chief Executive Officer of Oak Harvest Financial Group, which is one of the fastest-growing financial groups in Houston, Texas. He advocates the commonsense approach to retirement phase decision making such as how to remove risk from your portfolio without removing reasonable growth and how to choose the right advisor in your golden years.

Stephen, thank you so much for being with us today on *Words of Wisdom.*

WATTS

Hey David, it's been my pleasure!

Stephen Watts has been a "Retirement Phase Financial Specialist" since 1997. Throughout his career, Mr. Watts has been instrumental in developing retirement phase, educational business models for three large financial firms. He is currently the Co-Founder and CEO of Oak Harvest Financial Group, which is one the fastest-growing financial firms in Houston, Texas. They are successfully utilizing a system that is the evolution and culmination of his fifteen years of experience in the retirement industry.

Mr. Watts is the co-host of a popular talk radio program called *The Retirement Rescue Show*. The show broadcasts the educational spirit of Oak Harvest to a host of retirees throughout the Houston area.

He is also the author of *Retirement Rescue: The Book,* subtitled: *How to Protect Your Retirement in a "New Normal" Economy.* His book portrays the commonsense approach to retirement phase decision making, such as how to remove risk from your portfolio without removing reasonable growth and how to choose the right advisor in your golden years.

Steve Watts

Oak Harvest Financial Group
7670 Woodway Dr., Suite 165
800-773-1768
281-822-1350
info@oakharvestfg.com
www.oakharvestfg.com

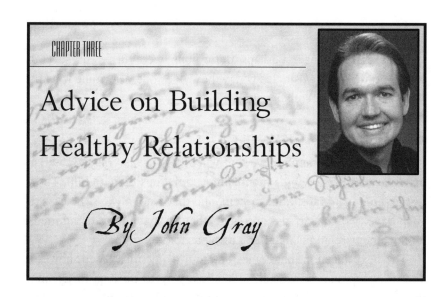

CHAPTER THREE

Advice on Building Healthy Relationships

By John Gray

DAVID WRIGHT (WRIGHT)

John, you've built a successful career as an expert giving relationship advice. I recently read a statement attributed to you: "A wise woman is careful not to pursue a man more than he is pursuing her." Will you explain why?

JOHN GRAY (GRAY)

When women make themselves too available to men, men get lazy. It's old-fashioned wisdom, but on a new level. We can understand it biochemically as well. Men bond with women when their testosterone levels go up. When there's a challenge, testosterone levels go up. But when things become easy, testosterone levels go down—so there needs to be a sense of the man initiating his own behaviors as to a woman doing it all.

The easiest way to make a man lose interest in you is to do everything for him. The most exciting thing to a man is when he feels that he is making a difference in a woman's life, as opposed to her doing everything for him.

WRIGHT

That makes sense. Perhaps definitions were different several years ago when I was single. Today, how does one determine if he or she is dating or in a "relationship"?

GRAY

Quite often women believe that when they are having sex with a man that they are having a monogamous relationship with him. They just assume that is his value system, and that's not always the case. I encourage women to assume that they're having a committed, monogamous relationship after a man has told them so.

The next question that comes up from women is, "Well, how do you bring up such a subject?" The best way to do it is to let him know at some point that you're not interested in having sex unless you're in an exclusive monogamous relationship. When he's ready to make that step she should tell him how she feels about it. That is certainly one approach.

WRIGHT

If someone is not sure that the person he or she is dating is "the one," how can that person get some help to sort through that uncertainty?

GRAY

Certainly feeling uncertain and doubting is a natural course of action in the dating process, and it's the first realization that's important. Sometimes people think, "If I don't know for sure, then maybe this is definitely not the right person for me."

One insight that is very important is that you could be with the right person for you, but still go through a period of feeling doubt and uncertainty. It's just a natural process, and while you are in that process it takes time before a part of you begins to sense that you're with the right person, or you begin to sense that you're with the wrong person. It just takes some time.

Couples who rush into making a commitment often make a mistake, and then feelings get hurt, so it's best to go slow when in doubt and not to assume that something's wrong.

WRIGHT

In the event of a cheating spouse or a lover, what should people do to learn to heal from infidelity in the relationship?

GRAY

It's an important concept to recognize that we all get our hearts broken, our partners make mistakes, and we experience disappointments. A part of growing in real love is the ability to forgive our partners for mistakes. People simply don't think sometimes and they make mistakes. By talking about it and sharing, people can understand what their mistakes are and make changes and grow from that. It's certainly a personal choice that some people make to simply exclude somebody who would ever cheat on them.

If someone has children I always encourage them to recognize that having an affair is a mistake, and people make mistakes—it's not a horrible, horrible mistake, it's just a mistake.

If someone's violent (that's more of a horrible, horrible mistake), even then it's forgivable if the person was to get help and recognize that he (or she) has a problem and overcome that problem.

The main question about being with someone is that after you have opened your heart and you've been hurt, if you take time to heal your heart, do you still want to be with him or her? That's the question. It's not for me or any other person to tell you whether you should be with that person; it's always an individual choice within the heart. The problem is that some people get caught up in this thinking that if someone makes a mistake then for sure I don't want to be with them. It's quite unrealistic to ever expect perfection in this world.

WRIGHT

In your writings you suggest using a relationship advisor or coach for those who need help. Will you explain the process?

GRAY

The process is simply talking with somebody who will ask you questions to help you to get in touch with your feelings. You can express your feelings without feeling that you're going to be judged or your feelings are going to hurt somebody or you're going to be held accountable and stand by those feelings. Often feelings need some room to flow and change as you grow in awareness. It's often not safe to show this with someone you're in a relationship with— the person might hold you to those feelings. So you go to a counselor to talk about those things.

Today it's becoming very popular to talk to coaches as well. One of the differences between a counselor and a coach is that a counselor is trained more academically in the process of analyzing what dysfunction you might have, and in providing a means to reflect on what's happening in your life related to things in your past. The counselor might even do more work on your childhood to rebuild self-esteem issues.

A coach is someone who is there to hold you accountable to do the things that you say you want to do by asking you questions. A coach can also become a sounding board who will ask you about what your feelings are, what happened, what you think should happen, what you think should not have happened, and what you think can happen. This type of exploration helps people find within themselves the wisdom to make better choices in their life. It also helps to motivate them to make better choices and follow up with action. So the coach tends to be more practically oriented.

A Mars/Venus coach adds to it an aspect of providing education as to the various insights of how men and women are different, how their emotional needs are different, and how they can motivate each other to be the best they can be in a relationship, rather than unknowingly pulling out the worst about the individuals in a relationship. I'm a big believer in education first, and then in coaching to motivate people. But often people don't even know what's going on, and some basic insights can help them make better choices and decisions. A coach can then assist them in staying motivated to achieve that end.

WRIGHT

I've heard the divorce rate is 50 percent. Is that true? And can a counselor or relationship coach actually help save a marriage?

GRAY

I've seen counselors ruin marriages, and I've seen counselors help save marriages. There are different forms of therapy. If you're in therapy and it doesn't feel right to you and you don't feel like you're making progress, you're probably in the wrong kind of therapy for you. There are some kinds of therapy where the opportunity is created for two people to sit and talk about how they feel with each other. This can result in arguments and fights in the counseling room just like the fights they have at home.

My Mars/Venus counselors are trained in ways to assist individuals in learning new ways of interacting, new ways of expressing their feelings, and new ways of avoiding arguments and fights. I think this is very important for a therapist to do. A Mars/Venus coach is going to focus more on assisting individuals in taking responsibility for how they're contributing to the problems in their relationship. This can simply be having someone to talk with to share what you're feeling. Sharing your feelings can sometimes bring about enormous insight into a situation, as well as helping you to feel better.

When you feel better you're able to respond in a more positive way. Our Mars/Venus coaches and counselors repeatedly receive stories and testimonials of couples who feel that their marriages were saved.

WRIGHT

I went on your Web site and I looked at some of the things that you're doing. I was really impressed. One thing that caught my eye was the Relationship Test. Does the Mars/Venus Relationship Test really work? What do you actually test?

GRAY

There are different areas of relationships which could be stronger or weaker. What a Relationship Test does is allows you to become more aware of what you're experiencing every day. Often people do not take the time to sit down and reflect on what's working here and what's not working. Our lives are often so busy that we're just going from the *next* thing to the *next* thing to the *next* thing, and we don't sit back and reflect on what's working and what's not working.

By doing the test and answering the questions, you're having to take that time and reflect upon what really is going on in your relationship. The irony in relationships is sometimes couples will be fighting in counseling or they'll be fighting at home, and they don't even know what they are fighting about. They don't even know how the argument started! Everything was fine, and suddenly one little thing happens and one or the other is flying off the handle and they just don't know what to do about it.

Often these flying off the handle experiences are like the water boiling and turning into steam. Long before it boiled, it simmered, and long before it simmered, the water was heating up. So there's a process that leads up to uncontrolled experiences in relationships. When you become more aware of what's not working in a relationship long before it's boiling, you have a chance to easily make adjustments in your behavior.

When taking a Relationship Test you're able to see many places where you have confusion or you don't understand what is going on. Talking to a relationship coach you can ask questions, particularly in the problem areas. You can talk about what's going on so that you can make sense of what's going on in your relationship.

Often when we don't know what's happening or don't know how to correctly interpret what's happening because it doesn't make sense to us, we then assume the worst rather than assume the best. And what our Mars/Venus coaches do is help to point out the *good* reasons why people do what they do, and strategies to help bring out the best in them.

WRIGHT

Every time I hear a talk show host ask a guest about the most important attribute a person needs to have when considering a relationship, the answer from males or females are always the same: "A good sense of humor." Is that really true?

GRAY

Well, that's what everybody says, but when difficulties arise in relationships the women then complain that the men are not serious. Or the man could complain that the woman isn't serious. Generally it's the number one thing on the list for women to say "a man's sense of humor," and when I hear that I want then to educate that woman to recognize that she's looking for the wrong thing. The last thing you need is for a man to entertain you. What you want is a man to provide security for you, to be attentive to you, and to understand you. In that place of safety, then you will naturally be expressive of your femininity, which is actually quite entertaining to men. It's the woman who brings joy to life, not the man. So when women are looking for men to bring joy to their life, women are often just feeling insecure as though they can't provide enough, and they are looking to a man to provide that role.

I have a wife and three daughters. When I travel with them it's amazing how entertaining they are! The nature of femininity is that women talk, they share, they look, they comment, they respond, they laugh a lot.

But what *is* good for a woman to look for in a man is not entertainment. She may think she's looking for that, but she'll find herself being disappointed again and again. What she should be looking for is a man's sense of humor in that he doesn't take things too seriously. That's extremely very attractive to women. Not taking himself too seriously means that he's not defensive about things and he doesn't claim to be perfect or expect or demand that she believes him to be perfect. That is a very healthy attitude and attribute in a man. If he can, in a sense, "lighten up," that constitutes a good sense of humor. That is what creates a sense of security for a woman.

If women want men to entertain them all the time, not only will they be disappointed, but it puts way too much pressure on men— they'll come on really strong and then women will lose interest because men are just not entertainers.

WRIGHT

Is it possible to be too cautious setting your criteria too high when choosing a life partner?

GRAY

I think the idea that you are getting at is very healthy to examine. I hesitate to say, "Lower your expectations and find your ideal partner." That sounds like you're not getting the best. What is going on today with both women and men is that they have very unrealistic expectations of what they require and what they want in a partner.

Life is often a gradual process of humbling them and helping them recognize what's realistic and what they are really looking for. We often look to the cover of a book rather than to the substance of the book, hence the old saying, "Don't judge a book by its cover." In our society we have become somewhat superficial in how we look for people. It takes a little maturing before we begin to realize who a person is is much more than how they look or how they react in certain situations or what they have or what they can do.

And yet those are all a part of the picture. I focus on helping couples change their expectations just in a sense of what a healthy relationship looks like. It doesn't mean that he's being romantic all the time, and it doesn't mean that she's happy all the time—two people really need to learn how to be happy on their own and then want to share that happiness with someone. That becomes the foundation of a relationship. When we are looking to someone to fill us up and make us happy, we will be disappointed later on. When we are somewhat happy and fulfilled in our own life, then we can find extra happiness through sharing our happiness with someone else. When that happens we are much less needy and our expectations tend to be much more realistic automatically.

WRIGHT

Almost everything you've said has hit me personally, especially the aspect of education. You see people who say, "This is my life-long partner" and they talk about all kinds of things, but it seems like you're talking about education.

GRAY

I feel that what's missing most in the world today when it comes to relationships is insight and education into understanding how to create healthy relationships. And why we need this education now more so than a hundred years ago, is that people didn't take courses even fifty years ago in improving their relationships. That's because there were hundreds of years of tradition where women had certain roles and men had certain roles. Men interacted in certain ways and women interacted in certain ways. As long as everybody acted according to those established patterns, everyone got along quite well.

Then the world changed. Now the world is different and yet no one has defined new roles and how men and women are supposed to interact and what works best for them. To a certain extent there is no "best"—it's a world of tremendous freedom and choice and we have to define those roles ourselves. But in defining those roles there's a certain amount of freedom to create those roles, and there's also a certain lack of freedom.

I might wish to walk through a wall, but I just can't—certain realities don't change. So in this world where we are "making up" relationships in a new way, there are certain realities that have not changed. There are certain ways that men interact and there are certain ways that women interact. There are certain needs that women have and certain needs that men have. The needs men and women have are different. By understanding those differences we can then realistically work with those differences to support each other better at this time of enormous change and enormous stress in our lives due to that change.

And what is interesting is that men and women react differently to stress, so most of the differences that cause frustration between men and women are simply differences that we don't understand, and those differences that we don't instinctively relate to are particularly how men and women react to stress.

For example, men will often become quiet or distant under stress, whereas women will want to open up and share and talk under stress. And then, taking another step that stresses even more, women will then *not* want to talk because they'll feel that they've tried to talk and no one listened so they begin to close up, and then they have no way to effectively cope with stress.

On the other hand, you've got men who tend to naturally pull away and mull things over to feel better under stress. If they are really under a huge amount of stress, these men don't even take the time to pull away. They go into a more talkative mode—they just want to complain and point out how they are victims in life. This becomes very distressing to women, and they go further and further away. That's what I would call "role reversal," which is another problem occurring today.

There are a lot of combinations in men and women and we just don't understand how to make sense of it, but by having a basic understanding of how men and women are different and how they cope with stress differently, we can then be better equipped to support our partners when they are under a lot of stress.

For example, if my wife doesn't want to talk about something, I can be helpful to her and be cooperative, which will lower her stress level. She will then begin to open up and talk, which will lower her stress level even more—as long as I make it safe for her to talk.

If a man is stressed and is complaining a lot and talking a lot, then what a woman can do is instead of trying to be a good listener, she can simply ask him to talk with his friends and give her some room to do what she wants to do. She should not encourage him to talk about all the things that are going wrong in his life. As she leaves him alone he will then be able to cope with stress better. He will then "come out of his cave" so to speak and be much more friendly to her. Women have to recognize that when men are in a bad mood or when they're stressed out, it's not up to her to do anything for him. Men have to come out of this primarily on their own, otherwise they tend to become weak.

So these are primary differences that a woman wouldn't think of. Another example is if a woman's feeling stressed out and he comes to her and asks her questions to help open her up and give her support, it will actually empower her. And doing so empowers the man. But when a woman is too much like a mother to a man, it will weaken him and she will resent it later as well, that's a no-win situation.

WRIGHT

I have known you for several years and I have always been impressed by your ability to stay on the leading edge of the subjects you are passionate about. Have you found any new information about relationship-building in the past few of years that might help people make fewer mistakes in the search for love and companionship?

GRAY

I think that in a sense I was touching on that a few minutes ago when I mentioned the subject of stress. Stress has become so high that not only do men and women have strong stress reactions, they actually go further into a role reversal where women are so stressed that they feel they have to do everything themselves and they become very much like a man. Men become so stressed that they begin to complain about their lives and feel like they're not responsible for their lives anymore. This is the wrong direction, and yet it's a natural stress reaction.

Today we are experiencing unprecedented amounts of stress with longer commuting hours and higher costs of living, balancing work and home life, increased information, and cell phones, talking, and being connected to work all the time. All this is putting a huge new burden on our lives and on our relationships.

What I have done is help to point this out, which can help couples enormously. Couples can recognize that there are ways to lower stress. If we are going to have more dramatic stress, there are more dramatic ways that couples can lower the stress levels for each other. Those ways happen to be women learning to ask for help—that's a real big issue—and men being more responsive to give help. That's not to say they have to do it every time she asks as if he's supposed to "jump to it." There are times when you are supposed to take your rest, so there needs to be understanding of that.

Women often resent having to ask for help, and that is something that has to change. She has to recognize that when you grow up in this world you have to learn how to ask for things, particularly in the business world. Likewise in relationships, if a woman wants her partner to change his natural mode of behavior she needs to *ask*. She shouldn't expect him to be like a woman who would just tend to think about everything that needs to be done until overwhelmed doing it—men typically don't fall into that role. So she needs to ask him, and when people ask others to do something, when they do it they need to let them know it's appreciated.

This is a new skill for a woman. While women sometimes resist this, once they practice it they realize, "Wow, this isn't that hard, and it works!" So that's one way to lower stress in life—if women are not feeling supported to *ask* for it in a way that will work rather than the way that they do ask, which often doesn't work. Practice "realistic expectations." Instead of complaining that "I can't walk through this wall" and "Why doesn't the wall open up for me?" you've got to find the door and learn how to open it!

The second important area to lower stress is in the realm of communication. Women want more sharing and more communication and men aren't providing that. There's a way that men can provide it—if women cooperate. As I said before, women should ask for what they want. Maybe a woman could say something like, "I'd like for you to listen to what is going on in my life." Let him know that he doesn't have to say anything. In fact, I encourage that in the beginning—he should say nothing, and let her talk for five or ten minutes. She then thanks him for listening, and then walks away. While this seems very unnatural, it is a super stress reducer once people start to experience it. It's quite amazing.

I didn't invent this—this is what has been going on for years in the therapy office. Women come in and they talk about what's going on in their lives and they feel better. The therapist doesn't say much at all. And the better the therapist, the less the therapist says and the more questions the therapist asks.

So the secret here is learning how to talk about what is bothering you without expecting a solution or without expecting your partner to "fix" you or fix the situation in some way. So she can set up that conversation and she will feel better; he'll feel better too because he helped her. And men like helping their wives.

The third area is romance. Again, in this area couples stopped having romance, and romance is actually one of the most strong and powerful stress reducers. It's just that when we're under stress the last thing we think about is romance, both for her and for him. Yet the difference is women will often think about how much they miss it. They're not necessarily feeling romantic, but they often complain that "he's not romantic," implying that she wants him to be romantic so she can feel good again. I understand that and I respect that. And I have a solution for that, but it's not waiting for him—you have to ask! Now, what woman would ever think to ask for romance? Well *you* can. It's a very simple thing.

To solve this problem women have to learn how to ask, and men have to learn how to respond. Women then have to learn how to appreciate that, and the solutions do occur. Women can't expect a man to be a mind-reader. He doesn't know what's going on inside her head and in her heart. Asking for romance is something so foreign that women need a few examples of it and then they can get the hang of it.

For example, she shouldn't say, "You're not romantic, we don't experience romance anymore, we never go out anymore, we're not having fun anymore." Those are just negative complaints. Instead she needs to focus more on what's positive. For example, "Hey, this particular band is playing in town this weekend. Would you get tickets for the concert?" The woman asks the man—that's it. It's a very simple thing. The woman could say, "Oh, we haven't gone out this week, would you get tickets for this or that?" or simply, "Would you pick a movie and we'll go see the movies?" or "Would you make reservations and let's go out to eat?" The man could say, "Where would you like to go?" The woman could say, "Whatever you want to pick."

Women can start defining romance as letting him decide where to go, her asking for it, him deciding, and her having a good time just being with him! And gradually that moves into more discretion about what you're going to do and so forth. This process will begin to restore the woman's confidence in the man. All the woman needs to do is to just ask and let him know that whatever he does will be fine.

Just as it was in the beginning when he was so romantic, men often become unromantic because they try, but after a while women start picking out what he did wrong. And men will think, "Well, she's so picky I'll just let her decide." And that's the end of romance because part of what reduces stress for women is that she does not have to decide. And when a woman comes back to the realization that having the man make some decisions and she doesn't have to decide will actually lower her stress enormously. It also lowers a man's stress enormously when he knows that whatever he decides she's going to like, as opposed to feeling that he's going to put his best out there and she's going to step all over it by pointing out what he did wrong. She doesn't mean to do that, but that's the net effect.

So these are extra additions, extra awarenesses, and insights that can help couples to cope with the extra stress they're experiencing in their lives today.

WRIGHT

If you had to "bottom line" the reasons for the success of your Mars and Venus books, products, ideas, and counseling help, what would the main reason be?

GRAY

I think that because the world has changed, people are eager and hungry to have a new way of understanding the world in a positive light. When we don't understand what is going on around us, we just assume something's wrong. By learning the new insights regarding how men and women are different, and how we look at the world differently in a *positive* way, they are released from having to blame their partners or blame themselves. They are motivated to find creative solutions that make their relationships better. So in one aspect, what I do is give people permission to make mistakes, and give them insight to solve the problems.

WRIGHT

An interesting conversation! I always learn so much when I talk with you. It's just incredible. I really do appreciate this time that you've spent with me today, and I really think the readers are going to get a lot out of it.

GRAY

Well thank you so much. It's a pleasure.

DR. JOHN GRAY is the author of fifteen books, including *Men Are from Mars, Women Are from Venus* (Harper Collins 1992), a number one best-selling relationship book. Over thirty million Mars and Venus books have been sold in over forty languages throughout the world.

Dr. John Gray, a certified family therapist, is the premier Better Life relationship coach on AOL. In 2001, he received the Smart Marriages Impact Award. John Gray received his degree in 1982 from Columbia Pacific University. He has authored fourteen other best-selling books. His book, *The Mars & Venus Diet & Exercise Solution* (St. Martin's Press 2003), reveals why diet, exercise, and communication skills combine to effect the production of healthy brain chemicals and how the need for those chemicals differ between men and women.

An internationally recognized expert in the fields of communication and relationships, Dr. Gray's unique focus is assisting men and women in understanding, respecting, and appreciating their differences. For decades, he has conducted public and private seminars for thousands of participants. In his highly acclaimed books, audiotapes, and videotapes, as well as in his seminars, Dr. Gray entertains and inspires audiences with his practical insights and easy to use communication techniques that can be immediately applied to enrich relationships and quality of life.

Dr. Gray is a popular speaker on the national and international lecture circuit and often appears on television and radio programs to discuss his work. He has made guest appearances on such shows as *Oprah, Good Morning America, The Today Show, The CBS Morning Show, Live with Regis, The View, Politically Incorrect, Larry King Live, The Roseanne Show, CNN and Company,* and many others. He has been profiled in *USA Today, Newsweek, TIME Magazine, TV Guide, People, Forbes,* and numerous other major publications across the United States.

Dr. Gray's nationally syndicated column reaches millions of readers in many newspapers, including *The Atlanta Journal Constitution, New York Daily News, New York Newsday, The Denver Post,* and the *San Antonio Express-News.* Internationally, the columns appear in publications in England, Canada, Mexico, Korea, Latin America, and the South Pacific.

Dr. Gray lives with his wife and three children in Northern California.

John Gray
www.askmarsvenus.com

CHAPTER FOUR

Open-Minded Relationships

By Ann Van Eron PhD

DAVID WRIGHT (WRIGHT)

Today we're talking to Ann Van Eron PhD. Dr. Van Eron is the Principal of Potentials, a global coaching and organization development consulting firm with more than twenty-five years' experience coaching leaders and teams all over the world to fully develop their capabilities. She specializes in creating environments where people have open-minded and productive conversations for unparalleled results in any situation, anywhere. She has developed a proven process to understand and work effectively with people with different perspectives, which includes everyone. Her clients include Fortune 100 companies, government and non-government organizations, health care, consulting, education, and privately held organizations.

Ann is a Master Certified Coach and teaches coaching. She provides leadership development and facilitates programs for managers on how to be effective in coaching their teams. She supports organizations in creating cultures of respect and open communication that facilitate achieving goals. Ann is an executive coach and leadership development expert.

Ann, welcome to *Words of Wisdom.*

DR. ANN VAN ERON (VAN ERON)

Thank you.

WRIGHT

Will you share with us a bit about the work you do regarding relationships?

VAN ERON

Sure, thanks for having me.

After seriously studying and being a practitioner in the fields of leadership, executive coaching, team building, organization development, and managing change for more than two decades, I am convinced that a critical factor for success is the ability to have open-minded conversations and to create positive relationships. Successful leaders know that respectful and trusting relationships are needed both in business and in the rest of life. As a coach and organization development consultant, I support people in forming relationships and having two-way dialogue to create agreements and results.

The effective leaders I coach are self-aware, and understand what is important to others in reaching agreements. Often those who are not effective are less aware about how they come across to others, as well as how to forge successful relationships.

For example, when I work with a team or coach a leader I interview those who work with him or her. In a recent situation, colleagues reported that a manager was cold and uncaring. People did not like working with her and her team was not producing high-level results. This leader was perceived to favor some people over others and to not listen effectively. The tension in the team was palpable and some key members resigned. The manager's reputation was less than positive and she was not in line to be promoted to the next level.

Unfortunately, the manager did not recognize the impact of her behavior, specifically her failure to develop positive relationships. She believed she did not have the time to focus on relationships since she had "real" work to do. Nowadays, many managers are required to manage teams and to also do the tactical or technical work. There is a pressing need to pay attention both to results *and* relationships.

After this leader received feedback and coaching, she began to change her behavior and pay more attention to relationships. She focused on listening more and learning more about her colleagues and their interests and needs. Within a short while, she was able to forge more satisfying relationships. She received more positive ratings and she was ultimately promoted. Most importantly, she and her staff began to enjoy working together and achieved greater results.

Poor or negative relationships take a lot of energy that could be devoted to achieving results. More than fifty years of research consistently shows that a person's relationship with his or her manager is critical. It is true that people join companies but they leave managers.

I see the same challenges in teams. I recently worked with a team whose leader was new to the organization. The teammates had known each other for many years and had fixed views of one another. They typically spoke negatively about each other and the department was perceived negatively by others. It was not until (through intervention) the team members got to know one another as individuals and began to establish more positive working relationships that the perception of the department shifted— internally and externally. They were able to find synergies that allowed them to achieve organization goals more easily and to realize greater results together.

When relationships are working, people have more energy to be creative and are ultimately more satisfied. It is human nature to want to be connected with others.

WRIGHT

Growing up in a business environment during the past five or six decades, I didn't hear a lot about relationships until recently. I know how hard change is, but do you see organizations paying more attention to relationships?

VAN ERON

That's a great question. You are right. Not long ago, most companies focused primarily on results. If a person got his or her numbers, there was not much focus on how the individual interacted. Now, organizations are realizing the importance of relationships for business success. There is too much wasted energy when people have poor relationships or create a negative environment. Strong performers, as well as clients, look for other alternatives when they sense that people and relationships are not a priority.

In our turbulent and global world, it is a given that people need to be creative and innovative, focusing their energy on the work and not on how they are being disrespected or mistreated by coworkers and others. Engagement is particularly important and challenging in our diverse workforces where there are four generations with different styles and interests working side by side.

When people feel valued and supported within the context of positive relationships with their manager and colleagues, they have more energy and more capacity to be creative and solve challenging business issues together.

Research shows that engagement and productivity are strongly correlated. Productivity and profitability increase by at least 50 percent when engagement is high. Retention of high performers is related to positive relationships where people bring more discretionary effort to the workplace. Sadly, in some organizations engagement is quite low. A lot of people do not know how to build and maintain effective relationships. We see this dynamic in families with the high rate of divorce as well.

A lot of my work is focused on supporting people who are challenged with building positive relationships within their workplace. This has become critical at all levels, but particularly for top leadership who are directly responsible for tangible results. They must set the tone and be explicit with expectations around behaviors that support engagement and collective ownership for what goes on in their organizations.

WRIGHT

It used to be that conversations about relationships were more about home and the focus at work was work, so is this divide not as important anymore?

VAN ERON

That's right. Let me offer you another example that illustrates how family life and work life cannot be separated. I coached someone in a major consulting firm who was frustrated because he was not being promoted to the partner level. He worked on large technical projects and he knew his area of expertise. However, he had trouble assembling teams for various projects. People did not like working with him. His colleagues excluded him from meetings and seemed to withhold important information.

He was also frustrated with his home life. His fiancé was reluctant to set a wedding date. He was working many long hours and did not experience fulfillment. In fact, his tenure with the prestigious firm was in jeopardy.

I talked with people who worked for him and with him. Each reported that he did not listen to them and he did not seem to care about their concerns. He had little patience for their challenges. Some reported that he devoted little time to understanding them and only demanded information. In this kind of environment, people do not feel valued as individuals and certainly do not feel innovative. They spend energy complaining and being frustrated.

After some coaching, this manager realized that he did not know how to be authentic in forming relationships at a very basic level. He tended to think of others as means to his end goals. He thought focusing on the people would slow down his productivity. This mind-set and patterned behavior was deeply ingrained.

What he gradually began to recognize was that in order to be effective he had to focus both on the task at hand and on building and maintaining relationships. He actually had to be willing to learn new patterns of behavior. As a manager moves from an analytical role to a more senior leader, forming relationships becomes even more crucial.

Research has shown that humans have mirror neurons that allow us to sense what others are feeling. A key to satisfying relationships is checking in with what others are experiencing/feeling and demonstrating understanding. This can be done by identifying how the other person is likely to feel or nodding and showing understanding through body language and offering support. When we give empathy, which is relating to people's emotions, they feel heard, recognized, connected, and acknowledged; they can relax and calm down. They then have more ability to see other perspectives and solutions.

My client took these lessons to heart and started practicing listening with his fiancée. To his surprise, she became more open and caring in return when he seemed interested in her and her challenges. As he gave her empathy, she became less angry and more interested in what he was experiencing. He then began focusing on paying attention to those around him at work—both colleagues and clients. He started listening and giving empathy to others. He began to pay attention to what he was noticing and he became more self-aware. He realized that he had just not paid attention to relationships.

Within a short time, he had turned around his situation at work and in his personal life. He got married and the skills supported him later with his children. He became a partner and an advocate for relationships. He became seen as a leader. Clients wanted to work with him and he had no problem forming teams for projects. He became skilled at listening, learning what is important to people, giving empathy and finding common ground. He became able to suspend his immediate judgment about others and was able to create agreements with others. They soon learned to trust him and reported that he was respectful.

Building successful relationships involves being self-aware and managing our reactions. We also need to be aware of others and learn how to create a shared understanding and agreement. Clearly we all have different backgrounds and see things differently. Understanding and accepting this reality helps us to be open to other perspectives.

It takes a number of actions and practice to build relationships; but most importantly, we need to be open and to connect with others. We need to have intention—the intention to be authentic and to honor our word. Then we need to listen, empathize, and create agreements and understanding with others. It is important to follow up on our commitments and to pay attention to the relationship as well as the outcomes.

WRIGHT

So what is it about connection that is all that important?

VAN ERON

Feeling connected and understood by others is a basic human need. It is natural to want to experience being understood and belonging to a group. When we feel misunderstood or on the outside, a lot of energy is expended trying to reclaim that sense of belonging.

We have all had the experience of feeling lighter and being more open to ideas and possibilities when we join people who are positive and who make us feel included and valued. We have also had the opposite experience when we enter a room and can feel the tension. Our bodies become constricted. We are typically focused inward and not able to access our creative energy.

The bottom line is that emotions are contagious. When we feel judged we are more closed and more self-protective, and we feel less connected. Neuroscience research is now supporting the idea that our brains are continually changing and there is a plasticity where we are influenced and changed by our relationships. When functional MRIs examine the brain of one person as they interact with another, it is clear that a neural pathway forms between the two brains. When we are connected with others, we influence each other. When we feel connected and are in a positive relationship, we are more open to possibilities, new ways of doing things, and more innovation. We are shifted and change as a result of our interactions.

Our emotions in relationships are more important than we once thought. When we feel judged or are in judgment, we tend to hold our breath, are less connected, and literally have less access to other parts of our brain and the ability to consider possibilities. Our world is smaller.

WRIGHT

When you were talking about entering a room and being lighter, it reminded me of something. There was a television show, *Cheers,* that made millions of dollars and was one of the most popular shows when it aired. The theme song for the show was titled "Where Everybody Knows Your Name." That song was based on basically what you just said.

VAN ERON

You're right. Norm, the character who was the bar's most frequent patron, was open to people and people responded by being open to him. They felt better just being in his presence and they appreciated when he listened to them and respected them.

Being present to others supports connection and is quite compelling. So often, we sense that people are not fully with us because they are distracted.

WRIGHT

So is it really about being respectful?

VAN ERON

A key is assuming positive intent with others. We are wired to protect ourselves and tend to jump to negative conclusions about others' intentions. When we can catch ourselves and be curious, we can be more respectful, identifying what others need and letting them know we are interested in understanding what is important to them.

Respect is a critical ingredient for successful relationships. The suffix, "spect" means to see and the prefix "re" means again. To show respect for others, we need to catch ourselves when we move to judgment and literally "see them again." We need to catch our natural disposition to see a person as a stereotype and shift to seeing the person as a unique individual.

We all want to be respected and valued for who we are. The challenge with respect is that we each have a different definition of what respect is. We each have different backgrounds and experiences that influence our perspective of what is respectful behavior.

I have been talking about respect with groups all over the world. It is the small things that seem to bother people the most. For example, I worked with a team where people did not feel respected. When I tried to identify what were perceived as disrespectful behaviors, the examples that were given ranged from people not saying hello to being late, talking too loudly, cooking odorous food in the microwave, and not knocking before entering someone's office.

If you grew up in a military family where being on time meant being exactly on time or earlier, you are more likely to be irritated when others come a few minutes after the designated time. If you grew up in a culture where time is more flexible, you don't see an issue with arriving a few minutes after the hour. Some expect to be called by their formal name and others are more comfortable using first names. The challenge is that people often assume that others should know what respectful behavior is and are offended when they feel that people do not honor their notion of respect. Often people don't even tell others that they feel disrespected, since the offensive behavior is so obvious to them that they can't even imagine someone else not recognizing it.

In one workplace situation a team member did not greet her colleagues, since she herself preferred not to be interrupted when people came into work at different times. She failed to share her intention. Her teammates considered her lack of greeting to be rude and talked with one another about this lack of respect. Soon cliques were formed and tension mounted. Some were positive about this woman and others were not. Colleagues picked up the tension and it spread across the department where small infractions were exaggerated and the atmosphere became negative.

After I interviewed members and brought them together, I supported them in understanding their different perspectives. We gave team members the opportunity to share with each other their view of respectful behavior and we developed a set of group norms. An important norm was to assume that each member had positive intent, and that it was important to talk about concerns rather than let them fester.

When I followed up with the team later, I could sense an entirely different atmosphere. People felt more respected and relationships were more positive. The more engaging environment supported greater results for the team. They produced more per month after our team sessions than they had the previous year. In addition, the team members reported more enjoyment because they worked in a more positive team environment where trust was increasing.

With the skills of talking about issues that concern us, we are able to create trusting relationships that support achieving greater results and make life more enjoyable.

I believe there is value in all teams and families taking time out to reflect on what they find to be respectful behavior and what each person needs, and then to follow-up to see how people are following through. I have facilitated such meetings with teams all over the world and they continually report value from the exercise.

It is often the small things that trip us up. For example, we may assume everyone knows who should be copied on an e-mail or how a person likes to receive information. It is helpful when people talk about when and how to enter another person's office. Some people say they have an open door, yet they become upset when interrupted. Two people next to each other can have different expectations about how to be interrupted when they have a meeting scheduled.

WRIGHT

I was having a conversation with myself as you were talking, asking how I would want to be spoken to. If someone walked by me and didn't say hello I would almost think they don't acknowledge that I'm here on Earth.

VAN ERON

Exactly. It feels obvious to you that your colleague should say "good morning." However, perhaps a person grew up in a family where people did not speak to each other until after their parents had their coffee, after 10:00 AM. I know that some of my neighbors did not teach their children to say good morning to people in my building. They thought it took too much time on their way to school. And it *did* take time. Sometimes my husband would take my daughter to the car using the freight elevator to avoid the greeting ritual with neighbors.

So people do have different views and it's important in organizations to make sure there is a collective understanding of what respect is for individuals and for the team. It is useful to have open-minded conversations with each other. We all have a tendency for confirmation bias where we assume the negative. Fundamental attribution error is where we assume negative intentions by others.

It is valuable to notice our assumptions and to check them out rather than believing we know the facts. I always tell myself, "I don't know what I don't know." Then I try to inquire and learn more. Ironically, if we do the same thing that bothers us, we are likely to make a positive attribution for our behavior. We are interesting human beings. We are wired to protect ourselves. Quite frankly, it is amazing we get things done with each other, given our different backgrounds and different ways of seeing the world.

WRIGHT

So if you are out and about in the corporate world teaching respect, how do you help people to be more respectful?

VAN ERON

I teach people how to have conversations after we acknowledge that we are all conditioned by our background experiences and are each seeing and experiencing the world and our situations differently. It is quite useful to adopt this perspective and to recognize that we all have quirks given our past experiences and dispositions.

I work with people to notice when they are making judgments and to learn how to shift into being more open-minded. This is challenging since we each experience the sensation of our being right and others being wrong. By noticing our physiological signal of being right, we can catch ourselves and shift to a place of being open and curious. With practice, this becomes easier.

In addition to supporting people in having conversations about what is important to them and developing group norms, it is useful for people to give and receive empathy about what is important. Empathy, as we noted earlier, involves recognizing another person's emotions and trying to understand the person's perspective.

Often people don't want to give empathy because they believe it means they are acknowledging that the other person is right and they are thus wrong. However, empathy is validating how a person is feeling—not that we fully agree. When we give empathy, the other person feels understood and generally becomes more open to hearing and understanding our perspective.

WRIGHT

Now I can give you an example. I can have an automobile accident and not really worry about it because I know I've got to fill out the insurance forms and it doesn't bother me. But if someone does not return my screwdriver, it really bothers me. I don't feel respected and it hurts my relationship with my neighbor.

VAN ERON

Yes. You have a standard or expectation that when someone borrows your screwdriver, he or she should return it immediately after using it. Yet the person borrowing it could have a different background and believe you will ask for it when you need it again or the person could assume that you have many of them and will not miss it. He or she may not be bothered if someone takes a while to return an item.

Yet, it seems obvious to you that the respectful thing to do is to immediately return your screwdriver. It may seem so obvious to you that you may not discuss it with your neighbor and instead withdraw or refrain from loaning additional items. Your friend my sense your judgment or withdrawal and not be aware of the concern. He may withdraw in return and the friendship can be impaired. It could be useful to talk with your neighbor. I support people in workplaces to have these open-minded conversations.

WRIGHT

You mentioned the divorce rate being high. Do you see respect as a large ingredient in that problem?

VAN ERON

Absolutely. When we live together, there are many things that can irritate us. We believe we are right and the other person is wrong. For example, we may know that our spouse should put the dishes directly in the dishwasher or wash them immediately. However, he or she may believe it is more efficient to wait until there is a pile to wash. Some of us have the disposition to fight in these cases and others withdraw. If we hold on to our judgment, the other person senses the disapproval and interprets it as a lack of respect or appreciation for him or her and his or her point of view.

We need to be self-aware and notice how unique we each are and be curious and open to differences. With open-minded conversations, we can show our understanding for different perspectives, share our view, and work out agreements that will work for everyone.

When my team or I offer workshops in organizations, we encourage people to try the processes immediately with their family members. People share their successes with delight. Sometimes people report they have the first real conversation with their family members. It is heartwarming to hear about successful conversations with adult children, too. Some report working out long-time disagreements. We can benefit from creating positive relationships in all areas of our life.

WRIGHT

You've mentioned open-minded conversations. What is that all about?

VAN ERON

Open-minded conversations is how I describe the process of being open to other perspectives and managing our reactions. When we are judging others and believe we are right and they are wrong, we typically constrict our breath and then literally have less access to other possible interpretations of another's behavior. When we are self-aware and can catch ourselves, we can learn to shift into a more open-minded and curious state. This supports others in staying open-minded as well. When common ground is found, and each party shares what is most important, it is easier to identify options and solutions that work best for all involved. It is, in fact, what we do naturally when we are not threatened or irritated with others. I call this process OASIS Moves®. The goal is to create the environment of an *oasis, a respite, or sacred space where agreements can be made without judgment and where individuals feel visible, safe, and acknowledged.* OASIS is an acronym to support recall of the basic steps of the process.

While we're at it, it is also helpful to manage our self-judgment since most of us can be pretty hard on ourselves. It is useful to check in to see whether or not we are experiencing a personal *oasis.* We are fallible human beings and are vulnerable. I think people are generally doing the best they can.

When we are in a positive relationship and we are open, we naturally communicate effectively. We are attentive and curious about what people are thinking. We are naturally empathetic and we can easily find solutions. It's in those more difficult relationships, where we are in judgment in the moment that it is hard to have a productive conversation or relationship. The more we make it our intention to have an open-minded conversation and a positive relationship, the easier it is. I have been testing and teaching OASIS all over the world for more than fifteen years. People report that shifting to an open and curious stance and being empathetic makes a big difference in enhancing environments and relationships.

WRIGHT

Do you think people are doing the best they can or do you think they're doing the best they know?

VAN ERON

That's a great point. While people may have good intentions, in the moment of judgment we can easily lose our capacity to establish and maintain effective relationships. Without reflection, most of us do what we've learned or what we have been conditioned to do. If you learned to go silent when there is a conflict or disagreement, this will be your default unless you are self-aware and work to shift old habits. Approximately 95 percent of our actions are habitual patterns. However, we can learn new ways of communicating and being. You could say, *people are doing the best they know how at that moment.* A critical factor of success is becoming self-aware and observing our emotions and thoughts and consciously choosing our actions.

A friend shared with me his reaction to an inflammatory question in a job interview. The interviewee reacted by making a negative remark about the interviewer's character. Needless to say, he is unlikely to be called back for a second interview. Of course, the interviewee said he did not mind; however, he would have had more choice if he had been able to notice his internal reaction and manage himself to respond in a nonaggressive manner and to be more open and curious.

It is useful to have the intention to be open-minded and to realize that humans are emotional and that if we can manage ourselves, we can stay open and learn more about what the other person is seeing or saying. Often we misinterpret others based on our own conditioning and experiences. Perhaps the interviewee misinterpreted the interviewer's question and he or she did not intend for it to be inflammatory. Perhaps it was a test to learn more about the applicant. I have seen many conflicts that were misinterpretations of what was actually said. Similarly, I've witnessed numerous conflicts due to misreading e-mails or misinterpreting statements. Once trust is eroded, actions lead to further mistrust. Often this downward spiral happens without a direct conversation. With open-minded conversations the spiral can be reversed with trust increasing and the relationships getting stronger.

WRIGHT

These open-minded conversations sound very important. Will you share some examples of tangible results?

VAN ERON

Sure. In a Fortune 500 firm there were low engagement scores and people felt that it was an environment where it was "every person for himself or herself." People were fighting each other and less focused on achieving results together. High performers were leaving the organization. After learning how to use OASIS and have an open-minded conversation, people started to work more effectively together. When members of the management team started to have open-minded productive conversations with each other, things began to change quickly. The leaders began to trust each other and were able to implement changes that resulted in dramatic savings and efficiency. They had invested in a lot of change initiatives. However, it was only when they were able to be honest and talk about what they really wanted and needed from each other that they were able to implement real change with greater results. The fighting at the top that had extended throughout the organization was reduced and a more positive environment spread throughout the organization.

The leaders practiced having open-minded conversations with each other and became confident in giving and receiving feedback.

After the leadership team saw the impact of open-minded conversations with each other, they supported the rest of the organization in learning the process and having two-way dialogue. Engagement scores soared and company results did, too. Fewer high performers left the organization. Conflict was addressed much more directly and was resolved effectively.

In another organization, the leaders across the organization were able to have open-minded conversations and take an enterprise-wide perspective rather than focusing on their silos. They were able to collectively agree to change the way they worked and they reduced the time required for some critical processes. They had been working for years to become more efficient and with the skill of talking openly, they were able to skip many steps and agree to make some changes that dramatically created more efficiency by speeding up critical processes. Some of the leaders reported that it was the first time they had truly spoken and listened to each other in more than a decade. Again, with the open-minded conversations, trust grew. The goodwill spread throughout the organization.

In a healthcare organization, after people learned how to have open-minded conversations, staff reported experiencing a more inclusive environment and patient satisfaction scores greatly improved—something that was critical for a heath care organization with a lot of competition.

In many organizations, I conduct "agreement meetings" where I work with different groups that seem to be in conflict and help them to understand each other's perspective and to develop agreements on how they will work together. These meetings have made a big difference in creating a more positive atmosphere in organizations. When people receive empathy and feel understood by others and relationships are formed, results are consistently much more easily attained.

Managers indicate that with open-minded conversations they are able to give feedback to staff and colleagues. Many managers report understanding staff and their needs and teams working more cohesively together. It is great to see the impact of assuming positive intent, suspending judgment, listening, and empathizing. When people understand each other and find common ground, they are easily able to generate solutions and create agreements.

WRIGHT

I can't help but think about the examples you gave us of the training you did and telling people to try this with their children. It sounds like they actually did what you asked them to do, and it probably changed the rest of their lives and their relationships. I can't think of a more noble thing than to change a relationship between a parent and an adult child.

VAN ERON

I always tell people to practice at home. They can't believe the impact on children of all ages. We all need understanding and empathy. When we feel cared for, we are healthier and more productive. People report using the process years after attending a workshop and the significant difference it makes in the quality of their lives.

We're all so busy nowadays. We think we don't have time to connect with others. But it is less about time. It is being attentive, present, and open-minded with our children and colleagues that make a difference.

WRIGHT

I'm energized just listening to the excitement in your voice about your work.

VAN ERON

Thank you, I do love it and I think it's really important for all of us to have these kinds of relationships.

WRIGHT

So what is your vision about what is possible?

VAN ERON

I worked in an organization that had significant polarization between the field and the headquarters and between management and staff and between business divisions. The tension took a lot of energy and exacted a high cost for all. I worked with a team of staff and the management team to have dialogue about how they each saw things in their organization. In a short while a relationship was formed between the taskforce and the management team and they worked to empathize with, connect, and understand one another. After learning how to assume positive intent and have open-minded conversations, people began to see themselves as one organization and began working together. They were able to find common ground and achieve goals together. I believe that through the OASIS process, people can achieve all kinds of goals to make organizations and communities work for all. I am committed to supporting people in learning these skills and having these open-minded conversations.

My wish is that we could make it a norm in our society that we assume positive intent rather than demonize or polarize. Ideally we would all understand that we each have different backgrounds and see the world differently. With effective communication skills, we can find common ground and create solutions together that will make the world better for all.

WRIGHT

What an interesting conversation. It's always a pleasure talking with you.

VAN ERON

Thank you so much, I appreciate you. I know you understand the concepts I've talked about here.

WRIGHT

Today I've been talking with Ann Van Eron, PhD, about open-minded relationships. Ann is the Principal of Potentials, a global coaching and organization development consulting firm. She focuses on creating environments where people have open-minded and productive conversations for unparalleled results.

Ann, thank you so much for being with us today on *Words of Wisdom*.

Ann Van Eron, PhD, MCC, is principal of Potentials, a global coaching and organization development consulting firm. She has more than twenty-five years' experience coaching leaders and teams all over the world for a wide range of organizations. Ann provides executive coaching, team building, and leadership development. She teaches managers how to coach and supports organizations in creating open-minded cultures that facilitate achieving goals and possibilities. Ann is the creator of OASIS® to support open-minded conversations for building relationships and realizing potential at work and in life.

Ann M. Van Eron, PhD

Potentials
195 North Harbor Drive, Suite 3707
Chicago, IL 60601
312-856-1155
Avaneron@Potentials.com
www.Potentials.com

CHAPTER FIVE

Living Your Dream

By Jennifer Powell

DAVID WRIGHT (WRIGHT)

Today I'm talking with Jennifer Powell. Jennifer has dedicated her twenty-five-year career to helping organizations achieve their goals through the growth and development of leaders, individual contributors, and work teams across entire organizations. Jennifer has more than ten years of coaching leaders at all levels of experience from CEOs to frontline supervisors. In 2003 she expanded her scope to include personal life transition coaching. In 2005 she launched Reflections, an independent coaching business focusing on leadership coaching and personal life transitions. In 2006 she began living her dream—working with dolphins at Dolphin Research Center in Grassy Key, Florida, where she currently serves as Senior Education Instructor. Jennifer is an active volunteer in her community. She is an avid reader and an accomplished ballroom dancer.

Jennifer welcome to *Words of Wisdom.*

JENNIFER POWELL (POWELL)

Thank you David; it's good to be here.

WRIGHT

So what does it feel like to be living your dream?

POWELL

It's that feeling of always enjoying getting up to go to work. I have worked at Dolphin Research Center now for a little more than six years and I don't think I've had a day yet where I said, "Oh, I wish I didn't have to go to work today." I've been lucky throughout most of my career to have always enjoyed the work I was doing, but I didn't enjoy any of them this much. I get to be outside a lot during the day; I can go out and see dolphins any time I want. If I'm working on an office project that doesn't seem to be going well, I can go out and watch the dolphins for a little while and shake things off. It doesn't seem to matter how hot and sticky it gets outdoors, I still enjoy the work.

I started out as a volunteer and, as a volunteer of course, you're not paid. We had to do fun things like separate the regular trash from the recycling and help to feed our tropical birds and clean their cages and various other duties. My friends always used to say, "You do that for nothing—you separate recycling and you're not getting paid?" Even before getting paid, it was enjoyable to be there.

WRIGHT

So how often do you hear people talk about their dream vacation, their dream job, their dream house, or what they will do if they win the lottery? How often do you hear them say that they are living their dream?

POWELL

Well, I don't know about you but I don't hear it very often. I don't hear them say they're living their dream very often. I regularly hear people say, "When I win the lottery, the Powerball jackpot, and so on." I hear people say something like this all the time, "Someday I'm going to take my dream vacation to Hawaii" or to the volcanoes or the mountains somewhere." They might say, "I'm going to build my dream home someday" or "I'm going to go across country on vacation" or "I'm going to scuba dive in the Great Barrier Reef." It goes on and on and on, but it's always in the future tense. I rarely actually talk to people who are saying, "I'm living my dream right now."

WRIGHT

So what happens to those dreams and why do so few people actually reach them?

POWELL

In my opinion, life happens, the dreams get lost, they forget about them, parents and teachers and loved ones can squelch them and criticize them. If you're referred to as a dreamer, that's not necessarily a flattering comment in our society. Others will tell you, "You've got your head in the clouds; you'll never make a living doing that." So that's what happens to dreams—people just lose sight of them when life happens and others discourage them so that they just forget about them. In other cases, I think people just don't know how to get there.

WRIGHT

Why are you so sure that you can help others live their dreams?

POWELL

Because I'm doing it—I'm living my dream right now. I can't tell you how many times people have said to me, "You're the first person I've ever met who's actually living her dream."

I'm a very practical person, so the concept of living a dream didn't come to me until much later in my life. I was almost forty and obviously my dream is living and working with dolphins. My actual introduction to dolphins, other than on television, was in my late forties. There are lots of self-help books and motivational speakers and they're all offering advice on how to be successful, how to make more money, work fewer hours, how to work from home, and how to be a free person. There is a lot of advice out there, but I still think there are many people who are giving up and not making their dreams happen.

I grew up in a middle class working family and finding a dream wasn't even a part of my equation when I was a kid, there was nobody really encouraging me to do that sort of thing, so I really had to find that path on my own. That's why I believe I can help others do it because I made it happen for me.

WRIGHT

When did you come to the realization that vacations are meant to make your dreams come true?

POWELL

It was the first time I came to Dolphin Research Center. In 1989 I came to a program called DolphinLab, which is a week-long program of study and interactions with the dolphins. I happened to be a member of the Baltimore Aquarium at the time and I saw it in their newsletter. It involved getting in the water with dolphins and all these other cool activities; I was convinced I had to do it. I signed up and came to the Florida Keys. That was a true turning point for me.

Prior to that, I'd done some traveling. I had been to the Bahamas and to Hawaii on vacation. I traveled a lot for my work in the past and had gone as far as India and Singapore for business. I took advantage of those opportunities and did a little sightseeing while I was at each location but vacations for me up until that point were just a chance to get away, as so many others who say, "I can't wait to get out of here for a week or two." That trip changed everything for me and it was when I decided that vacations are to make your dreams come true.

WRIGHT

People say they ought to follow their passion to make their dreams come true. How do they discover what they're passionate about?

POWELL

The first thing to do is connect with your passion, and I'm not talking about romance or intimacy or sex. I don't have anything against any of those things but that's not the kind of passion I'm talking about here. You need to find out what makes your heart sing, you need to be aware of when you start humming to yourself in the shower, singing a song as you're walking down the street, or smiling when you don't really even realize what you're smiling about. You have to find what makes the smile reach your eyes. I know a lot of people who will give you a big smile but it stops right at their mouth and it doesn't go all the way to their eyes. You don't see that sparkle in their eyes. That's what I'm talking about—when you find something that makes your heart sing and you feel an ache when that thing is missing in your life.

There is an author by the name of Mihaly Csikszentmihalyi who wrote a book called *Finding Flow* and in the book he describes that feeling. Other people refer to it as a calling; it might be that, but it's not necessarily a calling. Sometimes a calling is overwhelming and it's too all-encompassing for some, but whatever the passion is, it's important to discover it for yourself and know how you feel when it's happening. You've got to get in touch with your feelings and know that you feel differently when you're doing this. You lose track of time, you get lost in something, and you don't even realize that you've been working on it for hours. That's the kind of feeling that helps you connect with your passion.

WRIGHT

So what does it mean to connect with your passion?

POWELL

Passions are feelings and it's a big step to recognize the feelings but you can't stop there. You have to be tuned into what you're doing at that moment. Is it when you're on a boat or with your family or in your garden or on vacation? You can be anywhere, but the beauty of connecting with your passion is that there aren't any rules and there aren't any wrong answers. It's different for everybody and nobody can tell you that your passion is right or wrong. Some people try to tell us how to feel. They say, "Oh you shouldn't feel bad about that" or "You should feel good about this." The truth is, no one can tell anybody how to feel, any more than you can tell someone else what's right to be passionate about. The most important part is turning it into action.

WRIGHT

What's the active manifestation of one's passion?

POWELL

In the beginning it might just be an image in your head or a picture on your refrigerator and that's okay as a beginning because it will take shape as you keep working on it. You have to keep thinking about it. I'll give you an example. When I was first building this plan to go to the Keys from Pennsylvania, where I was living at the time, I mentioned my dream to one of my colleagues and what I wanted to do. I had a very fixed target; I had a specific date in mind. His advice to me was to make sure I had a picture of a dolphin on my refrigerator to continually remind me of my dream. I really shocked him by saying, "I've done better than that—I have a dolphin tattooed over my heart!" That's when he knew I was really committed.

So you've got to start taking steps to create something concrete of that vision. If it's just a picture on your refrigerator in the beginning that's okay, but you've got to do something more than just mull it over in your head.

WRIGHT

How important was having a clear path for you?

POWELL

For me it was very important. As I said in the beginning, I'm a practical person; I would have never been one who would be considered a dreamer. I was a hard worker, I worked long hours, I had several corporate jobs throughout the years and all that goes with them. Usually dreams require financing and I think some people get lost in the making money part. I kept my eye on the ball, I knew what I wanted to do and I knew when I wanted to do it. I worked at not losing focus on my dreams and not getting caught up with all the frills that money can buy. That's one of the traps people get into— they start earning all this money. It feels so good to be able to do whatever they want to do when they want to do it that making the money becomes the end in itself and not just the means to getting somewhere else.

I'm clearly not opposed to making money either. I worked in the corporate world a long time and I made a very generous salary that I never took for granted. I enjoyed all the benefits of working in a big company with a big salary and I loved my work; but seeing how it was getting me to something more important—my dream—kept me going.

WRIGHT

So why does one need a plan if it's all about dreaming?

POWELL

To me, what's worse than getting lost in the money trap is working so hard to earn it and not having the dream in sight. That's the real nightmare if you ask me. There are many people out there who are following the advice of their financial planners. They're starting early, they're saving wisely, they're investing smart, but they don't have any dream at the end of the rainbow, there is just a pot of gold there. I can't imagine working that hard and not being passionate about how I wanted to reap the rewards. That's when I realized that the next step was having a plan. I don't think most people know how to turn their passion and vision into reality.

In the corporate world, or in any kind of business, long-range planning and strategic plans or five-year plans and corporate goals and objectives are all very common language, but hardly anybody associates them with dreaming. It sounds like an oxymoron to say, "Oh, I've got a plan to get to my dream." But anybody who is living his or her dream (and I'm certainly one who can attest to it) knows that it didn't come from fairy dust and you can't just fall into it. That's why having a plan was so important to me and why I believe you need concrete steps that are going to move you in the direction of your dream and you have to work that plan. Simply putting it on paper isn't enough.

I knew that I would need to earn a living if I was going to move to the Keys and live my dream of working with dolphins; I knew Dolphin Research Center is a not-for-profit and salaries are pretty low. I knew that many people who work there had second jobs and I was going to need to have a second income source. That's when I started investing in my own training and development.

I had done a lot of leadership coaching inside organizations, so I decided to explore personal life coaching as an additional skill set. I enrolled in coach training school and I earned my Coach Certificate from the Hudson Institute. I thought I should also have a fall-back plan since establishing a personal coaching business would take time. The business would have to grow to support me. I also went to Mediation Training at Cornell University's Labor Relations Department. I thought I might be able to support myself working as a mediator because I also had skills in that area and needed mediator certification.

Those were the kinds of things I put in place for myself so I'd have a specific plan for making a living.

I also came to Dolphin Research Center about a year or so before I was ready to execute the plan. I talked with the people here I had known for years who were in a position to make decisions and advise me. I wanted to tell them I was serious about wanting to work here. Many people come through the center, fall in love with the place just as I did, and say they really want to work there but never follow through. I wanted them to know that I was serious and that I was planning to put my house on the market to get ready to move to Florida. I wanted to know what my chances were. Did they think I'd ever be a dolphin trainer? That's what I wanted to do initially. It's what everybody wants to do. I wanted to know if this was a pipe dream or if I really had a shot at a job. That's what you have to do to be willing to work your plan—you've got to be willing to make some changes and maybe do some things differently.

WRIGHT

You've written about the need to be open to reinventing yourself. Does one have to change that much to find one's passion and live one's dream?

POWELL

It depends on the individual. You have to ask yourself some questions about whether acting on your dream is going to mean going back to school and taking a new course(s) or getting some special education like I did for myself. Is there some other form of personal development you need to do in order to achieve your dream? Is it going to mean downsizing some of your personal possessions in order to do this? Will it mean relocating? Do you have a fallback plan? If one of the steps doesn't work exactly as you planned, is your plan flexible enough to adjust? Do you have a target date?

How that translated for me was in 2000 when I really committed to this dream, I set my target date as my birthday in 2005. My goal was to be living in the Florida Keys and working at Dolphin Research Center by my birthday of 2005. My birthday is May 10 and on May 3 of 2005 I was moving into my new house in the Florida Keys. I started volunteering six months after that, and six months later I was hired in the Education Department. I missed my target date by about ten months but to me it was pretty darn remarkable for a five-year plan to get that close with the kind of change that was required.

I went from making a six-figure salary to earning minimum wage. I went from living in a big four-bedroom house to a small, two-bedroom "conch" house. And I went from living in Pennsylvania with seasonal weather changes to the ever-hot Florida sun. I can't tell you how many times in those five years while I was working that plan and visiting Dolphin Research Center that I would say to myself when I got home, "I wish those dolphins were anywhere but Florida!" I had never liked the heat, I've always preferred the fall weather, and I was not looking forward to living in the hot Florida sun; but that's where the dolphins were and that's what I was willing to do.

I left all my friends, I moved to a place where I hardly knew anyone, but that's part of what I was willing to do to make the dream happen. So when you ask if it requires people to change that much, it depends on who is asking and how far from the dream he or she is living at the time the person starts connecting to his or her passion and planning how to make the dream a reality.

WRIGHT

What if the people who are reading your chapter in this book, are afraid to take the first step?

POWELL

That could be the hardest step. Everybody is going to recognize that all these questions I'm throwing out here are often part of a solid business plan or project. But the question is, why not apply that kind of thinking to fulfilling a life dream? If you have a good plan, that first step isn't going to be so scary and it doesn't have to take the fun out of dreaming. It can make your dream more real with each milestone you pass; each step is going to bring you closer. That clear picture you've developed in your head or put on the refrigerator door or tattooed on your chest, is going to be right there in front of you all the time.

Your dream may involve some risk, and most of them do; they don't come without some risk and change. But once you get right up to the door, you have to be prepared to walk through it. If you've done your planning it should be a piece of cake. What I encourage people to do is not let taking the first step stop them in their tracks. Joel Barker, another well-known author, has been quoted saying, "Vision without action is just a dream, action without vision just passes the time, vision with action can change the world." That's what I did for myself—I changed my world!

WRIGHT

So how did you avoid the money trap?

POWELL

You need to stay focused. You have to keep in touch with how you feel when you're "in flow" as Mihaly Csikszentmihalyi says, versus earning the money for the dream; you've got to stay in touch with those feelings. Let your family and friends in on it and get their support but don't let them discourage you. There might be skeptics in your family or among your friends who are jealous of your dream or who have never had a dream of their own or, if they do, they don't feel that they could ever accomplish their dream. Don't let them bring you down by saying, "Oh, you'll never make money doing that" or "That's a great hobby but what about a real job." Dreamers have to stay focused and not lose sight of where they're headed and how they're going to get there.

WRIGHT

How does a life coach fit into all of this?

POWELL

One of the primary roles of a life coach is to help you stay looking forward. They don't look back at what happened in the past and they're not trying to fix something that's broken about you; that's a role for counselors. Coaches look forward and they keep you moving in that direction. They can help you discover your passion by asking some of the right questions and getting you to do some self-reflection. They can help you deal with resistance, either your own or what you're getting from the outside.

For example, in 2004 there was a terrible hurricane season in Florida; it was all over the national news. The storms were hitting the West Coast of Florida in places that were hardly ever affected and communities were just being hammered. My friends all knew that I was planning to move to the Keys in the spring of 2005. They were all asking me if I was still planning to move here. My reply was always, "Yes, that's where the dolphins are and that's where I'm going. "

Staying focused and dealing with resistance is key. I could have let that barrier get in my way and decided it was too scary. I could have decided I didn't want to live where the hurricanes come but I didn't do that. I moved to Florida. And in my first season there were four hurricanes here. After that, I felt like a veteran. I learned what to do and how to keep myself safe.

The point is that I didn't lose sight of my goal and I didn't let that one thing scare me off. It goes back to the first step. If you're afraid to take the first step, sometimes a life coach can help you identify some scenarios, or some back-up plans to help you get through that first hurdle.

WRIGHT

Well, what a fascinating conversation. Living your dream, that's just something that I think all of us dream about but take very few steps toward accomplishing it. You've been very helpful and I appreciate all this time you've taken to answer these questions.

POWELL

You're very welcome. I want to add one other thing. A coach is committed to your success and a good coach leads from behind, meaning they allow you to move at your own pace but they always keep you facing forward and heading toward your goal.

WRIGHT

Today I've been talking with Jennifer Powell. In 2006 she began living her dream of working with dolphins at Dolphin Research Center in Grassy Key, Florida, where she currently serves as Senior Education Instructor.

Jennifer, thank you so much for being with us today on *Words of Wisdom.*

POWELL

You are very welcome. I've enjoyed the discussion.

Jennifer Powell has dedicated her twenty-five-year career to helping organizations achieve their goals through the growth and development of leaders, individual contributors, and work teams across entire organizations. Jennifer has more than ten years of experience coaching leaders at all levels from CEOs to front line supervisors.

In 2003 she expanded her scope to include personal life transition coaching. In 2005 she launched *Reflections*, an independent coaching business focusing on leadership coaching and personal life transitions. In 2006 she began living her dream of working with dolphins at Dolphin Research Center in Grassy Key, Florida, where she currently serves as a Senior Education Instructor. Jennifer is an avid volunteer in her community and she is also an avid reader and an accomplished ballroom dancer.

Jennifer Powell

Reflections
PO Box 522476
Marathon Shores, FL 33052
484-255-7785
jjpowell340@gmail.com
www.reflectionscoaching.net

CHAPTER SIX

Working with Family?

IT'S NOT PERSONAL—IT'S JUST BUSINESS!

By Rhonda R. Savage, DDS

DAVID WRIGHT (WRIGHT)

Today I am talking with Rhonda Savage. Dr. Savage served as a Lieutenant Commander in the U.S. Navy, Desert Shield/Desert Storm, attached to the U.S. Marine Corp. She is the CEO of Miles Global, an internationally known health care consulting firm.

She is the past President of the Washington State Dental Association and is an Affiliate Faculty for the University of Washington, School of Dentistry.

Dr. Savage was awarded the Navy Achievement Medal, the National Defense Medal, and the Expert Pistol Medal.

She is a member of the Institute of Management Consultants, the Association of Fraud Examiners, and the National Speakers Association.

Dr. Savage is a "straight" shooter: an author, a consultant, and speaks on women's health issues, leadership, and business management.

Dr. Savage, welcome to *Words of Wisdom.*

Rhonda, can a family who work together really separate the family history, emotions, and knowledge of the individual family members at a deeper level and also have a great working relationship?

RHONDA SAVAGE (SAVAGE)

Absolutely, David, but their key to success is communication. Successful family businesses have leaders and front line employees who know how to listen and communicate.

There are some very positive reasons to go into business as a family, yet also significant challenges that we'll discuss in this chapter. What are some of the positives?

- The family that works together in a business can be a tremendous asset.
- Family businesses typically enjoy more financial success.
- They also have a higher level of community involvement and more loyal customers.
- Family businesses are viewed as more trustworthy and willing to deal with concerns or consumer complaints.
- Most family businesses are conservative with risk and tend to avoid debt.
- Healthy families promote harmony and support of each other; however, for business to grow there needs to be healthy conflict and openness to change.

Even the most dedicated, hard-working family member can, however, experience or create tension, stress, and conflict in the business. The relationship is more complicated than the normal working relationship, and a dysfunctional business family can affect the longevity of the business and negatively affect employees.

I was coaching a family business client recently. Tammy, the Office Manager, groaned, "The undercurrent of family has been heavy lately. Employees feel like they're walking on eggshells. Nothing is getting done. The owners argue in front of the team. One shows up late and leaves early and sometimes disappears for a full day at a time. Communication just isn't there! If they do talk, they argue. It's so hard to be around!"

Tammy, a manager for twelve years, is used to resolving difficult situations with customers. But she feels it's not her place to address the relationship dysfunction of family in this healthcare business.

"One of the owners is responsible for the books, but he doesn't balance the bank statement and never looks at the credit card statement. I'm uncomfortable because I'm used to having accounts in order. There are boxes everywhere; nothing is ever filed. The other family members don't have anything to do with the books and that worries me." Tammy said, "Do you think we can ever have a more normal work environment? I'd like to come to work and enjoy my job, without all this stress and tension dragging me down."

Unresolved conflict can affect employees and customers. There are typically three areas where families disagree: task-related work (the goals), how the work should be completed and by whom, and relationship conflict. The worse of the three is the complex relationship conflict. As Tammy noted above, emotional conflict results in stressed employees and lack of productivity. The emotions run heavy—resentment, worry, and hostility are the rule of the day. Most families deal with this type of conflict by not talking about it or dealing with it. The result is that there is often ineffective decision making—decisions that are made can be irrational and result in a lack of commitment by other family members.

How work will be completed and by whom is often the second most emotionally charged source of conflict. Family members are often put to work who lack skills or desire. The old adage, "They have the right last name," creates resentment among employees. People become resentful when someone is unqualified or stands around and doesn't work as hard as the rest of the team.

Often, family members are put into a role with little or no experience. Or, worse yet, the person has little or no interest in the work; it's expected that the job is done. When resentment builds, morale drops. When morale drops, productivity goes down and gossip goes up. Commitment to the business and competency to do the work should be requirements of family who work together.

WRIGHT

In your opinion, Rhonda, what are the individual variables that affect the business?

SAVAGE

Communication differences are number one. Family history and willingness to take risk are variables that can also have a huge impact on the life cycle of a family business. Past business experience and each individual's work background, organizational skills, and work ethics do matter. In addition, gender and generational differences can be challenging, even in a non-family owned business. Difference in leadership styles, birth history, and continued traditions affect family business. If you consider all of these possible influences, plus the past emotional history of a family, you'll see that family firms are faced with unique challenges.

Another unique challenge to family businesses is the long-time retention of a low-producing employee or family member due to loyalty and family values. As a consultant, I see family-owned businesses are typically slower to make the hard decisions such as a termination.

WRIGHT

Is it possible for family to care too deeply? Do you ever find that a family can care so deeply about the business that one person, or group, holds back the growth of a company?

SAVAGE

Yes, this can be a concern, David. Every family has a history. Favoritism, sibling rivalries, and mistrust can sabotage a family relationship. Families that experience illness, death, or divorce can also affect how a member feels about the business. Sometimes, it's petty issues that build up over time in layers, like an onion. These issues cause deep-seated resentment that appears in different ways, on different days.

On the benefits side, there are definitely pluses to working in a family-owned business. Family that work together can strengthen the company. We'll explore the strengths and challenges of a family run business.

This chapter will face only a few of these challenges. It's not possible, in the framework of one chapter, to discuss legal, financial, investment, or accounting topics. And it's important to recognize that many frustrations and hurt feelings are wrapped around compensation of the family member. Instead, this chapter will focus on facilitation of communication, leadership, and conflict resolution.

WRIGHT

Rhonda, what are the qualities that facilitate successful family working relationships?

SAVAGE

Thanks for asking, David. Let's start with the traits of great family team members:

1. They don't gossip. Instead of complaining to others, they are respectfully direct and work to resolve issues.
2. Great family members are appreciative of differences in gender, generation, and speaking styles. They develop good listening skills.
3. There's a focus on goals and they stick to the issues. They communicate the goals and move forward with the decision-making process.
4. Personal and business values are clarified.
5. Work is appreciated and they give positive feedback.
6. They care about the interests of others.
7. Time matters—they are dependable and often early to work. They're respectful of their obligations and commitments.
8. Family members know it's important to lead by example and hold themselves to a higher standard; they communicate their standards and abide by them.

9. They pay attention to their work responsibilities and are accountable.
10. Their motto is, "I follow through." They keep others informed of their progress or hindrances. They don't make excuses.
11. There's a strong focus on having fun as a business and as a family.
12. They're encouraging and use the words "Absolutely!" and "Certainly!"
13. They're mentors of each other.
14. They take a lot of continuing education; they're excited and passionate about their business and communicate this with their employees. It's not just about the money.
15. Family members always speak positively about the family, especially in the office.
16. They know that communication is important and family meetings are held on a regular basis. If there's a difference of opinion, the family member doesn't attack the other person—he or she discusses the issue.
17. They have regular leadership meetings and family councils. They make certain everyone knows what's happening, decisions that have to or need to be made, and they gather opinions.
18. They're not adverse to diverse opinions. They have healthy conflict when communicating regarding the business. They're open to change.
19. Great family members in business offer advice when asked or ask first before discussing a concern.

A question for you, our reader: Do you have two family members in your business who don't get along? Maybe they get along sometimes but clash at other times. Are you and the employees uncomfortable by the resulting silence? If the behavior is allowed to persist, the conflict can actually "anti-market" your business.

Family members are often reluctant to address the "Elephant" in the room. No one talks about the issue directly, or the problem is addressed as a group issue versus individual behavior. In a group setting, everybody knows who's being talked about, except the person or people in question. It's human nature to want to brush issues under the carpet. Yet talking about and resolving the conflict is exactly what you'll need to do to have a harmonious atmosphere in your business.

WRIGHT

Rhonda, you just said that family tension could possibly "anti-market" a business. How could that happen?

SAVAGE

David, I believe, if you're in business, you're there to make money, serve your customers, and give back to the community. The question we need to ask ourselves is, "Are we meeting the needs of our customers? What are customers looking for in today's world?"

For years customers have wanted these four things:

- *Friendliness*—They expect this trait consistently.
- *A reasonable waiting time*—In an elective market, ten minutes is the maximum wait.
- *A good atmosphere*—If the family doesn't get along, you will not have a good atmosphere.
- *A relationship*—Does your client know you put him or her first? Clients won't feel this if you don't get along. Unresolved internal stress actually anti-markets your business. Clients feel or sense the tension. Tension or a bad atmosphere impacts customer service.

In this economy, we find customers are also expecting:

- *Price*—In this economy, price is important; however,

- *Value*—Women are twice as likely to choose value over price if they can afford to shop up.
- *Technology*—It's expected. If you don't have relatively current technology, it's time to make a wish list and develop a budget for technological acquisitions.
- *Convenience*—Important, but not as important as the rest, in the customer's eyes.

Unresolved tension and conflict affect the atmosphere of a business. Part of this lack of production will be a direct result of the lack of a good atmosphere and the perceived decreased value by the customer. Value can have many meanings and variables. When I ask audiences, "What do you look for when you go to buy something?" the response may be, "I look for a bargain!" Yes, a bargain is nice, but if you're treated rudely in the process, how much will you value that thing you just purchased?

In other ways, tension felt throughout the business drops energy and enthusiasm. Women, in my experience, are very acutely sensitive to tone of voice, silence, and the "feel" of a business. If there are unresolved conflicts within your business, you're anti-marketing your company.

The good news is: there's a systematic way to resolve these concerns, reduce your stress, and create a smoother, more professional environment.

WRIGHT

Rhonda, where do most problems in relationships begin?

SAVAGE

There are many ways interpersonal problems arise, David. Resentment, jealousy, how we say things (tone of voice), or lack of communication can result in misunderstanding. In fact, I would daresay that the key to success in family business, including the transfer of the business and continuation of the legacy, is communication.

Clear communication begins by defining the values of your organization. If I were to define the values of my business, I'd say I value honesty, hard work, education, a high level of customer service, having fun in the workplace and integrity. It's easy for me to write these words down, but what do they mean? What they mean to me can be different than what they mean to you.

A "Values Driven Exercise" can help clarify the values of your business, get buy-in from other family members and employees, and open up communication. Your homework, after reading this chapter, is to sit down and write the words that define your values and the values of the business. If you have a partnership relationship with parents or siblings, write down your words individually and then discuss them as a leadership team. Talk about what each word means to you.

Then, make a list of all the common values and agree on the driving values of your organization. Take this list to your team meeting. If you have a larger organization, you'll need commitment to this list of values from your leadership team first, and then work down through the company.

Do the same exercise within your company. Ask everyone to create his or her own list of values. Then pair people up to talk about what the words mean. As an example, I value integrity. What does integrity mean to me? It means following through with what you say you're going to do. It means coming to work consistently with a good attitude. It means honesty, timeliness, and hard work.

What does integrity mean to you? Have a group discussion and have the owner(s) put forth their list of words and talk about what the words mean to each as a leader. Then create a consolidated list of words as a group. This list of words determines goals, plans, and actions.

Everything you do, and all of your communication comes back to the values of your company. If your values include great customer service and a healthy business, then you can base your goals, plans, and actions around these two values. Whenever a decision is made, base it on those two values. It is also a great communication technique to use whenever conflict arises.

Conflict isn't always a bad thing. In business, healthy conflict can help vet out alternate solutions, weaknesses, and threats to the business or family. Emotions can get in the way of healthy tension created by conflict. Families who have a culture of respect, good listening skills, and the ability to respect differences do well with healthy conflict. If emotions take over, irrational decisions can be made, with little buy-in from others.

The easy way to take the emotional decision making out of the equation is for the leader(s) to ask these two questions:

1. Is "whatever is happening" in the best interest of the customer?
2. Is "whatever is happening" in the best interest of the business as a healthy business?

The best recommendation I can offer, as hard as it is to sit the offending party(s) down and address the problem(s) based on the two questions leadership questions noted above. I find that looking at these uncomfortable discussions with the eyes of a child can help! Children are often quite blunt and have the uncanny ability to say what needs to be said in just a few words.

My parents, both in the family business, had sniped at each other for years, bickering and creating uncomfortable moments. My siblings and I tiptoed around these tension-filled moments for years, hoping they'd go away, but they didn't resolve. One day, my quick-witted seven-year-old daughter cleared the way.

It was in the summertime and we'd flown to my childhood home in Alaska to visit my parents. Dinner was held on the outside deck that evening, overlooking the sunset, beautiful waters, and mountains. We'd just started eating dinner when—it happened!

"Bill, eat your salad," my mother snapped!

"No!" he said angrily. And congenial conversation died as the two began to argue.

Totally contrary to the moment, with a big grin on her face, my seven-year-old leaned back in her chair and said, "Oh! Dinner and a show!"

After a great belly-busting laugh, Mom and Dad apologized and acknowledged that they hadn't realized how their bickering made us feel. Our relationship deepened with the open discussions that followed through the years.

As adults, we often worry about putting our foot in our mouth. We don't want to say something wrong, so we say nothing at all. Or you don't like dealing with confrontation. You're sensitive to conflict and you hope the problem will go away. A word of advice: Conflict and tension will not go away, especially between women. Women take small things and worry about them, often mentally making the issue much bigger than it is.

WRIGHT

Why do you need to resolve the issue?

SAVAGE

Unfortunately, David, unresolved issues will cause hurt feelings to build up, layer upon layer, until silence or unexpected anger results. Explosive behavior and/or silence—neither is good for the business. The issues linger in the mind, waiting to resurface with the next confrontational moment. The problem with confrontation is that it happens when you least expect it. Have you ever thought, after a confrontation, that you could've handled it better? Or, have you thought you handled it well at the moment, but later thought to yourself, "Boy, that was stupid!"

I've had thirty-five years in small and large business, helping to resolve difficult situations. I've been in the dental industry since I was seventeen years old and I've been an employee, a boss, and a consultant. I've served on three Boards of Directors and on editorial boards. I've volunteered in numerous arenas and have worked closely with families in many settings. I have also had the opportunity to work with a zoo!

As a volunteer zoo dentist for twelve years, I love the study of animal families and would like to suggest a physiological reason for why we respond as we do during a confrontational situation. Above each kidney, you have an adrenal gland. The adrenal gland produces adrenaline in response to a confrontational, stressful situation. Adrenaline immediately courses through the blood stream during "the moment," re-routing the blood and oxygen away from the brain, into the arms and legs, creating what we know as the "flight or fight response." The amount of adrenaline produced varies from person to person. Unfortunately, depending on the person, during "the moment" you'll have less oxygen in your brain. At that moment in time, you may find you have the reasoning power and brain capacity of a rhesus monkey!

Here are some ways to be prepared for a confrontational moment, how to combat rash action, and deal with concerns as they develop.

The first step:

Be prepared for confrontational moments because they happen unexpectedly. Take several deep breaths and calmly say, "I need a few minutes. Let's talk before we leave today." Don't respond in anger. Cool off, but begin resolution of the issue that day. Instead of saying, "I'll talk about this tomorrow," consider approaching the person, if possible, that same day. If timing is poor, be certain to talk about the problem the next day. The longer an issue is put off, the less significance it seems to have. However, these unresolved issues have a way of building up. Unresolved resentment will reappear at unexpected times. Do not go to someone else to vent; this is called gossip. When you vent, you may feel better, but the person you vented to feels worse and the issue is still not resolved. It will resurface.

The second step:

When you approach the person, do so privately. There's a great communication tool you can use, called the "Feel-Felt-Found" method, and, clearly state your intentions.

For example: "Sarah, can we talk today? I *feel* upset about yesterday. I've *felt* hesitant to approach you, but have *found* that it's best to resolve issues right away. My *intention* is that we have the best working relationship, and I'd appreciate us sitting down to talk." Clearly stating your intention defuses the emotional defensiveness of the other person.

Be open to listening and do not interrupt. If the other person interrupts you, purposefully wait for the other person to finish and then continue. Continued interruption should be addressed calmly by saying, "Please let me finish."

The third step:

Mirror the other person's speaking style. If you're speaking with a reserved, quiet person, lower your voice, speak quietly, and be sensitive to the fact that this person is very sensitive to criticism and conflict. If you're speaking with a direct person, be direct.

The fourth step:

If you can't resolve the conflict, approach the managing partner, a majority owner, or a mediator. Sit down and work out the problem.

What do you do if the leader—the senior family member—is the problem? This is a more delicate situation. Approach privately and ask, "Is this a good time?" Clearly define your intentions: "My intention is that we have the business of our dreams! I want our customers to love our products. My concern is that customers and our employees are unhappy. Is this a good time to talk?" Then use the

"Feel-Felt-Found" method to decrease defensiveness, but clearly articulate the concern.

Perhaps the senior owner is continually arriving late to work in the morning and starts late after lunch. The staff is then stressed, trying to get caught up. Clients are unhappy because of the wait, and are leaving the business. The leader needs to know and then has to make a decision. I would say, "Sarah, the clients are feeling frustrated by the wait. I've felt pressured by the look in their eyes as they sit in the reception area. I've *found* that if we can control the schedule, especially by starting on time, the day goes so much smoother. I hope I've not offended you, but we need to start on time. We need your help."

For all family owners, whether you're all equal partners or in a generational hierarchy, it's important that standards of employment exist. This is a business. Family behavior can affect the business, the employees, and yourselves as family.

Agree to be coachable on a daily basis. Don't let your frustrations build over time. If you have a family member as an employee and there's a concern, don't save the issue for later or for a performance review, that is not appropriate. Never surprise a family member employee about past bad behavior during a review. Instead, use the "Feel-Felt-Found" daily and express clearly defined intentions to take the emotional concern out of the mix. Be clear about what you need and want, but also be careful about micromanaging.

The problem with micromanaging is that people give up. They think, "Why should I bother? I can never do it right." Then you'll get the silent treatment. The silent treatment means there are hurt feelings. Or worse yet, the silent treatment can mean they've given up. Begin by considering that if you're part of the problem and don't let the silent treatment continue. It's not professional behavior in a business setting. Watch your tone of voice and use good eye contact so the other person knows you're listening. Ask for feedback.

I recommend that as a family, you try working within a system of "up front" accountability. "Up Front" accountability reduces misunderstandings. If you want something done, don't say, "You might consider—" or "You might think about doing it this way" or "You should try this next time." Be specific. Say, "I need you to do this" or "I want you to do this now, as a priority."

WRIGHT

How would you lay out an accountability system that would work in all businesses?

SAVAGE

Here are some clear accountability system steps:

1. Sit down, talk about the plan of action with specifics about what you're looking for, and ask the other person to ask clarifying questions. Invite the other person to say, "So if I understand you correctly, you'd like me to take care of this project and these are the steps."
2. Create a time frame for the person to work within.
3. Have a due date for the project or job and then provide feedback as the work progresses.

4. For all work, have a "Plan-Do-Debrief" model in place. When debriefing, be non-confrontational. Talk about what went right, but what could be done better next time. There is no hierarchy in the debrief process. Family members are treated as equals; this encourages trust and openness as well as great discussion.

5. Every business can improve in communication, leadership, and teamwork. Lack of these three skills causes tension.

Don't let the problem continue and exacerbate over time. If the problem isn't resolved, you'll find one of three things will happen:

Other team members will become resentful. Some may start acting the same way. *The worst:* the leaders will lose the respect of the team members. Instead, look at the problem with the directness of a seven-year-old and resolve the issue! Conflict resolution by an outside third party may be helpful.

If you're like most family owned businesses, you have pet peeves and frustrations you deal with on a daily basis. What can you do to change these family behaviors so they don't affect the business negatively and you can maintain your relationship?

Let's look at some common frustrations and solutions:

Problem: The boss said, "Treat me as though it's my birthday every day! Why are they only nice to me on my birthday?" You know this isn't really true, but it's how you feel. You feel unappreciated for all you do; some days it seems like it's never enough!

Solution: Dial up the praise and appreciation in your office by personally making a daily effort to recognize the good efforts of your family in the business. Praise and appreciation, done well, is genuine, specific, and timely. The more you dial up the praise and appreciation, the more the morale of the business will go up! When morale goes up, production goes up.

Problem: You explode in anger and you're trying to get better control of your emotions.

Solution: At your business meetings, let your family members know what you're personally working on changing. Ask for their help. Let them know you want to change the office environment. The 90:10 rule applies: If your boss's behavior or behavior as a family member is good 90 percent of the time, but 10 percent of the time you "blow" it, by acting in silence or exploding in anger—the employees and family—remember the 10 percent that's bad.

Ask for feedback by saying, "I've been working on this. How am I doing?" When the person responds, he or she will immediately think of the positive and may say, "You know, you've been doing better! There was a time last week, thought, where you—" Your job is to say, "Thanks for the feedback. I'll try and do better!" Don't criticize the criticism, or he or she will stop giving you feedback. Your goal is to have the person focus on your positive efforts. Will you be perfect? No, but all you can change is yourself and your reaction to a situation, and be proud of your progress.

Problem: I hate her brushing their teeth in the hallway! I've told her about it but she still does it! Other pet peeves could include a dirty break-room, clutter and personal items lying around, and family not following through with directions or job responsibilities.

Solution: Asking for something repeatedly will lead to frustration. Small things matter! You need to be careful to not micromanage, but if someone isn't doing what he or she needs to do, respectfully discuss the issue and come to a mutually agreed upon resolution. If you're the boss, or majority owner, make certain the person knows what he or she needs to do and ask the person to write it down. Set a date for him or her to report back to you (a mutually agreed upon deadline) and then you won't have to wonder whether or not the task was accomplished.

Most leaders believe they over-communicate. Statistics show that leaders actually under-communicate by a ratio of 1:10. Family employees, just like regular employees, need detailed, specific instructions, coaching, feedback, and appreciation or correction. If someone doesn't do what's needed, despite your efforts, the next step is to sit down with the family member one-on-one and resolve the issue.

At work, your team is like a big family. All need to pull their weight and respect others' concerns, or they're disrespecting others or the place of business.

> **Problem:** The personal use of cell phones and Internet at a family member's desk. Cell phone use, texting, and personal Internet use are a form of time embezzlement. Not only are these habits detrimental to the business and the customer, but resentment will build among the employees who are hard workers. When resentment builds, morale drops. When morale goes down, production goes down. People who are working hard become resentful when someone (especially family) is standing around and not working, or surfing the Internet.
>
> **Solution:** All family members need to be held accountable to the same or higher standards of the business. How many hours a day are you losing to personal cell phone and Internet time during business hours? Are you as the leader personally on your phone/Internet during business hours?

These problems may seem small, but often it's the small, unresolved annoyances that often lead to bigger misunderstandings.

> **Problem:** I hate it when they cry!
>
> **Solution:** Sam Frasier, a small business owner, told me, "Dealing with my family at work is so complex; I get frustrated and feel inept. My sister cries when I try to talk with her about my frustrations. And then, I get even more frustrated, and I know how I act is making the situation worse!"
>
> If your sister is crying, the foundational question is why? When our brains get tired, it's much harder to control an emotional response. Ask her to take a break, then talk again when she is more collected. Ask her to write up a summary of her concerns as talking points. If she needs to, have her

write out how she feels and read the letter to clearly express her concerns. Schedule a time to talk the next morning; don't postpone the discussion too long. It's best to deal with any situation as quickly as possible rather than letting a situation stew.

At times, tears may also be from frustration, anger, or fear. Does your sister feel intimidated? Family members who act out in anger by yelling or punishing with silence will have more dissolution of the family business than those who can practice healthy disagreement.

WRIGHT

What kinds of different issues do businesses experience with family in the business?

SAVAGE

David, there are so many potential concerns. Being prepared and recognizing possible scenarios is the responsibility of leaders in a family business. Some of the issues I see on a regular basis include taking work home, pay issues, and micro-management.

The issues:

Loyalty leading to micromanagement: Often, family members are more dedicated to the success of the business than employees. The old saying, "blood is thicker than water" is often true, and yet too much "caring" can cause conflict.

Example: Bernadette, the mom, felt the front office staff wasn't diligent enough in collecting money from the patients at the time of service and they were inconsistent in their insurance processing methods. Bernadette was clashing with Sarah, the lead front office person. She also clashed with Casey, the dental assistant in charge of supplies. She felt they weren't doing a good job and needed to pay more attention to detail.

Dr. Greggs, her son, had difficulty enforcing his policies because of the conflicting views between Bernadette and the other team members. His mom was a micromanager. She told everyone how they should be doing their jobs, in detail. The stress drove the morale of the practice down.

Taking work home: Dr. Frank Collins had been in practice for twenty-six years. His wife is part of his front desk team. He has said, "I love working with my wife!" Dr. Collins is a very nice, quiet, reserved person. He dislikes conflict and struggles to grow his team and his practice. He's worked very hard through the years, taking a lot of continuing education. His primary goal is to educate his patients and provide quality dentistry. His wife, Emily, is frustrated and concerned that the team members aren't held accountable for their work. Emily holds her thoughts in during the business day, but her frustrations spill over into the evening hours, resulting in silence or explosive behavior.

The solutions:

Both Bernadette and Emily have skills, talents, and strengths. They are incredibly loyal to the doctors and want them to be successful. But their strengths, if overdone, will create problems that should not be ignored. Deferential passive-aggressive behavior and the opposite, micromanaging, will create conflict and tension in the dental practices as well as in any other business.

If you're a family member with a micromanaging or passive-aggressive tendency, here are steps you can put in place to empower your employees:

1. Reassure the employee that you have confidence in their ability.
2. Clarify your expectations. Ask the employee to clarify by paraphrasing. Give them permission to say, "So if I understand you correctly, you'd like me to—"
3. Be professionally direct. The younger generation does not like the passive-aggressive approach. Tell them what you need specifically.

4. Increase the avenues of communication and feedback, but again, don't micromanage. If need be, set up a communication tracking system for the project. Do not make the tracker too detailed (or you'll find the employee spends his or her time working on the tracker and not the project!). Use text-messaging, e-mail, Excel, MS Word via e-mail, calling, or writing.
5. Have step checks and give feedback, both positive and negative.
6. Have a due date.
7. Set aside time daily, as spouses or family members, to debrief prior to going home.

Family gets paid too much or too little:

Some owners try to help their family out by paying more than the average wage for that employment category, which can impact the total staff overhead. Lack of raises for the team members will cause resentment. The opposite of too much pay is too little. If your family member is paid at a lesser rate, is there a concern about resentment? Honest, open discussions are important to be certain this isn't the case.

How do you communicate these emotionally charged concerns, regardless of your side on the issue?

Again, there are two questions you can ask yourself that will help take the emotional side of the problem out of the equation:

1. Is "whatever is happening" in the best interest of the customer?
2. Is "whatever is happening" in the best interest of the business as a healthy business?

If the answer is no, or no for both, something must change.

Problems in family business arise from unclear communication or lack of communication. Lack of communication or miscommunication causes worry, frustration, built up resentment, anxiety, and worry.

WRIGHT

What are other causes of communication issues in a family business, Rhonda?

SAVAGE

David, besides leadership and communication styles, we also need to be concerned about generational differences and gender differences.

From a gender standpoint, men and women are often different in how they communicate, as well as in their leadership styles. Women are involved in family business at an increasing number annually. They enjoy flexible working hours and the focus on family and business goals.

Women tend to have a participative leadership style that is very effective during these tough economic times. Women can be more inclusive, sharing information and building a sense of self-worth. Yet, being too inclusive can be seen as unsure or indecisive or perceived as the need to be liked. There's a balance that's necessary in effective leadership.

Inclusive leadership works well when there is a need for fast growth and fast change, which is great for these tumultuous times. Sharing information gives employees the ability to solve problems and see the need for decisions made. Male leaders can also be inclusive, but often have more of a transactional style. Men are more bottom-line thinkers—cut to the chase, make the decision based upon facts, and "let's get it done."

Obviously, some men and women have both transactional and/or inclusive leadership styles, but as a gender, there are tendencies that can cause frustration in the decision-making process.

WRIGHT

What about generational differences? I understand there is the potential of four generations of family members in the family business work force.

SAVAGE

Yes, David, and the major differences are due to time, loyalty, and technology.

The senior family member was born before 1945. This generation worked hard to climb the business ladder and loyalty mattered. This was the era of World War II. It was a time of frugality, hard work, discipline, and certainly less technology. There were no cell phones or personal computers; technology can make this group feel uneasy or incompetent.

The Baby Boomers were their children. Highly educated women became a major part of the work force. Motivated by hard work, and a driving need for success, the Boomers sacrificed family and friend time, only to be faced with recessions and layoffs. Technology was rapidly developing, but computers and cell phones belonged to the Generation X.

Generation X, the latchkey kids, value family and personal time. They watched their parents lose jobs and have less trust and loyalty to the company; it's loyalty to the boss that matters. They assume companies lie and are skeptical of media hype. They thrive from recognition as an individual, but work is not what identifies them—they also value flexibility in the work place.

The fourth generation is Generation Y, also called the Millennials. Fast-paced, multi-tasking, computer-skilled individuals, they expect directness. They like you to make a plan together and they want to know and respect their boss. They change jobs easily. Work is about getting the money necessary to travel. The Millennials want you to talk with them privately, directly, and in a neutral language.

WRIGHT

Rhonda, we've talked about many factors that can cause stress for family in the business. Earlier you discussed the traits of a great family team member. How do you know if a family is in trouble?

SAVAGE

David, signs of stress that I've seen include arguing, avoiding family meetings, or worse, no arguing at all. Silence is crippling for the employees, the business, and the family. Other signs include substance abuse, depression, and other stress-related conditions. Hurtful things are said, in unkind, defensive, angry ways. The breakdown of the relationship can cause a family member to move away and be distant.

How do you prevent this kind of progressive breakdown in the family business and instead, thrive and grow in your business? Communication is the key to the success of a business. Recognize that you can't change other people, but you can change yourself and your reactions. Sit down as a family and talk about your differences in communication styles, gender differences, and generational differences. Discuss how the family interactions are hurting or hindering your business. Work together on the family business, not just in it, and respect the differences that make your family unique and strong.

We all dread the drama of family stress and tension in the business. Your team's needs and clients' expectations should come first, for the business to succeed as a healthy business. Conflict resolution and crucial conversations are not only necessary, but imperative.

Miles Global works with growing health care firms to improve its business, increase client satisfaction, and retain valuable employees. We believe that all businesses want to be more productive, increase efficiency, and have all team members understand the crucial numbers that ensure the business's success.

Dr. Savage and her firm can help you grow your business.

Dr. Savage is the CEO for Miles Global, formerly Linda L Miles and Associates, an internationally known practice management and consulting business. She is a member of the National Speakers Association and the Institute of Management Consultants. Dr. Savage is a noted speaker and lectures on practice management, women's health issues, and zoo dentistry.

Rhonda R. Savage, DDS and CEO

Miles Global
3519 56th St NW, Suite 240
Gig Harbor, WA 98335
Rhonda@MilesGlobal.net
www.MilesGlobal.net

CHAPTER SEVEN

Making Meaning on Multiple Levels

By Irena Yashin-Shaw, PhD

Strategies for Building a Three-dimensional Relationship With Your Audience

DAVID WRIGHT (WRIGHT)

Today I'm talking with Dr. Irena Yashin-Shaw, an international professional speaker, expert corporate educator, and dedicated life-long learner. Before becoming an entrepreneur with a global business, Dr. Yashin-Shaw was an academic at Griffith University in Brisbane Australia. She has an eclectic array of qualifications including a doctorate in Educational Psychology, a master's degree in Adult Education, a Bachelor of Arts as well as qualifications in teaching speech and drama as well as mathematics and science.

A specialist in cognition, problem-solving, and knowledge design, transformation and application, she is expertly placed to partner with organizations seeking to improve professional productivity and effectiveness through creative thinking and communication. A formidable combination of deep academic knowledge, practical business acumen, and fun theatricality, Dr.

Yashin-Shaw works with leaders in government departments and large corporations to transform people into masterful thinkers and communicators who can get their message across clearly, persuasively, and with impact. The result is enhanced reputation and branding in the marketplace, increased client and customer engagement, and a wonderful sense of satisfaction for people who are nurtured through Dr. Yashin-Shaw's tailored corporate programs.

Dr. Yashin-Shaw welcome to *Words of Wisdom.*

WRIGHT

Your chapter is titled "Making Meaning on Multiple Levels: Strategies for Building a Three-Dimensional Relationship with Your Audience." First, give us your take on what you mean by building a relationship with an audience.

IRENA YASHIN-SHAW PHD (YASHIN-SHAW)

Sure, David. The relationship I want to discuss is the relationship we form with people when we share information with them. Think about all the different occasions in the course of our professional lives when we find ourselves in the role of information disseminator. It could be in the form of prepared presentations to stakeholders or at conferences, briefings during meetings, debriefings after projects, delivering individual coaching or mentoring, group strategy days, planning meetings, or even just at the water cooler, elevator, or corridor. Information sharing is at the core of much of what we do in the workplace.

We live in the knowledge age where knowledge is the new currency. Therefore, when it comes to sharing information, I advocate being not an information *disseminator* but rather a knowledge *entrepreneur*. Entrepreneurs are those who are innovative about how they conduct their business, those who create opportunities where they didn't previously exist, and those who seek to multiply the investment of their time and resources. So by knowledge entrepreneur I mean someone whose content, when shared, prospers, multiplies, and flourishes. It creates value for the people receiving it, fulfils a purpose, and is transformed through the application of that knowledge in a new context. When sharing knowledge we should seek to not only inform but inspire. If we can do that then the recipient will take that investment of knowledge, time, and resources and multiply it, synergise it, optimise it, grow it, leverage it, propagate it, combine their own experience, understanding and perspective, and put it to good use.

The sad part is that in most workplaces, information is still treated like a static commodity, delivered in a one-way direction without thought of how it could be packaged and delivered in a way that makes it come alive. This is particularly the case in contexts where the information being shared is of a technical or complex nature and the person delivering it is a technical expert with a very deep knowledge and understanding of his or her topic but not necessarily of how to communicate that knowledge.

The relationship we create with those with whom we share this information will, to a large extent, determine how effectively that information is assimilated, recalled, and subsequently used. For example, if we give people too much information at once in a disorganized way, then they will go into overload and feel frustrated. If we bore them, they will not want it, if we deliver it in a disrespectful way, they will resent it. So the way we create the relationship will influence people's receptivity to our message.

WRIGHT

Then the obvious question here is how do we do that and how do we do that on multiple levels?

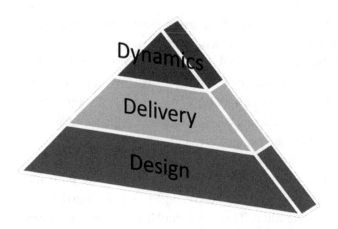

YASHIN-SHAW

There are three key ways in which we can ensure that our message is well received, and that is through the artful management of the design, the delivery and the dynamics we create around our information sharing experience: Design, Delivery, Dynamics—the *3Ds of presenting*. When we have all 3Ds working well, we create a three-dimensional relationship with our audience.

There was something seriously wrong with that sentence. Expert design, delivery, and dynamics engages people on an intellectual level, an emotional level, and a social level. This is a relationship that has depth, texture, and meaning. And that's a relationship worth having. Sure, it might take a little longer to craft, and may require a little more imagination, and it does demand a little more care and commitment. But, as with all good relationships, it is also very rewarding. So it is time well spent.

WRIGHT

Design, Delivery, and Dynamics. Let's unpack each of those Ds in turn. I've heard of graphic design but what do you mean by information design?

YASHIN-SHAW

Design in its broadest sense refers to any process of carefully moulding or strategically planning for a particular outcome. It means to artfully structure something for a specific purpose. So in relation to knowledge or information, it refers to the creation of an elegant structure for information so that it can be clearly shared and easily remembered. This is a topic close to my heart as an educator and a cognition specialist. I have spent much of my adult working life in my various roles as educator in different contexts engaged with the question of how to make learning meaningful and memorable through expert knowledge design. Let me share three principles around this.

Firstly, *organize information.* Clearly organizing information effectively engages the intellect. It is referred to as "chunking." This is where you as the presenter do the work before hand in the preparation stage to categorize the content you'll be sharing so that you don't overwhelm people with too much information too quickly or confuse them with poorly structured content.

When information is delivered in a barrage of isolated pieces of information, it is difficult to remember. So anyone telling you about the twelve reasons why you should do something or buy something is just too much information. It would be much more effective to categorize those twelve reasons into three overarching categories or principles with four points in each, or four categories with three points in each.

When I'm delivering information to people, I always try to do it in chunks of three. That is not always possible, of course. If you are talking about the quarterly reports for the year, then that has to be in four sections. The human brain is very receptive to the magic number three because so much of our life is organized in threes— morning, noon, night; before, during, after; too hot, too cold, just right; stage 1, stage 2, stage 3; plan, execute, evaluate; early, mid, and late career—you get the picture.

This is a great strategy for people who have a tendency to give either too much or too little information. I use this principle when coaching executives for interview panels or managing a question-and-answer session. Think of three key points and expand on those systematically.

I often work with technical experts who have to present dense, often dry, complex content sometimes to other technical experts but also sometimes to non-technical people. While they, themselves, may be expert engineers, programmers, academics, and so on, they are not necessarily steeped in the finer arts of how to communicate that expertise elegantly and succinctly. There is sometimes a tendency to drown people in a torrent of information. Teaching them how to begin with a simple but effective structure is a great starting point.

So chunking is a good way of engaging the mind without overwhelming it.

Secondly, *craft creative stories or analogies.* Building in creative analogies and stories when sharing knowledge aids in memorability. It has the benefit of switching on pictures in people's minds and encourages them to put themselves into the stories and consider how they would feel or react in the same situation.

For example, I recently worked with an IT specialist who had the daunting task of rolling out, within her organization, a new platform that would become the new business management system. The new system represented a significant change in how people went about doing their business. As we all know, it can be difficult to encourage people to embrace change and do things in a new way when they are really busy, time poor, and battling with the demands of heavy workloads. So she knew that there would be challenges in getting people to become familiar with and use the new platform.

Her task was to inspire people to *want* to use the new portal, not because they had to but because they wanted to. So we worked together to come up with creative ways of getting the message across. In the end, she used a creative metaphor about going shopping. She started her presentation with a picture in PowerPoint of an old corner store. Back in twentieth century Australia, the corner store was an iconic place—usually cramped and dilapidated. It sold staples such as bread, milk, or cigarettes.

She told a humorous story of how back in the '70s she had scraped the hub caps of her dad's brand new car on the curb right outside that particular corner store when she had gone there to buy cigarettes. Then she showed a picture of the brand new, amazing huge Dubai Mall, which is absolutely enormous in size, all gleaming in gold and glass, with every possible kind of product from a global marketplace.

After people had had a chance to take in the dramatic differences between the two images, she asked, "Where would you rather shop?" This then became the metaphor for comparing the old IT platform with the new one. She went on to cleverly extend the metaphor as she unpacked the advanced functionality of the new system.

For example, the Dubai Mall has multiple entry points from all the different car parks instead of just one small front entrance like the corner shop. Like the new Mall, the new IT platform was so spacious you could even have your own "shop" in the mall to keep track of all your business in one place.

Throughout the talk, she engaged her listeners with rhetorical questions, inviting them to imagine themselves in the spectacular surroundings of the beautiful, innovative architecture of the Dubai Mall. It was brilliant and very effective!

WRIGHT

That's a great story and very creative. How was it received?

YASHIN-SHAW

Very well. It was a wonderfully engaging way sharing of information that energized everyone and motivated them to want to learn and use the new system, instead of a dry and difficult-to-digest, one-way presentation that left everyone feeling overwhelmed by the complexity of the change. The other benefit of this was that it gave her colleagues the opportunity to appreciate her as a warm hearted, three-dimensional person with a wonderfully quirky, off-beat, sense of humour and not just as the IT guru. That's good content design and it is a wonderful vehicle for relationship building.

The story engages the *emotions and the imagination* and thus brings an extra dimension to the relationship.

The third and final principle in relation to knowledge design is *"Mix it up."* By mixing it up you can build in a number of different ways for people to interact with you and with each other. This provides the social dimension of the relationship and creates a sense of conversation, collaboration, and connection.

Let's take, for example, someone who has been given the job of briefing a client group about a new product. Usually what happens is that the people gather all the information they want to present and then deliver it in a lecture style to people. This becomes an exercise in talking *at* people. Yet this is exactly what must be avoided. For many people, it is the model with which they are most familiar because it may have been their school or university experience. So not surprisingly, they may resort to the institutional learning model when they find themselves in the role of information disseminator. This happens especially when given short notice for a presentation or if they are feeling nervous. This kind of design is boring. My recommendation is for people to do these two things to create the social dimension:

Ask questions—Ask questions either rhetorical or otherwise. It creates a sense of being in conversation with people rather than a one-way talkfest.

Interaction—Have people interact with each other in different ways or do some quick activities in pairs or small groups. What you can do here is limited only by your imagination.

WRIGHT

Do you have some examples of what you do to mix it up to bring in the social dimension?

YASHIN-SHAW

If I'm teaching a course on presentation skills, I'll often start a session with a series of questions such as, "Has anyone had the experience of sitting in a presentation and been talked at solidly for forty minutes?" "How did that make you feel?" "How much of it did you remember?"

Everyone can relate to that one. And everyone has his or her own stories about "the presentation from hell." And sometimes it was his or her own presentation!

A great way of getting people connecting with each other as well as sharing their knowledge is to give them a single-page content matrix and have them gather the information from other people in the room to fill in the cells.

	What works	What doesn't
Hand gestures		
Posture		
Stance		
Facial Expression		
Movement		

For example, if the topic is gestures and body language, I give them a page like the graphic above, get them into pairs, set the timer, and they have to fill in the first two cells before the timer goes off in thirty seconds. Then they have to change pairs. This is almost like a speed networking activity except that people are eliciting information from each other in a short time and in the process getting to know each other. This principle can be used with virtually any kind of content.

If I am doing a presentation about creativity, a simple but fun activity is to get people to draw a light bulb on their index finger and then to put that finger on three other people's heads and say to them,

"You are full of bright ideas." And of course everyone just laughs while they are doing it because it is such a strange thing to be doing. I've given them permission to do something absolutely absurd, so they're loving it.

WRIGHT

That sounds great and a lot of fun. There are probably many more examples you could give us, but let's move from the first D, which is design, to the second D—delivery.

YASHIN-SHAW

Sure. Delivery comes in two categories, vocal and physical. Let me talk about each in turn.

The overarching is that we make it easy for people to engage with us and our message. So we need to speak clearly, project our voice, and use good vocal modulation where we vary the pitch, pace, pause, and power (volume) of our voice. I call them the 4Ps. These are the basics of good vocal delivery. If people can't understand us or hear us or are completely bored by us, then we can't attend to the finer details until we take care of those basic aspects. But let us assume we have that under control. What are the more subtle ways that we can use our voice to improve delivery?

First, we can facilitate cognitive comprehension of our material when delivering complex information by using the 4Ps like a *vocal highlighting pen.* This means we can emphasize to listeners the important words and points in our message by using our voice. Effective vocal modulation can actually help people to understand and process complex material. This is particularly important for technical experts when delivering complex material. Effective use of modulation "predigests," so to speak, information and makes it easier for listeners to assimilate it quickly. Lift the pitch or make your voice louder or pause before really important words phrases or concepts. This subtly alerts listeners to the fact that something important is being said.. When you read something, you have the luxury of going back over it and rereading it if you didn't understand it the first time.

This is not the case when someone is listening to you speak. People have to get it straight away. So make it easy for people to understand you by using subtle changes and nuances in your voice to effectively convey meaning, flag what is important, and hold interest.

Secondly it is important for us to realize that the tone of voice we use will elicit emotional responses in people and subsequently effect their behavior. Malcolm Gladwell reported some interesting research about this in his book, *Blink*. Amazingly a doctor's *tone of voice* is a strong indicator as to whether or not he or she will get sued! The book presented research showing that doctors who use an overly dominant tone of voice, suggesting a lack of respect, were sued more often than doctors who sounded less dominant and more concerned. So the *tone of voice* we use with people can influence their attitude toward us. If our tone of voice suggests lack of respect (even if unintentionally) it can have very negative ramifications. For example, a team leader or boss or manager who uses a tone of voice that suggests a lack of respect, may not get sued as in the case of the surgeon, but may inexplicably find progress heavy going, or more than a fair share of projects that don't run on time, and not know why. The reason could be subtle sabotaging or passive aggression on the part of the team members because they are not feeling respected.

So far we've talked about how to use our voice to help deliver our message effectively; however, building a quality relationship with your audience when presenting to them involves the *whole person,* not just the voice. We also need to attend to the physical delivery of our message. The building blocks of good physical delivery are effective use of gestures, posture, stance, facial expression, eye contact.

David, audiences today are very sophisticated. We can watch the great orators on YouTube, and we see our politicians on television. People know all the basics of what works and what doesn't. Most people know that to present well we need to use different kinds of hand gestures without being repetitive, to stand up straight so we don't look sloppy but still relaxed, keep our weight evenly distributed and not sway or rock back and forth, to face the audience full on so we look confident, to convey warmth and sincerity through our facial expression, and to connect with everyone through good eye contact. These are the kinds of things that create a polished and professional delivery and people respect that. It is great to see someone in action who ticks all the boxes when it comes to good presentations skills.

However, what I'm discussing today is about making meaning on multiple levels and building a multidimensional relationship with the people with whom we are sharing our message. We're talking about how to connect in a way that goes beyond their admiration for a set of polished and highly honed skills. What we're after here is a deeper connection through our physical delivery that engages people's hearts and minds and creates a personal connection.

Bill Clinton was and is a master of this. There are so many accounts of people who, after meeting him personally, were completely entranced by his personal charisma and presence. He has the ability of making them feel as if they are the only person in the room through unwavering eye contact and facial expression that sends the message, "I'm paying attention to you."

Something we can all learn from this is that when we find ourselves in the privileged position of presenting to a group, we need to ensure that our body language says that we are fully present. Even small things like looking at the clock, adjusting our clothes, adopting a closed face, or our stance can undermine the relationship we are trying to build because such gestures signal disinterest rather than interest. Nothing will turn people off faster than if they think we're not there for them, only for ourselves. So the key message is to ensure that people can see we are present, authentic, and ready to give of ourselves. Building the relationship is more important than any refinements we may make to our speaking style and manner. Let me give you an example of where I saw this principle of *relationships before refinement* in action recently.

Just last week I finished teaching a leadership program to a group of emerging leaders. It was a five-day course and we met one day a week for five weeks. Now this was a blue-collar group, not a white-collar group and it would be fair to say that they were rather rough around the edges. But they were highly skilled young men used to doing physical, dirty, and sometimes highly dangerous work.

Their final activity was to deliver a ten-minute presentation about what they had learned in the program, how it had benefitted them, and how they were going to apply what they learned in their respective workplaces. Many of them had never stood up to present in front of a group before. So they were way out of their comfort zone. To raise the bar even higher, I took them to a large auditorium for the final presentation and away from the training room that they were used to. And to be honest, I wasn't sure how it would all turn out. But what I saw happen was truly amazing and served to remind me yet again why I love this work so much. Despite less-than-perfect physical deliveries, every one of them shared a powerful message of transformation and personal and professional growth that was utterly compelling. I was so captivated by the power and authenticity of each one's story that the occasional hands in pockets, unnecessary weight shifting, or overly long pause, was completely irrelevant. What was palpable was the connection the group had made and the desire they had to see each other succeed. In this case, the relationship was more important than the refinement. There will be plenty of opportunities to develop refinement over time. Right now they were establishing their purpose, which is the cornerstone of good communication.

WRIGHT

So we've covered Design and Delivery, now what about Dynamics?

YASHIN-SHAW

I want to make a clear distinction between the words "dynamic" and "dynamics." Dynamic refers to someone who is energetic and vibrant, especially relating to being a speaker. Many speakers see this as a complementary way of being described and indeed it is.

The term "dynamics," on the other hand, refers to the subtleties of an interaction, the undercurrents of a situation, and the interplay of the underlying, unseen forces at work in any context involving human beings. It is to this that I refer. How we as communicators manage these subterranean influences is the third dimension of that relationship.

WRIGHT

Okay, I understand the difference between these two concepts. How do you create good dynamics when you are presenting information to groups?

YASHIN-SHAW

Number one is to meet their needs. Number two is help them to feel good about themselves. Number three is to help them feel good about being there. Let's see how each of these work.

Meeting peoples' needs means giving them what they came for. We have to be clear about the benefit we bring to any group. Any time people are receiving information, they are asking themselves, "What's in it for me?"—the famous WIIFM principle that every salesman understands. If we strategically remind people about the benefits of our message, then they will be much more receptive. This is really important, especially if you are presenting to a difficult group and there is some resistance or even hostility in the air. Clarifying benefits will help to diffuse negativity.

To help people feel good about themselves, create an environment where people feel safe, valued, relaxed, respected, confident, engaged. People learn and develop more effectively and more quickly in those sorts of contexts. A surefire way of doing this quickly is through the use of humour—tasteful of course. If you can get people laughing, everyone relaxes, the energy level in a room goes up, and people are immediately more engaged.

To help people feel good about being there, give them more than just information—give them an experience. We will create a good experience for people if we make meaning on multiple levels and build three-dimensional relationships. Use this matrix as a guide for doing that.

Making meaning on multiple levels: Building a 3-dimensional relationship	Intellectual	Emotional	Social
Design (Structure)	Organize material by chunking content	Stories and Analogies	Mix it up
Delivery (Vehicle)	Vocal and physical highlighting for cognitive comprehension	Relationships before refinement	Pay attention
Dynamics (The unseen forces)	Meet their needs—clearly identify the WIIFM	Help them to feel good about themselves	Help them to feel good about being there

The dynamics we create around the entire experience will determine the effectiveness with which people will receive our information, comprehend it, remember it, and be motivated to use it. If we share information or knowledge that is never used or makes no difference, then it dies. If we share it in a way that it takes root, multiplies, and generates more knowledge, then we have done our listeners a great service and fulfilled our role of *Knowledge Entrepreneur.*

To summarize:

Design is what you do *before* you are in front of an audience. If you do good work there, you will make it easy for them to "get" the message and for that, they will *appreciate you.*

Delivery is what you *do to* an audience—you deliver to them using physical and vocal vehicles. If you do a good job with that, you will look and sound very credible and they will *respect you.*

But Dynamics is what you do *with* your audience. And if you attend well to this dimension, then they will *like you* so it becomes a rewarding experience for everyone.

WRIGHT

That's a useful way of thinking about all the different aspects of creating a meaningful presentation. Cater for the intellectual, emotional, and social component in the design, delivery, and dynamics of presentations. Just a final question, Dr. Yashin-Shaw: do you think these principles apply to all presenters?

YASHIN-SHAW

Indeed. I believe that these are overarching principles that are relevant to presenters at any point in the spectrum, from an informal briefing session by a leader to his or her team, to a technical expert presenting at a high-powered conference, to classroom teachers, trainers, and facilitators, to salespeople, to speakers at networking meetings, and business breakfasts.

WRIGHT

I've been talking with Dr. Irena Yashin-Shaw PhD, educator, and entrepreneur. If you wish to continue the conversation with Dr. Yashin-Shaw, follow her on twitter @IrenaYS or connect on LinkedIn.

Dr. Irena Yashin-Shaw PhD is an educator, and entrepreneur with a unique blend of academic and business experience, which makes her the ideal partner for organizations seeking to improve productivity and effectiveness through high-quality professional development for their people.

Dr. Yashin-Shaw has devoted her professional life and research to the field of learning and development and understands what works and why when it comes to helping people and organizations achieve their full potential.

Before starting her own consultancy, Dr. Yashin-Shaw was a Senior Research Fellow and lecturer at Griffith University in Brisbane, Australia. A highly-respected international expert in her field, Dr. Yashin-Shaw has been invited to deliver keynote presentations and workshops in many countries around the world including the UK, Russia, China, India, New Zealand, Malaysia, the Middle East, and Australia. She has authored and co-authored numerous publications.

Irena's presentations and programs are a unique blend of in-depth academic knowledge, practical, real-world business experience, and fun theatricality and humor, which have made her a favorite on the professional speaking circuit.

Visit Irena's website listed below for a variety of free resources. E-mail her office to find out more about her programs.

Dr. Irena Yashin-Shaw

Speaking Edge
PO Box 65 Mansfield LPO.
Brisbane. QLD. 4122. Australia
info@speakingedge.com.au

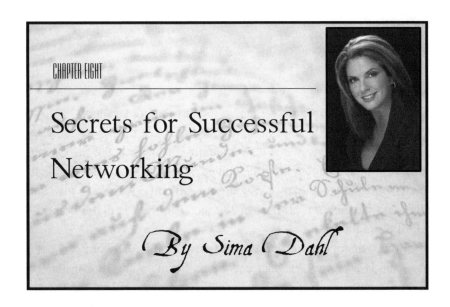

CHAPTER EIGHT

Secrets for Successful Networking

By Sima Dahl

DAVID WRIGHT (WRIGHT)

Today I'm talking with Sima Dahl. Sima is a social media strategist, trainer, and speaker, and well known for her Sway Factor™ system for social networking success. Sima has delivered hundreds of sales training programs, keynote presentations, and workshops nationwide to teach executives, rainmakers, and business owners how to forge a strong personal brand and generate referrals.

Sima serves on several industry boards, is a bylined columnist for *Marketing News* and *Social Media Marketing Magazine*, is the Cofounder of MarketMyCareer.com, and a faculty member at Lake Forest Graduate School of Management. She earned her BA from the University of Illinois and her MBA with Distinction from DePaul University.

Sima, welcome to *Words of Wisdom*.

SIMA DAHL (DAHL)

Thank you. I'm delighted to be a part of this project.

WRIGHT

So what does personal branding mean to you?

DAHL

That's a great question. I'd like to start the conversation by first discussing what a business brand is. When I ask people to define a brand, they may say it's a visual identity, a logo, or the packaging that brings a business to life. Others say it's the messaging that underscores the company's value, and still others say it's just the way you feel about a product or service. The truth is that a brand is all of those things.

I think the one word that best defines brand is the word *promise*. A brand is a promise or pact between a business and its consumers that a certain level of service or quality product will be delivered. Brands are very emotional—people can have strong feelings about a brand, even if they have never interacted or experienced it directly. For example, you may not have ever volunteered for Greenpeace, purchased anything with a Versace label, driven a Mercedes Benz, or conducted business with Accenture, but you may have a strong opinion about those organizations based on word-of-mouth marketing or peer influence. Even cities such as Chicago and Miami have brands.

Big brands spend big bucks to establish, enforce, and evolve their brand story. In the digital age, people are brands, too. A personal brand is simply who you are, what you do, and what makes you special. It's how you want to be known, remembered, referred to, and how you want to be referenced, especially when you're not in the room. You know you have a strong personal brand when the phone rings and someone says, "You were referred to me as somebody who can help me do X," where X is something you really can and want to do.

Personal branding is not an entirely new phenomenon. We've always had industry gurus and pundits, but those titles were often reserved for professionals at the very top of their game. Now, with the advent of social networks, we all live in what I call the Age of Referral. And each of us has an enormous opportunity, dare I say responsibility, to forge a strong personal brand that enriches both our professional and personal lives. As your personal brand value becomes clearer, and the emotional ties within your network stronger, the more opportunities will come your way.

WRIGHT

Is personal branding important at all stages of your career?

DAHL

Absolutely. I like to think of professionals in three broad categories: job seekers, ladder climbers, and rainmakers. These categories, however, are not mutually exclusive. The days of working for forty or more years for the same firm are long gone. Most professionals I know are either actively looking for a new job, trying to move up the ladder, or in some sort of business development or rainmaker role. That may be as a business owner, Realtor, insurance producer, or attorney. A rainmaker is anyone responsible for bringing in new business. In all these scenarios, having a strong personal brand makes it far easier to stay top of mind, generate referrals, and attract new opportunities.

I worked for many years as a corporate high tech marketer and it was a volatile industry to say the least. I worked hard to craft a strong personal brand and cultivate my network, and that helped me navigate from one job to the next. It wasn't always seamless, but it was far easier for me than it was for others who were relatively unknown and not well connected within the industry.

In my most recent corporate position, there were five thousand employees scattered around the globe, and I worked remotely from a field office. At that time, I was a ladder climber, and my goal was to elevate my name within the organization so I would be considered for exciting new assignments or opportunities.

Now I have my consulting and training firm so I'm a rainmaker, and my personal brand is how I attract new clients. What's more, I know several professionals who have recently retired from corporate jobs but are not quite ready to call it a day. To stay engaged professionally, they're leveraging their personal brand to seek out consulting opportunities, board positions, or other ways to offer advisory services. Personal branding is a lifelong endeavor.

WRIGHT

Do you have any tips for professionals struggling to articulate their personal brand value?

DAHL

It's not easy for everyone to articulate his or her personal brand story. When my clients have difficulty succinctly explaining who they are, what they do, and why they're special, I encourage them to think about the end goal first: What does a golden opportunity look like? In order to position yourself for a positive outcome, you have to first define success.

For a job seeker, that is the equivalent of asking, "What is your dream job?" For a ladder climber, success might be an invitation to speak at an industry event, serve on a board, or move into management. For a rainmaker, success can certainly be a new client, but it may also be uncovering a potential strategic partner or connecting with a referral source. Entrepreneurs may be seeking venture capital or looking for new channel partners. By painting a vivid picture of what you want to have happen, it is sometimes easier to work backward and determine how you want to be known.

Another exercise I invite people to try is this: Imagine you are the star of a thirty-second television commercial and the only people who will be watching are those who can help you achieve your goals. What would you say in those thirty seconds? Don't edit yourself. Just dump it on a piece of paper; you can wordsmith it later. Once you have refined your "commercial"—your brand story so to speak—your aim is to practice telling it over and over again. No marketer airs a commercial just once—it's about repetition. A clear and compelling message, told consistently, will help you stay etched in my mental Rolodex for later recall.

I have an acronym I like to use: WISE. When you're developing your story or your personal brand it should be WISE. The W stands for *Well-rehearsed.* Your story should roll off your tongue with ease. The letter I is for *Intriguing.* Why are you unique? Come up with a hook. The S is for *Simple.* You have to be able to explain your general expertise in plain English without lingo. And E, finally, is for *Exciting.* If you're not excited about who you are and what you do, how can you expect me to be? Think about what you want to have happen at the end, how you would leverage that thirty-second commercial, and come up with something that is WISE.

WRIGHT

So what advice do you have for recent graduates who don't yet have much work experience?

DAHL

It can be difficult when you're just out of school and much of your work history is in jobs that have nothing to do with where you want to land. However, more and more graduates are getting savvy about obtaining meaningful internships before they graduate. I advise recent graduates to be aspirational in their personal brand, to envision the future clearly, and be prepared to speak with passion about their hopes and their dreams. Nobody expects you to know exactly what you want to do when you're fresh out of school, but you should be able to express your intentions in a meaningful way. If you make a positive first impression, you'll have an easier time asking for referrals and support in your job search.

For example, you might say "I really enjoy working with people and I'm extremely organized," or "I love managing complex projects so I'm exploring career paths in association management, but I'm also considering management tracks at big companies like General Electric." The point is to give people a sense of what your interests and intentions are. Be articulate, crisp, clear, and passionate about what you're seeking.

WRIGHT

What are some simple ways to reinforce your personal brand?

DAHL

There are some very simple ways to promote your personal brand or your positioning statement. For example, when you are introducing yourself at a networking event, rather than simply giving your name, you can give a brief "pitch" about what you do and what makes you unique in a crowded room. Job seekers should aim to reinforce what makes them uniquely qualified on all their marketing materials including their resume, cover letter, and thank you notes.

I've seen some great examples of business cards that reinforce personal brands with just a few key words on the card's reverse side. I have also seen some good e-mail signatures and out-of-office responders that do the same. Professional bios present another opportunity to articulate what makes you unique in your industry. I like to see professionals leverage their social networking profiles and status updates too.

WRIGHT

You mentioned social networking. What do you say to people who think it's a waste of time?

DAHL

There are a lot of naysayers out there. I think many people simply don't understand the full potential of smart, intentional social networking, the operative word being *intentional*. It's not about logging onto Facebook and playing Mafia Wars; this is about reinforcing your personal brand. I know a lot of people just don't know what to do once they log in.

The first thing I do is remind people that we live in the Age of Referral, and every member of their network, regardless of what industry they may be in, is a possible referral source. As a lifelong marketer of business-to-business products and professional services, I know firsthand that the old adage is true: people buy from people they know, like, and trust and you know what? They refer them too!

Before social networks, we relied on in-person networking, some phone calls, and an occasional e-mail to stay connected to one another—to stay top of mind. Social networks amplify that person-to-person interaction. When done correctly, a digital exchange can be just as intimate or as powerful as an in-person interaction, only with greater reach, speed, and scale. Smart social networking allows you to stay connected to friends, partners, clients—everyone in your network, without ever leaving the comfort of your home.

When I left corporate America to start my own consulting practice, I essentially rebranded myself from perennial job seeker/ladder climber to newly minted rainmaker. Much of the early success I achieved was a direct result of social networking. It took time, and persistence, but my business is 100 percent referral based and I now regularly attract new opportunities to write, speak, and teach through the actions I take in social networks.

WRIGHT

What about in-person networking? Is it still a viable way to make connections?

DAHL

Without a doubt. However, people forget "networking" is an action verb. In my opinion, far too many people don't prepare appropriately or leverage networking opportunities to their fullest. If you are going to take precious time out of your schedule to attend an in-person event, having a game plan is critical. You have to know what you want to have happen as a result of attending that event. That might mean meeting a particular individual or making a certain number of new connections.

Be sure to practice your personal positioning statement so when you're shaking those hands, your WISE statement comes out well-rehearsed, intriguing, and simple. Come prepared with plenty of business cards. Even if you don't have a job, print business cards with your contact information so you can take part of the ritual of exchanging information. Stand near the door and meet as many people as you can as they enter the room. Extend your hand and be fearless, then follow up and reinforce those new connections online so you can stay connected until you meet again.

WRIGHT

These days professionals frequently change jobs, switch industries, or even embark on a brand new career path. How can they keep their personal brand relevant as their career evolves?

DAHL

That's a great question. Years ago, one of my favorite supervisors advised me to take stock of my resume at the start of every calendar year. He said it's important to pause and take note of what you've accomplished, the value you're delivering to the organization, and be prepared to ask for an increase when it's warranted. I never forgot that advice and I think it's the same with your personal brand.

Every year (or twice a year or even quarterly depending on where you are in your career trajectory), I encourage you to take a look at what you have achieved, what you still aspire to accomplish, and make sure your brand story is in sync. If you have new accomplishments or your aspirations have changed, then your personal brand may be due for a tune-up.

Industry lingo also changes. I'm a lifelong marketer and early in my career, the hot topic was integrated marketing communications. My resume and my online profile were sprinkled with references to integrated marketing communications (IMC). Then the emphasis shifted and recruiters were looking for marketers who could talk about lead generation and return on marketing investment (ROMI). It shifted again and digital marketing was sexy, social media was hot.

Believe it or not, we're now coming full circle and I'm starting to see more and more references to IMC.

Paying attention to those cues in your industry is another reason to update your personal brand. When you're switching gears or chasing new dreams, it's time to refresh your story. The more passionate and articulate you are about who you are and what you're seeking, the easier it is for me to know how I can help you, and that's what it's really all about.

WRIGHT

When it comes to the top social network sites, which ones do you think are the most effective at reinforcing a personal brand and generating referrals?

DAHL

There are so many out there—there is literally a new social networking site popping up every month. The big three that most of us have tinkered with at some point are LinkedIn, Facebook, and Twitter.

LinkedIn is like the professional networking event—you have on your professional attire, business cards in every pocket, and you are there for business purposes.

Facebook is more like a backyard BBQ and more social. While you might be dressed in flip-flops and jean shorts, hopefully you still have a business card on you somewhere because the topic of work does come up on occasion. That being said, you don't want to be the person standing in the corner at the BBQ talking about work the whole time or you'll never get invited back.

Twitter is more akin to a cocktail party with short snippets of conversation. Don't arrive empty-handed—bring something to talk about, almost anything will do! But don't forget to make sure the other guests know who you are and what you do. In other words, they should know what a good opportunity looks like for you before you call it a night

I would force rank them in that order, LinkedIn first because it is the most professional platform. Facebook comes second. The platform is particularly useful for establishing, sustaining, or reigniting close relationships. The interactions on Facebook can be quite personal and those connections, over time, can become fierce brand champions. Twitter falls in last place because it takes serious stamina to attend that many cocktail parties. And while I have generated business leads from all of three social networks, I find Twitter the most difficult to sustain during busy periods.

Which social network you choose depends on how much time you have and what your intent is. If you're not yet engaged in social networking, I encourage you to start with LinkedIn and/or Facebook; Twitter really is a different beast.

During my first year in business, one of my largest clients was referred to me by someone I went to high school with ages ago. I hadn't seen him since graduation, but we reconnected on Facebook and through our exchanges he came to know who I was and what my business was all about. Since then I make a point not to discount any social connection, regardless of social platform.

WRIGHT

What are the biggest mistakes you see novice networkers make?

DAHL

Remember that networking is an action verb! Each of us has an opportunity to drive results out of every networking exchange. The biggest mistake I see is that people are generally too *passive*. You have to tell people what you need in order to garner their support. I think perhaps people are afraid they will appear overly aggressive. My advice is not to do or say anything online that you wouldn't in person. Get comfortable making the first move. I once heard someone say that life is an opportunity—you have to rise to it—and social networking is no different.

Another mistake I see is people trying to be so buttoned up and professional that they lose their *personality*. When that happens, there is no passion in the interaction. The most engaging networkers are those who readily show their true voice—their authentic self. Be passionate and be personable.

A third mistake I see is a lack of tenacity or *persistence*. E-mail can get lost, voice mail misplaced. Respectful persistence is a dying art. The general guideline I use is three attempts, after which I will reach out to other people who might be more willing to help me move toward my goal.

Finally, novice networkers are well-served to maintain a *pay it forward* mind-set. The best networkers know that you have to give to get. When I make a new connection I first consider how I might add value to that person's network personally or professionally, and I know it will come back to me. Too many people are willing to ask but not give; that behavior is a sure way to tarnish your personal brand.

WRIGHT

How do you respond to disbelievers who think they don't have enough time for social networking?

DAHL

There are plenty of those people. I encourage everybody to think of themselves as the chief marketing officer of their personal brand. There is no one responsible for your personal brand other than you. If you're serious about advancing your career and attracting new opportunities, you will find five minutes a day or thirty minutes a week to practice intentional social networking. It doesn't take technical skill but it does take tenacity; it only works if you work it. Half the battle is just logging in; the second half is making the most out of the time you have available to you.

I have a proprietary approach to social networking that I call the Sway Factor™ system. It's precise and it's quick and it's intended to help busy professionals know what to do if they have just five minutes, even if it's in front of the television or on a smartphone on the train each morning. The first tenet of the Sway Factor system is

Practice Consistent Indirect Marketing. You don't want to overly sell or overly promote, but gently reminding people of your character, competence, and charisma is perfectly acceptable. The second tenet is Make Frequent Digital Deposits. This is the means by which we stay top of mind. A simple act such as giving a friend's status update a "thumbs up" can raise your visibility. Tell someone congratulations on a job well done, or share an article with a note saying "I read this and thought of you." These simple acts take just seconds but leave a lasting impression.

The last tenet is Pledge Unwavering Personal Commitment. As I said earlier, it only works if you work it. I ask people to take a twenty-one-day challenge to see if they can form a daily or weekly habit of social networking. More often than not they come back and say, "You know what? I *can* do this and what's more, it *really* does work!"

WRIGHT

Will you share with our readers some best practices for making the most out of their social profiles?

DAHL

I'll give you three. The first best practice is to leverage keywords. A keyword is any search term that defines your professional space. It's not enough to say I'm a marketer; that doesn't mean anything anymore. You have to refine a broad term with words that describe your area of focus, industry expertise, or geographic reach— anything that helps people understand your unique value or ability. Using our marketing example, you might say you're a search engine marketer with expertise in Google analytics and pay-per-click marketing, and you have experience in consumer packaged goods companies. Notice all the qualifying keywords. Your social profiles should be optimized around those keywords. That's how people will find you and remember you. Those people may be recruiters, they might be hiring managers, potential partners, clients, or consultants.

Even the media are looking for experts to quote in magazines. Keywords count.

Second, puffery is permitted. If ever there was a time to gently boast about your accomplishments it's on your social profile, especially LinkedIn. Showing up small doesn't serve anyone. Nowadays, first impressions happen online. Your LinkedIn profile is indexed by Google, which means that if I search for you online I will likely find it, along with any other content you've contributed to the World Wide Web. This is your digital footprint, and it's a very powerful opportunity to underscore your accomplishments, skills, and expertise.

Finally, remember *the brand is you*. If you want to build a network of brand champions, tell them what you do, what you want. Do this consistently, with clarity. Be aspirational. Treat your personal brand with the utmost respect and you will attract opportunities that will help you move forward. Remember, you cannot get from the universe that which you're not willing to ask for. Go for it!

WRIGHT

What a great conversation. I've really learned a lot more about social networking than I've ever known before and you gave it to me in a very palatable way; I appreciate that. Our readers are going to get a lot out of this chapter and I appreciate your being in the book.

DAHL

Thank you David, the honor is all mine.

WRIGHT

Today I've been talking to Sima Dahl. Sima is a social media strategist, trainer, and speaker. Known for her Sway Factor system for social networking success, she has taught hundreds of executives, rainmakers, and business owners to forge a strong personal brand and generate referrals.

145

Sima, thank you so much for being with us today on *Words of Wisdom*.

DAHL

David, my thanks to you.

Sima Dahl, President & CEO of Sway Factory, is a social media consultant, trainer, and speaker. When she's not advising clients on social media strategy, you'll find Sima speaking about her Sway Factor™ system for social networking success. Through her keynotes and training, she has taught hundreds of sales professionals, business owners, and executives how to forge a strong personal brand and generate referrals on popular social platforms such as LinkedIn.

Sima is a bylined columnist for *Marketing News* and *Social Media Marketing Magazine*, is faculty at Lake Forest Graduate School of Management, and is the cofounder of MarketMyCareer.com. She earned her BA from the University of Illinois and her MBA with distinction from DePaul University.

Sima Dahl

Sway Factory, Inc.
2020 N. California Ave., #7–167
Chicago, IL 60647
312-884-1888
info@swayfactory.com
www.SwayFactory.com

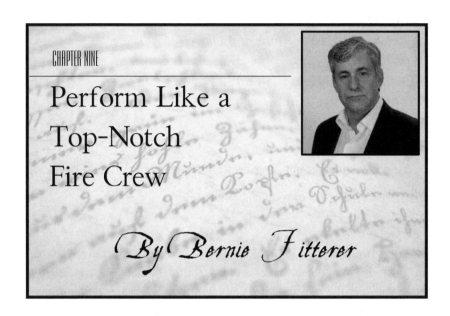

CHAPTER NINE

Perform Like a Top-Notch Fire Crew

By Bernie Fitterer

How would you like your team to be able to perform like a Top-Notch Fire Crew: Complete a rescue in 3 minutes of arrival, have the fire out in 8, and be back in the station in 45 minutes?

DAVID WRIGHT (WRIGHT)

Today I'm talking with Bernie Fitterer. Bernie has worked in various business sectors and at different levels in organizations. As a firefighter, Bernie decided to obtain a bachelor's degree in Adult Education where he blended his practical experience of worker behavior with his studies. He learned that by putting people first, some of the most discordant work groups began to work better together.

Now, Bernie speaks to audiences on how to build leaders from the inside out. He coaches and trains business leaders and teams by breaking down barriers to learning, which results in sustainable improvements of productivity and profitability.

WRIGHT

Bernie, welcome to *Words of Wisdom.*

BERNIE FITTERER (FITTERER)

Thank you, David.

WRIGHT

How does performing in a firefighting setting relate to a business setting?

FITTERER

As a fire fighter, I learned how to manage other people's chaos. In business we often have regular routines that we engage in; however, it is the unusual situations that require greater commitment to time and creativity to solve these issues. To put this into context, if you wanted your team to perform like a top notch fire crew, they must be trained and coached. Training is not only about skills that they have but it is also about how to assess and prepare for a variety of situations that may never occur. What is required is just-in-time training and just-in-case training. Too often it is too expensive to train everybody just in case something may happen. Problems need to be identified and then it is important to identify who in the workplace has the specific skills to deal with these irregularities. Then the teams need to be coached to allow leaders to emerge in specific situations.

As we move between being a leader and a follower, we actually become a facilitator of leadership. Issues that appear to be chaotic to some are routine to other individuals. When these individuals are given a leadership role related to their skill sets they respond to the situation rather than reacting to it. In this way, what appears to be chaos is routine for those who are skilled. More importantly, learning what skill set is needed and which individual on the teams is most skilled in this area is essential for developing leaders. Collectively, most teams have most of the skills needed. However, the best skilled individuals are not always called up to perform in the appropriate situations.

WRIGHT

How does a fire crew perform?

FITTERER

Let us look at a story of a fire incident where the crew's performance was at its peak. Imagine you are the Captain of 7A Pumper. The truck is speeding down the road. The siren is blaring! The air horn is going off! Your driver is moving in and out of traffic, your heart is racing, you see smoke, and you know that this alarm will put you to the test. Hundreds of thoughts are passing through your mind. Are you ready? Is your crew ready? How good are they, really, how good? You question yourself. Will you remember everything that you have been taught? Do you need to remember or just respond? You have trained. You have practiced. You feel the edge, the excitement, the terror. You are ready!

You arrive on scene and hop out of the truck. You raise your radio to your mouth calling dispatch and saying, "50 from 7A, 7A has arrived at Wallace Street, we have a two-story house with smoke coming from the attic, balloon construction; 7A is in Command and preparing to attack the fire."

Dispatch responds, "7A arrived, in Command, from 50."

You turn to your crew who are at the back of the truck and shout, "Advance two lines to the front of the house."

A teenage girl is waving her arms to you to get your attention. She tells you that she was babysitting when the fire broke out. She then tells you that there is a baby in the front bedroom on the second story. You ask her if she knows where the fire started and she confirms that it started in the basement. She indicates that everyone else is out of the house and was glad she took the babysitter's course.

The intensity in now up a thousandfold! Yet, as calmly as you can you thank her and ask her for her name. You request that she stays on the sidewalk and waits for someone else to talk to her. She agrees.

You raise your radio again and say, "50 from Command, the babysitter of the house just confirmed that there is an infant in the second floor front bedroom. The fire began in the basement. Command will begin rapid fire attack and primary search. Command is offensive."

"Primary search and rescue," from 50.

"7B," from Command, "upon arrival catch a hydrant, then become the Back-Up team."

"Command," from 7B, "10-4, set up water supply and back-up."

"7 Ladder," from Command, "set up a ground ladder to the second story front bedroom window and begin to ventilate."

"Command," from 7 Ladder, "10-4 set up ladder and ventilate."

You and your crew prepare to enter the second-story window. You get your masks and face pieces on. Then, you confirm with your crew that everyone is ready to enter the building.

You raise your radio to your face piece and say, "50 from Command, on the air, entering the building."

"Command," from 50, "10-4, on air, entering building."

You climb up the ladder with your crew and fire hose. You listen to your own rapid breathing in (tssuuu) and out (toooo). Then you listen for your crew members' breathing as well and note that everyone is breathing fast and deep (your air will not last long). You crawl into the window.

Inside the room you cannot see anything. The smoke is so dense that you cannot see your hand two inches in front of your face. You can hear windows breaking in other rooms of the second story and smoke starts to move away from the window and into the hallway. The nozzle person opens up the hose to push the smoke into the hallway and the heat is drawn away as clean air comes into the room.

Everyone is on their hands and knees and the third crew member finds the crib and yells out, "Over here! I found the baby!"

You raise your radio to your face piece and say, "50 from Command, victim found, and exiting the house."

"Command," from 50, "10-4, victim found, exiting house."

The nozzle person climbs out on the ladder and receives the baby from the other firefighter. The second firefighter climbs out the window followed by you.

Back on the street, you take your face piece off, shut off your air supply, and you radio dispatch, "50 from Command, we are all out of the house, passed victim over to Emergency Medical Services, victim has burns to face, neck, and arms."

"10-4," from 50, "Command out of building, victim with EMS."

The Assistant Chief arrives on scene and announces that AC is on scene. The Chief asks, "Command do you wish to transfer, command?"

You respond, "10-4 transferring Command. 7B, 7 Ladder have assignments, remaining units are standing-by."

You then hear the AC say, "AC assuming Command, all units PAR [Personnel Accountability Report]."

At this point you settle back a bit. You go to the back of your truck with your crew and sit on the tailboard. With your head in your hands, you breathe for a moment, just to collect yourself and reflect on the events that just happened. From the time of arrival, you developed a plan of attack, set up a temporary organizational structure, gave commands to leaders on the fire ground, talked with the home occupant, revised your strategy, fought a fire, and performed a rescue within three minutes of arriving on the scene. Wow!

The fire in the basement was extinguished by other units within another five minutes. Then in just over forty-five minutes from arriving on scene, the equipment was all packed up and the crews were back in their stations.

Investigators were called to the scene and talked with the babysitter. It was determined that the fire was started by an eight-year-old playing with matches in the basement.

WRIGHT

How does this story apply in an office or business setting?

FITTERER

Before we go on, it would be good for the reader to take a moment and get a *feel* for what is going on in his or her own body after this vicarious experience. Be mindful of the feelings you are having. The awareness of these feelings is really important. In a work setting, whether it's an office or business, you often get into situations that create emotional intensity, yet you may not be aware of them in a given moment.

In the heat of the moment it is not always advised to check your feelings when you are in the intensity of the situation or when it is escalating. However, as soon as the situation stabilizes and it is safe to do so, it is essential to connect with your emotions. By being aware of your emotions you can respond to the situation, rather than react because of them. This emotional awareness is a part of what good coaching identifies. It allows you to shift from reacting to responding to situations.

Back to the story, the fire department was called to the scene because somebody was in a place of chaos and needed assistance. In your business, when things are not going right, it is important to call someone to provide the assistance, perhaps a coach or a trainer or both. I will use some fire terminology and give some explanations as to how it all fits together.

Upon arriving on scene a *size-up* was conducted that looked at the whole situation. Command was established, assignments were given, more information was gathered by actively listening, then more assignments were given—water supply, back-up and laddering. All of these assignments were given to leaders who had the ability to perform precisely. Three crew members entered the building, performed a rescue, and attacked the fire while the other leaders were performing other tasks (the windows breaking indicated ventilation was occurring, and so on). The rescue was performed and the victim was turned over to medical professionals. Finally, the function of command was transferred and timely reflection occurred.

In your business, *size-up* is similar to having a coach arrive. First the coach will talk with your managers. Although coaching services do not require organizations to be in chaos, usually there is a recognized need for assistance—a situation that is beyond the current capabilities of the leaders. With a size-up, an initial report is offered upon arriving on scene. A multitude of things are considered in a fire situation—conditions, the type of building, time of day, and so on. Similarly, with a business, a coach or a trainer will be gathering information through the initial phone call then with follow-up calls. Some factors that are considered may include the nature of the business, how many staff members, customers (local or long distance), types of customers, is the business a boutique or a thrift type of service or a product provider, and so on? By understanding these factors, it becomes possible to quickly identify areas of concern and appropriate questions to ask at a first meeting.

In the story, evidence was given that something was burning because smoke was showing as the Pumper was en route. The amount of smoke indicated that more than a small extinguisher will be required. Likewise, arriving at your office the coach or trainer would be talking to the front end staff, listening for attitudinal comments, identifying any concerns, watching the staff and customer interaction, and so on. These factors would be used for developing a plan of action.

In talking with the babysitter on the street, the Captain was given critical information. There being a baby in the house, the location of the baby and where the fire started required a shift in plans. If the Captain had not talked with the babysitter, the crew would have attacked the fire, which would have had devastating results for the infant. Similarly, a coach or trainer who actively listens to people in various positions in the business can develop a plan that can be more effective than just talking with a select group of executives or managers who share a positional perspective. This inclusive approach will result in better outcomes and greater success.

By having a coach come in to the business, the coach may be able to determine individuals who have skill sets that are required in certain situations that the managers or supervisors have not considered. These individuals may be overlooked because the managers are sometimes too close to the situation to consider them. A plan of action could be developed that would identify these individuals' strengths without the bias of workplace history.

Communication is a key issue to address. In the story, messages were given and then repeated back to confirm understanding. The communication style was very directive and repeated back. In your business, it is important that this approach be used. Managers and the supervisors who take time to listen to their staff and their concerns will be able to make appropriate changes to their plans and convey concise messages.

Imagine that you are in a sales company. You realize that sales are down. Your first thought might be to change your marketing plan. Without listening to your staff, you could spend large sums of money on this strategy. However, if you listen to your people you may find out that there was a defect in the product. No matter how good the new marketing plan was, sales would not improve. By listening to staff members, you would be able to address the product defect and then you would be able to market an improved product more cost effectively.

As the fire crew entered the building, they had a plan and a *back-up* plan. A back-up crew was established in case something went wrong and the first crew needed help. For your business it is important to have contingencies whereby you have people who are ready to step up and support each other. Each one of the members on a team need to be cross-trained to a functional level in order to confidently provide support. If a back-up system is not in place and a change is introduced, pushback can result. Some people may feel threatened while others may feel that they are being pushed into additional work. Skillfully done coaching and training can support a healthy transition that will identify the value of supporting others while still recognizing the specialist on the team.

Ventilation was required in the story. Windows were broken that allowed smoke and heat to escape. A water stream was used to help push smoke out and draw in clean air, clearing the view. In your business, there needs to be a place where people can safely say what they need to say. A coach can provide such a safe environment. At times it is important to strategically lead the ventilation process by sharing stories you as a leader have experienced that relate to other team members.

Upon exiting the building, the victim was removed and turned over to Emergency Medical Services. The fire crew knew what their primary responsibility was and also their limits. They had a strong network of specialists who could provide specialized assistance. In your business, when ventilation occurs it is important to have a strong network of coaches and trainers as well as special service providers. For example, if drug or alcohol problems are identified or possibly bullying or harassment concerns may be exposed, there may be a need to engage an employee assistance program or other specialized service providers.

WRIGHT

How do business leaders determine if they need to bring in coaching to their business?

FITTERER

Let us look at a few tough questions that would be good for business leaders to ask. These would include:

- How happy is your staff?
- Is your staff engaged?
- Are your people disengaged, or even actively disengaged?
- Are you clear of the reason for staff absenteeism?
- Do you have a high rate of staff turnover?
- The really big question is: Would your staff agree with your answers?

If your answers and your team members' answers are not completely consistent, you could well benefit from coaching.

To get greater depth on the status of your organization, ask the following questions:

- How do you perceive your people—do you look at them positively or do you look at them questioningly?
- How well do you trust your people?
- How do you coach your people?
- How do you lead your people?
- Better yet, how do your people see you?
- Do they trust you?
- Do they follow you or others who are providing a positive example?
- How well do your people lead on their own?
- How aware are you of their leadership abilities?
- Do your people trust you enough to engage in honest dialogue?
- Do they follow your lead or do you need to continually check with them to make sure they are doing what needs to be done?
- As a business leader, how comfortable are you with these questions?

The greater the disparity between your answers and those of your staff would be an indicator of your staff's level of engagement. The greater the disparity, the more coaching and training may be needed for you and your organization. In working with staff, supervisors, managers, and executives most of these people recognize the problems. However, they often do not know what questions to ask or even when the right questions are asked. Moreover, they are not sure how truthful the answers are.

WRIGHT

How do business leaders bring about these changes when they have busy schedules?

FITTERER

With a busy schedule it is not always possible to look at the situation from a whole picture perspective. In the fire story, the Captain of 7-A was also the Commander. The most critical assignments were given out, then the Commander became committed to the rescue effort. When he entered the building, he needed to be concerned for self and crew preservation and what was happening inside the building, the temperature, the color of the smoke, and so on. He was not able to deal with this information and stay connected to what was happening outside of the house let alone what was happening on the street. When the chief arrived, he was able to transfer command and then focus on his immediate needs. By that time, what was needed was rehabilitation and reflection. A person can only work at extreme intensity for a short period of time.

One of the most important lessons I learned as a firefighter was to protect myself first and then take care of others. This is similar to the message told when you get on an aircraft. You are told to put the oxygen mask on yourself first and then assist another person. If you become unconscious, you add to the list of victims, which results in fewer people who can support others. Similarly, as a leader it is important that your needs are taken care of, then you can look after the needs of others. An objective perspective on dealing with people in organizations can save time and money both in the short-term and long-term. A coach/trainer who can work with individuals and teams alike is imperative. The coach/trainer must be available for a sufficient period of time so that the whole work unit can engage in the change until new habits are formed.

WRIGHT

What advantage do leaders or teams have by embracing coaching and training services?

FITTERER

Team and individual coaching can assist your business by being objective and offering suggestions to tough choices. Coaches can address the *white elephants* because they are not directly a part of the workplace culture. Managers may need to make tough choices and the coach can support these decisions while providing dialectic feedback. Once dealing with the aforementioned questions, the following question needs to be asked: Does each team member actually contribute to the workplace?

Likening this to a fire situation, if there were three people on the tenth floor of a building who were in extreme need of being rescued, yet you had twenty-five people who were on the second floor, not quite in immediate danger. You need to make a choice and determine what is doable. Sometimes you have to write people off. You have to let go of the ones who cannot be helped.

This is often one of the toughest choices a manager has to make. However, if no decision is made, all can be lost. A coach can provide objective feedback during this decision-making process. Once the decision is made, appropriate action must occur quickly. The key to making and acting on these decisions is to do it in a manner where everyone is treated with dignity.

After a decision is made, suitable *training* can be provided. In our story, the babysitter called the fire department and waited outside the house because she had taken a babysitter's course where she learned her job was to protect the children who were with her and get them out of danger. She called 911. Her rapid action allowed the fire fighters to arrive quickly before the fire grew out of control. She knew what to do because she was trained and she had developed an escape plan.

For your business, plans such as policies and procedures need to be practical, easy to understand, and most of all they need to be practiced. How well are your policies and procedures practiced in your business? Do you have training to support these documents? Solid training can turn this information into healthy habits by your people.

Additionally, an independent coach or trainer can identify signs of *leadership*. In the fire story, leadership took on many forms—officers knew their crew members and provided assignments to individuals who could take the lead in executing these tasks. All of these leadership issues required that a strong organizational structure was in place and recognized leaders at various levels. Great commanders know who their leaders are and they depend on their leaders to provide accurate information so situations can be dealt with in a systematic manner.

Coaches can also establish needed *trust*. In the fire story, the leaders passed on information to the incident commander who assessed and prioritized the information, and the commander needed to trust the information was accurate. Leaders needed to trust the commander that their concerns will be addressed as they became a priority. The rescue became the initial priority. Putting the fire out in the basement became secondary. If trust is not established in your business, communication will break down and tremendous loss will occur. When trust is not present on a fire scene, people die and parking lots are created where houses or places of business stood.

Coaching and training can support the building of trust by identifying communication blocks and addressing these issues with new information. Training done skillfully can support transitioning information into knowledge through reinforcing awareness of the information. Knowledge can be transitioned into wisdom by supporting a practice that uses the new knowledge. As the wisdom is practiced, it becomes new habits. These new habits or behaviors, when applied in appropriate situations, can result in a competitive advantage for the business as it moves forward.

Coaching and training, when delivered skillfully over a period of time, will develop people within the business who will generate a lasting system of internal support so that desired habits can be sustainably reinforced and supported. The effectiveness of coaching and training can be measured by how well the habits stick once these service providers have completed their work in your business. Can you imagine your business with people that are hired to be problem solvers, to be engaged, to want to be productive as they work in teams with customers, and clients to achieve a win-win mind-set and work with suppliers for everyone's benefit? Imagine them being committed to community and the environment with a desire of enhancing shareholder's value. Coaching and training can support these outcomes.

WRIGHT

What tools can you offer to leaders or team members so they can get started right away?

FITTERER

Five basic tools from firefighting can be used immediately. These firefighting tools and terms will be presented and then applied to a business setting.

In firefighting *PPE* stands for Personal Protective Equipment. This equipment protects the firefighter from being harmed and from the extreme conditions they work in. In business, PPE stands for a positive *Personal Protective Environment.* It is important to protect yourself from negativity both externally and internally. As a manager or a leader, it is critical that you come to work every day with an attitude of loving yourself. This position is not from a self-inflating egotistical perspective but from a perspective of being grounded and able to deal with issues from a subjective and objective perspective at the same time. Practice taking at least a half an hour of personal time each day for reflection and introspection, preferably first thing in the morning.

The next tool is a *hydrant wrench.* This tool is used to open the hydrant so water can flow. Water cools and protects as it puts fires out. In your business, rumors can cause people to get upset and angry. It is important to open the communication flow that will cool down rumors with truth that develops into trust. Truth will nourish your people. By providing this support, they will feel the opportunity to be creative in the workplace. When they do a good job, genuinely let them know. Give acknowledgements in front of the team. *Make a habit of giving acknowledgements publicly to everyone at least twice a week.* This action will raise the standard of work among all team members. However, if an individual needs to be addressed for underperformance, do so privately (no one wants to be burned).

The next tool is the *beale tool*. It is used for forcible entry into buildings. It is handy for breaking windows and breaking down doors. Using this tool can expose the firefighter to physical threats of smoke, flames, or shards of glass that cause firefighters to be physically vulnerable.

Being vulnerable to your team can be done skillfully. To be an effective leader, you must be able coach people. By being vulnerable about yourself with your team, you can share the fears you experienced in challenging situations that relate to their current challenges. As you open to being vulnerable about your challenges, your team members will become inspired to turn their challenges into successes.

The next tool is a *tarp*. Although it is a simple tool a tarp is used to protect people. When people are trapped in a car crash, a tarp is used to prevent them from being splashed or debris hitting them until they can be rescued. A simple barrier can be used to minimize damage.

In your business, if there is alleged harassing or bullying behaviors, it is important to set up barriers to minimize the effect of negative behavior until it can be resolved. An example would be to use a temporary communications barrier such as e-mail. If alleged harassing messages are being transmitted, a temporary system could be put in place to carbon copy an objective supervisor. The barrier is put in place to ensure inappropriate communication does not continue.

It is important to remember that this is a temporary measure so larger problems can be addressed. Too often *Band-Aids* are applied to problems in business, the acuity of the problem is reduced, which can lower its priority, and the situation can be forgotten by managers. Use this tool only as a temporary measure and deal with the major issues to their completion.

Finally the fifth item is a *two-way radio*. These are communication devices that allow for closed-loop communication where messages are received and sent. On the fire ground, the incident commander must place a priority on receiving information. The information is evaluated for relevance and priority. Then, decisions are made and messages are sent out. In your business it is important to share pertinent information. However, it is essential to continually gather information and prioritize it. This information can arrive by conversation, e-mail, blogs, or chat rooms. If internal blogs and chat rooms are available, inform the users that comments will be monitored and when appropriate managers will provide comments and feedback. To get honest feedback from people, you may want to consider having these systems set up so people can access them anonymously. Getting people to work with and learn from one another is crucial for businesses to survive. Electronic forums are excellent to achieve peer-to-peer learning, especially when people work in satellite locations.

As good as electronic communication is however, what is even more important is that managers and especially executives are visible to their staff. These leaders must always take time to listen and interact individually with people from all levels of the organization. *Staff members will pay attention to the work that they perform and the company they work for in direct proportion to the amount of attention they feel is being paid to them.* The more your people feel heard by a leader the harder they will work.

WRIGHT

What can business people do right now to see if a people first approach will work in their organization?

FITTERER

Often executives and managers are busy dealing with moving the business forward and ensuring the financial concerns are being addressed. Without money a business will not survive. Many times managers and executives are like entrepreneurs. All usually have great technical skills that their business is based on. However, many times there is a lack of essential interpersonal connection when leading their people. It is imperative that owners, managers, and executives meet with their people. *Undercover Boss,* a television show on CBS, provides examples of executives who work along side front line workers to learn about their businesses and their people. The executives are amazed at how creative their people are and the staff is impressed that an executive would spend time on the front lines with them. These staff members feel valued. They feel empowered and many workers gain a deeper dedication to the business and ultimately produce more.

Leadership programs in universities teach about the *Hawthorne Effect.* About eighty years ago, research was conducted to determine the best way to improve speed and productivity on the manufacturing floor. Some people were given specific body motions to perform while others were a part of a placebo group and not given any instructions on how to improve productivity.

The findings were interesting. Both of the work groups increased in productivity during the study. After the study the productivity dropped back to pre-study rates of production. It was realized and later confirmed that people produce more when they feel that someone is paying attention to them.

A simple approach that you can take in your business immediately is to *spend some time with your staff on a regular basis* and see if there is a change in productivity. A note of caution, if you have not spent much time with them lately; be prepared that the first few encounters these people may challenge you, especially if there are outstanding concerns. However, you will likely see an increase in productivity immediately. As you continue to be with the people who work for you, you will see these improvements last and become habits. *Your present workload will actually decrease*, because your people will be dealing with your clients, your suppliers, and community in a way that puts out the business fires before they even start.

Caution: When using this approach, be genuinely interested in your people. If your intentions are not genuine, your people will figure this out quickly. They will determine that you are attempting to use a technique on them and then productivity will decline. Using a technique approach to training is often why most behavioral training programs fail. *Be genuinely interested in your people.*

WRIGHT

Bringing Spirit to Business is the tagline for your business. Can you explain what it means and how it applies to this message?

FITTERER

Bringing Spirit to Business is best defined by breaking the phrase down into each of the words.

Bringing means *to cause* something, to enter the mind, cause something to enter somebody's body or cause something to happen. *Spirit* means *enthusiastic, energetic, animated life force* that shares the universal state of mind that serves the common good of individuals, groups, and humanity.

Business is *a risk-taking* commercial organization or *activity* that involves *exchanging money* for goods or services.

In a sentence, *Bringing Spirit to Business* is to cause an enthusiastic energetic, animated universal state of mind that shares a common good for all humanity in commercial organizations or activities that involve risk-taking exchanges of money, goods, or services.

By *Brining Spirit to Business,* whether it is in a commercial venture or in an emergency service, the key is to stay people focused. To perform like a top notch fire crew, the following factors must be present: There needs to be time for *introspection* and *reflection* on a regular basis, preferably daily. This practice will *cause* people to show up powerfully because they have the *faith* and *confidence* to act with *creativity* and *discipline.* Leaders who use this approach evoke *a discerning vision* that others are willing to participate in. The team members will develop a *passion* for *serving* each other and step into *leadership* roles when situations arise. When combining these factors, the benefactors of this *people's first mind-set* are the customers, clients, and shareholders of the organization.

I offer this message to all business leaders, whether you are a front line worker, a supervisor, manager, or executive. Skillfully performed expert coaching and training that focuses on causing a genuine connection with you and your people is essential for moving your career and business forward now and into the twenty-first century.

WRIGHT

Bernie Fitterer is a speaker, trainer, and coach. Bernie speaks to audiences on how to build leaders from the inside out. He coaches business leaders and teams by breaking down barriers to learning, which result in sustainable improvements of productivity and profitability.

Bernie, thank you so much for contributing to *Words of Wisdom.*

FITTERER

Thank you very much.

Bernie Fitterer began working in the construction industry at an early age and had his life threatened by one of his crew members. This experience put him on a path of learning how to engage people in extreme situations as a firefighter, and how to use a collegial approach as a college instructor and in business settings. He has developed a practical approach to working with people and now offers training and coaching to individuals, teams, and corporations on ways to improve productivity and profitability.

Bernie Fitterer

Inspiring Developments
Calgary, Alberta
Canada
403-390-1201
Bernie@inspiringdevelopments.ca
www.inspiringdevelopments.ca

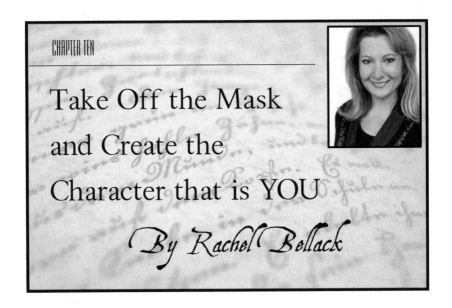

CHAPTER TEN

Take Off the Mask and Create the Character that is YOU

By Rachel Bellack

DAVID WRIGHT (WRIGHT)

Today I'm talking with Rachel Bellack. Rachel is a certified coach, trainer, workshop facilitator, professional actor, and speaker. She is the Founder of Aspire Coaching, Cofounder of the Improv Advantage, and Managing Director at Michigan Actors Studio.

Her focus is on helping corporations, small businesses, and individuals in the areas of communication, leadership, emotional intelligence, and how to generate and create a life of their dreams. After years of teaching acting and improvisation skills to adults, as well as coaching and training in business, she has developed a unique experiential methodology that includes coaching skills along with the tools and processes that actors and improvisers use, plus a dash of NLP. The result is a quick highly effective process that retrains the brain for sustainable success, enhances creativity, and helps to create an extraordinary quality of life.

Rachel, welcome to *Words of Wisdom*.

RACHEL BELLACK (BELLACK)

Thank you so much; it's really exciting to be here.

WRIGHT

So what does it mean to take off the mask and create the character that is you?

BELLACK

Well, taking off the mask means that we've all learned to wear masks or play roles to fit and be accepted by the groups that we belong to—families, peers, workgroups, religions, countries, and so on. When we remove the mask, we allow our authentic selves to emerge, though sometimes we've been wearing the mask for so long that we don't even know who our authentic self is. This is where creating the character comes in—we have to recreate or reinvent ourselves. So get ready to meet someone new—*you!*

WRIGHT

So why is removing the mask so important for success?

BELLACK

It's very important for a number of reasons. When we wear the mask we're not being true to ourselves or to our core values. What we think and feel doesn't match what we say and do and the result of that is being incongruent. This leads to miscommunication, lack of trust, and lack of connection with others. So wearing a mask and the absolute vigilance it takes to keeping it in place is a big factor in chronic stress and the low level anxiety and depression so many people are experiencing these days. In acting, congruence is what makes a character believable and authentic, what the character thinks, feels, says, and does is in perfect alignment. So the character's motivation (people always make fun of that—"what's my motivation?") is what begins the process of discovering what the character thinks, feels, and believes, which leads to how they behave.

An activity we use to help students express emotion and to illustrate the value of congruence is to have them recount a personal story that affected them emotionally. I'm often struck by what happens; it's usually the females that do this. They will recount a personal painful story but they'll have this huge smile on their face. They've been taught that nice girls don't get angry and they've unconsciously accepted that, so they're surprised when I point out that they're smiling. With no awareness of what they are putting out to the world, it's no wonder they often feel misunderstood because what they're saying and what they're doing are two different things. Observers are left very confused—do they react to the words that are being spoken or to the smile they see on the person's face? Which one is true? Which one do they trust? The other factor is that when we cover being upset with a smile, it's a form of suppressing our emotion. These internal feelings they are not expressing are being continually pushed down; that's what builds up inside and creates stress and ultimately disease.

Studies show that the words we speak only represent about 18 percent of our message.. The meaning is actually being derived from the tone of voice, body language, and the energy around the speaker. So it's very important to remove the mask to create effective communication, trust, connection, and definitely to reduce stress.

WRIGHT

Why use acting and improv skills to help people learn to be authentic? Isn't acting about pretending to be someone else or putting a mask on?

BELLACK

That's a common misperception that acting is about pretending or being fake. Acting is actually about communication, connection, and listening. To elicit an emotional response from an audience, the character has to be authentic. We've all seen bad acting, right? What made it bad was that it wasn't believable or true to anyone's life, so it elicits the response of, oh I don't believe that, that seems so fake. Acting and improv activities help people shift their perceptions, communicate congruently, connect emotionally, and listen without judgment. These are definitely skills that come in handy in real life.

Improv in particular helps people develop the right side of the brain, the side where creativity lives. As their creativity develops and expands, people become aware of infinite possibilities and get glimpses of their potential to create even more. They then have the opportunity to choose what they want rather than automatically reacting to their circumstances or situations. So acting, far from being fake, is truly all about authenticity and being real.

WRIGHT

How does one begin to remove the mask?

BELLACK

The process for removing the mask begins with the decision to do so and even though it might sound simplistic, these masks are in place for a reason. They've been there for a long time, so it's natural to encounter some internal resistance and fear at the thought of allowing ourselves to be seen without our mask and to be vulnerable. From the very first time we were told we "should" do something, we're given the message that what we think and feel is unacceptable, that we have to hide who we are to fit in and be accepted. What if who you are is truly your gift to the world? When we wear a mask and play a role, we are not at choice; we are in reaction, even though we may not even realize it. We may think we are choosing what we really want, but are we?

A great example of this is one of my clients, Aaron. Aaron's father is a successful lawyer, both his grandfathers were lawyers and one of them even became a judge. So of course it seemed natural for Aaron to go to law school and become a lawyer. If you asked Aaron at the time if this is what he wanted to do, he would have told you that it was. His family did not put any pressure on him to attend law school, though they were pleased with his choice. Aaron believed he was doing what he wanted to do and that he had chosen it.

He went to law school, graduated with honors, and joined his father's firm. He was dating a wonderful girl and they were talking about marriage. His life was perfect—or so it seemed. Aaron wasn't happy. He hid it well, though, because he felt embarrassed and was making himself wrong about how he felt. He had a great life (he told himself), everything was wonderful. What was wrong with him that he wasn't happy?

It was about this time that Aaron walked into one of my workshops seeking some fun and relief and secretly hoping that he would gain some clarity on his situation.

Early in the class, Aaron shared his love of music and his ability to play multiple instruments with ease. He had done so since childhood and said that nothing brought him more joy and that when playing his guitar he felt he was truly "in the zone." When asked why he hadn't pursued music as a career he responded, "Oh it's just a hobby; you can't make a living doing that!" When he was asked what he would love to do if money wasn't an object, he immediately responded that he would love to play and teach music. This was the beginning of clarity and real choice for Aaron.

After a few months and whole lot of questions and trial runs Aaron decided to take off his mask and step into his authentic self. He still practices law, but only part-time. The rest of his time is devoted to playing and teaching guitar. He's never been happier or more fulfilled. So as you can see, deciding to remove the mask is the first step and it's a big one.

WRIGHT

How do you discover and create the real you?

BELLACK

Well, once you decide to remove the mask, the next step is to define who you are and what you truly desire. Now this also may sound very simplistic, but so many people have been wearing a mask for so long they don't know who they are, what they would like to have, or what the possibilities and potential are.

A great way to discover who you are and what would bring you joy is to examine your values. If you look at what your core values are, such as love, wealth, freedom, security, peace, and so on, and how you've been living those values day to day, you'll probably find that they don't match. We spend a lot of time doing things every day that we don't really care about and that don't reflect our values.

So ask yourself what actions you could take to live your values more fully. If you have a hard time with that, think about what you wanted to be when you were five years old or eight years old or twelve years old. What did you love to do? What brought you joy? What are you doing or being when you're "wasting time"?

Often, when we judge ourselves for "wasting time," we are actually allowing ourselves just to *be* instead of doing, doing, doing. These things will help to start you on the path to deciding what you really desire.

Once you have an idea of what that is, ask yourself what's standing in your way of having it, believing it, or doing it. The first thing people point to as obstacles are the externals such as time, money, commitments, and so on. These things are seldom real obstacles—it's more our thoughts and feelings about it that hold us back. Many people object when I say that it's not about money or time, "My bank account is empty—I have no money!" they'll say. Think about it, though—if you remember the times that you have truly wanted something—to the point that it was a must—you found both the money and the time. Money and time are what hold us back from beginning the process because we decide that if we don't have those then we may as well not even think about moving forward.

What actually keeps us from having, being, and doing what we want are not outside of ourselves, but inside. These internal obstacles block our energy and hold us back from having what we want. The four main blocks that keep us stuck are Limiting Beliefs, Interpretations, Assumptions, and Gremlins. Awareness of them is the first step to minimizing the blocks, so let's talk about what these are and how they stop us.

First is *Limiting Beliefs.* A limiting belief is a belief that we develop about how something exists in the world. We often use it as a reason we can't have what we want and allow it to limit us in some way. Some examples of limiting beliefs are: "Women aren't good at math or science." "You can't get ahead unless you graduate from the best college." "You can't start a new career if you're over fifty," and the list goes on. So you can see how, if you had these beliefs, they could hold you back from even attempting to do something—they just keep the doors closed. Limiting beliefs cause us to make decisions that dictate how we live our lives. There were very good reasons for creating those limiting beliefs at one time, but now we may find that they no longer support the new things we want—they are beliefs by default, not by choice. So it's time to make a new decision based on our values and new beliefs.

Next is an *Interpretation.* An interpretation is about what we decide something means—it is simply our point of view. Usually what we do is take a few facts and a whole lot of judgment and opinion and put them together to form a conclusion of what something means—and it's rarely something favorable for us.

An example would be that you are sitting at your desk at work and your boss walks past you and completely ignores you—doesn't make eye contact or greet you in any way. This is out of character for the boss, so right away we start our story. "What's her problem? Oh she must be mad at me—I must have done something wrong—she doesn't like me" "Maybe he's going to pass me over for promotion or even fire me." The things could be true of course but we don't know if they are. The problem comes in when we decide that our "interpretation" is the "truth," and then take action based on that.

So how would you behave differently if you decided you were going to be fired? What about when you find out that the boss's attitude had nothing to do with you, and he or she had been in an argument with his or her spouse, or had just returned from the dentist and been distracted?

An improv game we use for this is "What Else Can it Mean?" You have to come up with ten different reasons for something, whether you believe them or not. It's really helpful to expand perspective and help us see other points of view.

Moving along, the next one is *Assumptions.* An assumption is about how the past influences our present and future. So for example, if Sally believes she has never been successful in business in the past, she will not even consider starting another business. Or if someone has a string of unsuccessful romantic relationships he or she may make the assumption that because these relationships didn't work in the past that they won't work in the future either. So an assumption is the belief that the past equals the future. It stops us from having what we want because we close doors to so many possibilities based on our expectation that it's not going to work because it never has. This creates a self-fulfilling prophecy and it also discounts our experience and learning that could serve to create a new and different outcome than in the past.

Viewing this from the perspective of an actor is helpful. When we look at the idea that the character's "script" is already written, it would be easy to assume that the character is always the same. Nothing could be farther from the truth. If you've ever seen more than one actor play the same character, you'd see that each actor chooses different things for their character. The script is the same but the character's motivations and choices are very different. You can't make assumptions just because you know how it ends. For our lives we act as though we know how it ends—in fact we are creating it, moment by moment.

Finally we have *Gremlins.* Many people remember the movie from the '80s—*Gremlins.* They appear as cute, fuzzy creatures with big eyes, but our personal gremlins are not so cute. A gremlin is that voice that speaks to you and tells you, "You can't do that," "You're going to fail," "Who do you think you are?" and, "You're not good enough."

Gremlins can be very powerful when they are allowed to be and have a nasty characteristic of seeming to get stronger if we try to ignore them or resist their message. Gremlins are often developed in childhood and have been with us for so long that some people mistake the voice of the Gremlin for their own inner knowing and allow it to stop them from having the life they want.

The first step in managing the gremlin is to understand that it is not us but is separate from us and we have a number of fun and creative activities to help people to do that.

These four energy blocks of Gremlins, Assumptions, Interpretations, and Limiting Beliefs we refer to as GAIL. So if you don't have what you desire, one or many of the GAILs are likely standing in your way.

So discovering and creating the real you is about examining values and what brings you joy, while overcoming the internal obstacles that stand in your way and then taking action on those choices.

WRIGHT

What methods do you use that can help someone move through this process?

BELLACK

Well, it's actually a combination of different things that are put together to help people create clarity and effect change. It consists of a combination of activities and information that are drawn from the Acting and Improv world coupled with coaching skills and NLP. The focus is on discovery and asking the questions that will help people to know they are at choice and begin to see what infinite possibilities are available to them. This will allow them to contribute to their own life and live in a way that brings them ease and joy. Acting and improv activities and skills build confidence, creativity, choice, and communication and help people to see the infinite possibilities. NLP, often called the science of success, is a great tool for retraining the brain and creating and helping change to occur very quickly. Coaching is the thread that runs through it all, creating clarity and propelling people forward while offering support and producing results that last.

WRIGHT

What examples do you have of people who went through the process and got results?

BELLACK

So many people come through my workshops and find their lives transformed by using the tools, doing the activities, and just trusting the process. It's so exciting to share their stories. I have a couple of examples here, so let's start with Tim.

Tim is in his early forties, works as a skilled tradesman, and he lives in a rural area here in Michigan. He's what you'd call a "man's man"—he hunts, fishes, and he plays lots of sports. Tim never went beyond high school but he has a natural cleverness that sometimes got him into a little trouble in his youth. Tim always wanted to be an actor but no one around him could ever accept that because only sissies are actors, according to the group he belongs to. Tim wanted to belong and be accepted so he buried his dreams and even began to consider them "stupid and childish." So by the time he came to my workshop he was a regimented, responsible stress-filled, angry man. He was also a heavy smoker because everyone around him was a smoker and that's just what people did. During class he said that one of his goals was to quit smoking and that he'd tried before but just had not been successful and he always went back to it.

During this workshop, Tim took off the mask; he used the tools, and had a huge shift as he realized what he truly valued. Doing this created the opportunity for a number of ah-ha moments. He left with a completely new perception of himself and that perception did not include smoking. His new character was so compelling to him that he never picked up another cigarette and what's quite amazing is he didn't suffer any of the challenges he had in the past when he tried to quit smoking—he didn't have withdrawals, or have the urge to go back to it. The new Tim was a nonsmoker and that was that. It's pretty amazing.

Another example I have is Stephanie. Stephanie is a fifty-year-old woman and she was in a long-term relationship that was just not serving her. It was making her very unhappy and was not what she wanted for herself. When she first showed up in the workshop she was playing the blame game and was very angry. She blamed and judged her partner and took great relish in her story of how awful he was and all the things he did that made her mad. She was "sticking it out" though—not because that was truly her desire but because she was worried that she'd be alone forever. Not only that, she had limiting beliefs that there were no good men left out there and that people over fifty couldn't find a mate. On top of this, she had an assumption that because she'd never been able to find anyone great, she never would. Plus her gremlin was whispering that she wasn't young enough, pretty enough, thin enough, or smart enough to deserve a great relationship in the first place. With all that going on, it's no wonder she was feeling stuck in her relationship.

So she went through the process and by asking a lot of questions, she started to realize that it wasn't about someone else's behavior—it was about choice and possibility. She had made decisions in the past about what was true for her and held that old point of view for a reason; however, she discovered that it wasn't what was true for her now. She ended up choosing to leave the relationship, not with blame and anger but with a knowing that it no longer served her and she is excited about her possibilities for the future. The last we spoke to her, she was taking a trip around Europe and is truly living her life and enjoying herself.

There are so many stories, like Tim and Stephanie, and the biggest challenge people have is making the initial decision to take that mask off.

WRIGHT

So what do you think it is that keeps people from making the decision to take off their mask?

BELLACK

You know it's mostly fear—fear of what others will think, of being judged, feeling that people won't like them or that they'll leave them. It could be fear that if they start to explore who they really are, they won't like it, and they'll have to make too many changes and face uncertainty—that their only option is to leave the people they love behind. On the contrary—discovering who they are and accepting themselves is the first step to accepting others and creating even better relationships. Often there is a lack of awareness that they're wearing a mask in the first place, which causes them to look outside of themselves rather than within. It takes a lot of courage to look at ourselves and contemplate change. The rewards are worth it for sure.

WRIGHT

In your experience, what are the signs that someone is ready to take off their mask?

BELLACK

The biggest thing I hear from people who are ready to take off their mask is that they feel like there is something missing in their life but they don't know quite what. There is a constant feeling of vague dissatisfaction and anxiety; they feel they are in a rut. They're not in *agony* because if they were, they would have done something about it already. Everything is just "okay."

Does this sound like you? Do you feel that some days you're on autopilot, just going through the motions and having constant low level stress that's just always there? If you can't remember the last time you felt passionate and excited about something, if mild depression or anger are constant companions and you know (or hope) that there really is something more out there for you, then you're ready to take off the mask and to begin creating the character that is you. You are right, there *is* something missing in your life and that something is you—the real you, the authentic you.

WRIGHT

When would be the best time for someone to start the process?

BELLACK

As we say in NLP, when would *now* be a good time? What if you could be, generate, and create everything you desire right now. If you had someone to give you the tools, what would stop you? Why delay happiness and success waiting for the right time that never comes? Why run the risk of exiting this life with your song unsung? Your unique and authentic self is your gift to the world, why hold back that gift any longer? Now is the time. Claim the life you were meant to live and be who you were meant to be. Your life is up to one person—*you*—the *real you.*

WRIGHT

Do you ever have clients who think that now is not the time because they just don't think it will work or they don't think they can make it work?

BELLACK

Yes, a little of both; it's pretty common. A lot of people say, "Oh, it's really great and I would truly love to *but* I have to wait until, until my kid leaves for college, I change jobs, I lose twenty pounds," and the list goes on. I call it the good dishes syndrome—it's always saving the good dishes for company instead of using them and enjoying them right now. It's like waiting for the "right time" to change your life. If you wait for the right time, it never seems to show up. There is never a right time, there is only now.

The other thing is people think, "Oh, you don't know my life and all the things I've done. Maybe for me this is all there is. That may be fine for all those other people but not for me. I'd rather stay as I am rather than try and be disappointed." So understand that is the gremlin talking and that gremlin is highly invested in keeping things the same as they've been. As I said before, it takes courage. The question I ask is, "What will it cost you if everything stays the same?" That's one of those questions that propels people into action.

WRIGHT

So what can someone do to begin to make a difference right away?

BELLACK

A great place to begin is something you can do on your own to start to open yourself to possibility and potential. There is an activity called "Ideal Day" that helps to start that process so I'll explain what that is. Write a description of your ideal day, from the time you wake up until the time you fall asleep. It should be as detailed and descriptive and as specific as you can make it. It includes things like the environment you would like to live in—an urban loft or a country farmhouse for example? With whom would you like to share it? You don't have to list the specific person here, just what his or her characteristics and relationship to you would be. What do you eat? What do you wear? What do you drive? (Or do you have a driver?) what do you do, feel, enjoy? How do you contribute to the world? Keep in mind this is the ideal day of your wildest dreams—you could make up a fairy tale, go over the top. So many people base what they want on what they believe they can have or what is realistic based on their current circumstance. It's important to get out of your head and into the realm of possibilities and really have fun with it.

So once you've completed that, then look at what you've created. Notice what themes show up. Is it full of adventure and daring or rest and relaxation? What things are included and what's absent? What's the rhythm of your day? Look at how this relates to your life today and how it aligns with your values. Ask yourself, "What is one small step I can take today that will bring me closer to my authentic self?" You can also go to my website for more resources and activity ideas. It's time to take off the mask and create the character that is uniquely you, your gift to the world.

WRIGHT

Well, what a great conversation. I think that a process is a lot more helpful than just wanting to be something and not having a way to accomplish it; at least it would be for me.

BELLACK

That's an important distinction. Many people will tell you *what* to do or *what* to be or not to be, but what they don't give you is the *how*, and knowing the *how* is the key to change. When you're given the *how* you have the tools and can experience the shift yourself rather than just listening to someone else tell you about it. That way it isn't about something you have to believe—you can test it out and see the results in your own life.

WRIGHT

I've always had problems with the word "passion." People always told me I have to be passionate about something—"follow your passion into your work life." I've always found that whatever I did in my work I found passion in it, so I find passion in almost everything I do or I don't do it.

BELLACK

That's a great point, David. So many people are looking for their passion and what they don't realize is that they can't find it outside of themselves—they have to look within. By choosing to take off the mask and discover their authentic self they'll be living with passion and experiencing joy, regardless of what they are doing. So if you feel that there really is something missing in your life, then get ready to take off the mask and create the character that is you. *You* are what is missing and your uniqueness is a gift to the world. Consider this an invitation to the life you always knew (or hoped) could exist, yet never knew how to make happen.

WRIGHT

I certainly appreciate your taking all this time today to answer these questions. This is going to be a marvelous chapter in the book and I know that our readers are going to get a lot out of it.

BELLACK

Thank you so much; it was fun.

WRIGHT

Today I have been talking with Rachel Bellack. Rachel is a certified coach, trainer, workshop facilitator, professional actor, and a speaker. Her focus nowadays is on helping corporations, small businesses, and individuals in the areas of communication, leadership, emotional intelligence, and how to generate and create a life of their dreams.

Rachel, thank you so much for being with us today on *Words of Wisdom.*

BELLACK

Thank you.

Rachel Bellack is a native of Canada where she received her Bachelor of Arts and MBA degrees. After moving to the USA she became an instructor at the Second City Detroit Training Center and in the Performing Arts Department of Oakland Community College. Rachel is currently the Managing Director and a lead instructor at Michigan Actors Studio and success coach and workshop facilitator at Aspire Coaching and The Improv Advantage as well as a credentialed member of the International Coach Federation. She serves as a Mentor Coach, a professional public speaker, and a licensed trainer of NLP. She is a graduate of the Second City Conservatory, a member of the Company at the Detroit Ensemble Theatre and is a member of the Screen Actors Guild (SAG).

As a coach, speaker, and trainer with a performer's unique flair, she offers stimulating and entertaining workshops and signature programs that apply acting and improv methodology to "real world" leadership, presentation, and communication training.

This unusual mix of creativity, combined with business acumen, makes Rachel the coach to help you discover infinite possibilities for success in all areas of life.

Rachel Bellack

Aspire Coaching
248-546-6690
Rachel@AspireCoachingGroup.com
www.AspireCoachingGroup.com
www.TheImprovAdvantage.com
www.MichiganActorsStudio.com

CHAPTER ELEVEN

Sustaining Meaningful Relationships

A Pathway to Harmony

By Mary Beth Carlson

DAVID WRIGHT (WRIGHT)

I'm talking with Mary Beth Carlson, songwriter, performing and recording artist, author, and inspirational speaker. Mary Beth moves audiences throughout the country with her message of hope and encouragement. She has produced and recorded twenty-three albums of internationally distributed piano orchestral music and has written and performed music for the Billy Graham Evangelistic Association, International Special Olympics, Arc, Children's Cancer Research Fund, the Alzheimer's Association, and Joni and Friends, the disability ministry of Joni Eareckson Tada.

In 2009, Mary Beth collaboratively created a comprehensive music experience program for residents in Memory Care for The Goodman Group Inc., LLC, a company that owns and manages senior living, health care, and residential communities throughout the United States and Europe. Due to its overwhelming success, Volume II was completed in 2012. She and her husband, Kent, have raised three daughters and reside in Eden Prairie, Minnesota.

Mary Beth, welcome to *Words of Wisdom.*

MARY BETH CARLSON (CARLSON)

Thanks, David. I appreciate the opportunity to share ideas about this topic!

WRIGHT

What qualifies you as an expert on mastering life and business relationships?

CARLSON

Developing, nurturing, and sustaining meaningful personal and professional relationships require significant time, commitment, and a whole lot of heart. The rewards are well worth the effort. Aspiring to be successful at this process and experiencing the joy of mutually satisfying partnerships is more of a journey than a destination. It's a life-long growth curve along which I'm an eager participant.

The subtitle of this book places life relationships ahead of business relationships. If we apply what we've learned about investing ourselves in building lifetime bonds with family and friends, these endeavors will be infused into all walks of life, whether in business, volunteerism, or other opportunities in which we relate to each other.

Rather than consider myself an expert, I credit individuals in my sphere of influence who demonstrate exemplary relationship-building skills. I'm continually inspired by others with character qualities I greatly respect regarding how they thoughtfully react and respond to the words and actions of people in their environment. Deeply grateful for extraordinary life experiences that have led to developing meaningful partnerships, it is a blessing and a privilege to help encourage hearts and enrich lives throughout the journey.

WRIGHT

How do you begin to strategize your way through establishing a meaningful relationship?

CARLSON

As a composer, I view the big picture of every piece as a passage from its initial inspiration to its debut performance in a concert. Sharing an analogy of musical themes and glimpses into the procedure I use in writing music to the progression of developing, nurturing, and sustaining a relationship will hopefully help to remember some key elements. There is indeed a beginning to every building and bonding process. A reasonable place to start is in utilizing effective communication skills.

The Introduction—A Prelude to Harmony

When discovering a potentially positive connection, pursue and identify common threads.

The most engaging, interesting conversations involve an intentional purpose to *ask questions* that search beneath the surface. If we truly desire to become better acquainted with someone who is like-minded and "like-hearted," we'll nurture this connection by exploring these commonalities.

Have you ever walked away from a conversation and surprisingly realized you weren't asked a single question? It can feel a bit like a flat and shallow encounter, don't you think? It's certainly possible to enjoy a stimulating discussion during which each is contributing opinions and ideas. But isn't the conversation taken to a deeper level and greater dimension when probing, thought-provoking questions are exchanged that invite a sharing of reflection and experiences?

Three reminders for effective communication: *Ask* questions. *Listen* patiently with an attentive mind. *Respond* thoughtfully with a perceptive and honest, yet compassionate heart. When people communicate a sincere interest in learning about that which is valued and important, trust and respect is born in that relationship.

"To listen well is as powerful a means of influence as to talk well, and is as essential to all true conversation."

—Ancient proverb

189

Most passionately inspired to compose songs about the value of relationship, I wrote "Music of My Heart" with gratitude for those who truly care about who and what matter most to me. It's a song of sharing in each other's lives through a mutual interest and concern about matters of the heart. The lyrics evolve from listening to understanding as precious time is given to get to know each other intimately.

> *"Listen to the music of my heart*
> *There's magic in the way you hear my song . . ."*

A simple message: if we ask, listen, and respond with the quality of compassion that seeks a deeper understanding of the needs and desires of our relationship partner, the journey leads toward a richly fulfilling bond.

What's "magic" in the way *you* hear a song of the heart? We each have the capacity to create our own. And this is a pleasing prelude to the music of hearts in harmony.

WRIGHT

The relationship has begun to acquire the kind of character necessary for substantial and satisfying growth. Describe a key element involved in moving forward to more enriching subsequent levels.

CARLSON

In this world of increasing tension and uncertainty, relationships built on trust are vital to our emotional, spiritual, and even physical health. If we have one true companion, we are richly blessed. When we find someone with whom to share our innermost thoughts, convictions, and even dreams with a comfortable confidence and intimacy, we've been given a rare gift.

The Purposeful Partnership—A Harmonious Duet

Cultivate a companionship of trust. Invest the time necessary to nurture growth toward a mutually gratifying partnership.

Trust is learned as a result of prioritizing time to get to know and understand each other. Trust is a gentle strength that lifts a relationship to a place of comfort and contentment, assurance and confidence. We intuitively know when we have reached that place.

Trust is earned by being increasingly committed to giving supportive encouragement, successfully resolving conflict, keeping promises, being honest, and putting another's needs ahead of our own. Consequently, we gradually experience a decrease in tension, inhibition, competition, and self-centered goals. Conversation is not forced, dialogue flows with ease, and even a sustained silence or pause is welcome. The peace experienced in this safe place to "just be" allows our spirits to breathe and expand together.

Trust grows as a new level of maturity develops in which we are free to speak our mind and share our heart without concern of being judged or misunderstood. We are released to confide without reservation and openly give of ourselves without condition or expectation.

An attitude of *partnership* prevails as a result of mutual trust. Focus is diverted away from ourselves and drawn toward actively encouraging our relationship partner. A spirit of genuine interest in the other's well-being and a depth of quality in the interaction intensifies, creating a sense of purpose and fulfillment.

There are many parallel principles throughout reaching goals in partnerships within both personal and professional connections of our lives. Mutual trust is essential to the integrity of every partnership.

In addition to the foundation of trust, what are other characteristics of a carefully nurtured and thoughtfully cultivated partnership?

~ *Mutual admiration and respect* affirm that each person is valued and validated.

~ *Authentic compassion and sincere empathy* assure that commitment to the well-being of both persons involved is a priority.

~ *Action-oriented, unconditional giving of self* fosters enduring gratitude.

~ *Honesty and humility* reveal our humanness and reinforce the partnership.

~ *Cooperation and compromise* avert unhealthy competition.

~ *Humor* proactively prevents potential tension or smooths a bumpy path.

During my concerts, an audience can expect a wide variety of entertainment. I most often play solo piano, but occasionally perform with an orchestral ensemble. I particularly enjoy performing in a duet. Whether with a virtuoso violinist, cellist, guitarist, woodwind artist, or vocalist, I love the harmony of a musical partnership with a fellow artist. Because I choose gifted guest musicians who also "play by ear," we enjoy the freedom and spontaneity of listening and responding to each other to create something "off the page," fresh and uniquely inspiring. Our unified goal is to stir the hearts of listeners with a passionate, even healing performance. We purposefully complement the other, allowing both time to shine and time to support. We often become so interwoven in each other's artistry, it seems we are performing as one—a true partnership.

Who is your most trusted friend? What attributes do you highly respect and admire in this person, and how does he or she influence the lasting integrity of your relationship?

A partnership anchored by trust is the most crucial key development in the journey to achieving deeper levels of fulfillment.

WRIGHT

Share another interesting analogy to introduce other key elements of building partnerships.

CARLSON

Only the rhythmic thumping of my exuberant heart permeates the silence in an auditorium filled with anticipation. I hesitate another moment, wondering if the respectfully patient audience is expecting to hear the "signature song" featured in many of my concerts. For the faithful attendees, this is the performance to which they most enthusiastically respond, enjoying a new and surprising arrangement every time, custom-created by each of my gifted guest artists and me.

The piece begins as a piano solo to introduce the simple yet elegant theme, a tender musical conversation between five strong, beautiful chords. Their structure is sequenced in a way that builds expressively throughout eight bars and pleasingly resolves beginning with the subsequent repeated pattern.

The audience quickly recognizes Pachelbel's "Canon in D," and I smile at their appreciative response. Excellent! They've been waiting for it and are looking forward to this tradition. After presenting the melodic theme and then weaving variations of that melody within repeated structures, the sweet strains of the violin join me, beginning a new variation on the theme. One by one, the other string and woodwind instruments contribute their individuality, expertise, and soulful interpretation to the Canon.

The beauty builds dramatically throughout this musical story. The depth of passion in the performance is dependent upon the uniquely exquisite, richly varied color and texture of the instruments, and most important, the talented creativity of each artist. The rousing response from our audience indicates a favorable lasting impression. Bravo!

Color + Texture + Creativity + Superb, emotive performance =
Timeless artistry

Hopefully, you can "read into" my passion for creating and performing music. I am equally enthused about investing necessary elements into a relationship to accomplish a meaningful outcome— an enduring partnership. To keep a partnership alive and assure that it thrives require growing deeper roots by applying and building upon three specific character strengths.

Endurance in Partnership—The Canon: Variations on a Theme

The goal of a purposeful partnership is to sustain its quality and ensure longevity. Keep the relationship alive and make sure it doesn't merely survive, but energetically thrives.

Resilience + Patience + Perseverance = Endurance

The maturity of these three character qualities within each member of the partnership may be the strongest indicator of whether or not a relationship endures the test of time and its many challenges. The combination of these strong personality characteristics is not unlike the strength and durability of a three-stranded cord. Woven together to remain secure, the cord will withstand extended use and wear. If somehow it does weaken and a strand breaks, it may continue to hold together, but will not be as long-lasting. Resilience, patience, and perseverance work most effectively together in achieving endurance when facets from all characteristics are applied. Experience in overcoming seasons of adversity is the best teacher in developing and honing each one, and successfully rising above times of difficult change and challenge can reinforce each virtue.

"Patience and perseverance have a magical effect before which difficulties disappear and obstacles vanish."
—John Quincy Adams

People with resilience typically also demonstrate patience and perseverance. As creativity, character, and quality of variation build

194

within "Canon in D" to crescendo into a memorable masterpiece, resilience, patience, and perseverance work together in varied configurations of balance and intensity to build upon each other and create the desired result, endurance. There are several variations of characteristics in people with these strong traits. They are often independent, determined, confident, empowered, adaptive, insightful, moral, and spiritual. Possibly most important regarding their contribution to partnerships is their indelible optimism. They create successful pathways to harmony and expect positive outcomes.

If these qualities are not inherent in our personality, what can we do to learn, develop, and foster them? Mentors and life coaches can be excellent resources. There's also a plethora of self-help books, articles, and even webinars available on this topic.

Ultimately, attempt with conviction to meet adversity head-on and use challenges as opportunities to learn lessons and apply them in daily interactions with people.

"A trial is not just an assault to be withstood, it is an opportunity to be seized. With this perspective, life becomes inspiring; not in spite of the trials, but because of them."

—Joni Eareckson Tada

My dear friend Joni is my favorite life example of resilience, patience, and perseverance, to name just a few of her many attributes. A diving accident in 1967 resulted in quadriplegia. Despite her initial fear, anger, and depression, Joni persevered. With God's leading, she was determined to live not only a productive life but an inspiring, resilient life. In 1979 she founded *Joni and Friends*, an organization dedicated to accelerating Christian ministry in the disability community throughout the world. Joni has received numerous awards for her passionate work advocating for individuals with disabilities. She is internationally recognized and respected as a best-selling author, speaker, and artist who learned to create magnificent works of art using a paintbrush between her teeth. She also hosts a radio outreach ministry program with a weekly audience of more than one million listeners.

In 2010, Joni was diagnosed with breast cancer, which is gratefully now in remission. She continues to demonstrate perseverance and resilience and exudes radiant joy with an unyielding faith in God as she faces each new challenge.

Are you willing to give what it takes and engage the qualities of character that elevate and enrich your most valued relationships without giving up during a struggle with adversity? Striving toward endurance is arduous work, but well worth the persistence to attain and maintain this partnership theme of lasting significance. Consciously choosing and practicing patience, perseverance, and encouraging ourselves to rebound from negative situations and get on with life can be a huge step toward personal and partnership growth.

WRIGHT

What do you consider to be the most important component in sustaining meaningful relationships?

CARLSON

A large capacity to freely forgive builds the bridge that leads to healing, restoration, and success in sustaining the relationship. It is the most vitally integral attribute supporting the journey. A critical, unforgiving spirit can extinguish the flame of a vibrant future in which individuals grow and thrive together. Consequences can be devastating and adversely affect the physical, mental, emotional, and spiritual well-being of both the unforgiven and the unforgiving. Conversely, a warm and genuine gesture of grace and forgiveness will strengthen any bond. Forgiveness is the greatest challenge but also the greatest gift to the partnership.

Forgiveness—The Bridge

To endure the test of time, forgiveness must be of utmost priority. Learn the art and share the heart of forgiveness.

We've all had plenty of opportunities to refine the art of forgiving. It's a life-long learning experience, and the most important factor is that we put it into practice whenever necessary. If we grasp an understanding and appreciation of the process, it helps with the motivation to initiate forgiveness. The result can be as significantly freeing as a conscious release of bitterness, resentment, or a festering grudge, and a letting go of a need for any kind of revenge. We may not see it this way initially, but forgiveness can be a valuable gift we give ourselves.

"To forgive is to set a prisoner free and discover the prisoner was you."

—Lewis B. Smedes

We must first acknowledge and confront the nature of our personal pain from the injury and betrayal of trust. Embrace the thought of forgiving, knowing it will bring freedom and healing; if not to the forgiven, certainly to ourselves and hopefully to the relationship. This frame of mind will provide an anticipation of emotional release and relief.

Most helpful to me regarding an instance in which the other did not recognize the need to be forgiven or accept wrongdoing was to pray that the disappointment that had begun a path to resentment would be replaced by compassion.

"Life becomes easier when you learn to accept the apology you never got."

—Robert Brault

Look forward to reconciliation unless, in an exceptional case, there is a carefully considered decision to not continue the relationship beyond the act of forgiveness. Remember that forgiving doesn't mean we are excusing the hurt inflicted. Forgive without judgment or harsh accusations; rather, extend the same grace we've appreciated in a reverse situation. We are taking responsibility to help influence a positive change and direction. We will avoid defining the relationship by how we've been hurt.

When do we know we have truly forgiven someone? When the pain is replaced with peace. When that gripping hurt is relieved by an increased desire to turn what we feared was lost into something found that is of greater, sweeter significance. Lost: Trust. Found: An opportunity to jointly rebuild the trust toward not only a rebirth of new and stronger trust, but a renewal of compassion and a sincere hope for contentment and well-being for the person who betrayed us. Do we have hearts big enough to forgive the grandest of transgressions and avoid burning a bridge?

When I am the one who betrays the trust of a partner in a life or business relationship, a sincere apology free of excuses, along with a request for forgiveness is essential to healing as well as prevention of further harm. Preserving trust requires a mutual commitment to give and receive forgiveness and move forward together. This is the heartbeat of a healthy relationship.

"Forgiveness is the fragrance that the violet sheds on the heel that has crushed it."

—Mark Twain

Like the bridge of a song that leads the listener to a place of satisfying resolve, forgiveness in a relationship is the bridge toward reconciliation.

Following is a list of parallels comparing the functions of a musical bridge to the purpose served in the act of forgiveness.

Bridge

1. This songwriting technique is an artistically constructed connection between movements in a piece.

2. A distinct advantage to the bridge is that it offers a departure from the main theme to rest, reflect, and allow for a resurgence of new energy.

3. The most important function of the bridge is to lead from an anticipatory segue to the resolution, which is the subsequent movement in the piece, most typically a return to the familiar chorus with increased emotion.

4. The end result is a fresh beginning and often a new direction for the remainder of the song.

5. A song without a bridge can inhibit exciting movement toward the highest point of a song. The form of the song remains constant in its pattern and possibly less interesting.

Forgiveness

1. The act of forgiveness is a crucial connection between developments in the relationship.

2. Both members of the partnership need to take time to reflect on the personal injury that requires forgiveness, then commit to resolution to allow for movement forward.

3. The most significant purpose of forgiveness is that it leads to conflict resolution, reconciliation, redemption, return to a familiar and safe comfort zone, and a renewal of energy to pursue a greater dimension to the relationship with deeper rewards.

4. A fresh beginning is breathed into the partnership and perhaps with an exciting new direction. Trust is restored.

5. Without a timely act of forgiveness, a relationship is inhibited from moving forward and may even lose its initial purpose and motivation.

"After the Rain" is a musical message of hope and promise found in a new beginning:

Like a friendship starting over
When forgiving lights the way
A rose about to bloom
At the dawn of a new day

Finding love once lost
Hearts mending through the pain
There's a whole new world of promise
In a rainbow after the rain
©Lyrics and Music by Mary Beth Carlson

Every relationship faces a myriad of obstacles. When challenges are conquered and the bridge of forgiveness is sturdily built, the reward is crossing over to a newfound hope, resilience, strength, and stamina in a partnership filled with purpose.

WRIGHT

Describe your most uniquely fulfilling, meaningful relationship.

CARLSON

Blessed to enjoy a rich history and hopefully a future filled with meaningful relationships, there is a friendship that uniquely stands apart. I've learned that an ordinary encounter can grow into an extraordinary relationship when we're open to the vulnerability in freely welcoming a new friend into our heart. Receiving and experiencing all that results from giving our hearts completely and unreservedly can be a beautiful blessing with a treasure trove of wonderful surprises.

Heart and Soul—A Sweet Refrain

The heart and soul of every true friendship is a familiar, consistent theme of mutual unconditional love and support—a treasure beyond measure.

Upon meeting Annie during an event at which I was the speaker and performing artist, she recognized and identified the potential for a relationship built upon many common bonds she learned about from what I shared in the presentation. Annie began keeping in touch regularly, and we both soon realized this would be a connection worth developing.

I marvel at how God wove together a friendship so strong and so deep in so short a time. Annie and I could only surmise that He brought us together to enjoy a relationship filled with many layers and levels of mutual respect, trust, commitment, and loving companionship "for such a time as this." "This" remained to be seen and understood after we'd met that evening in December of 2010 and quickly discovered common threads in our families, careers, personalities, values, and particularly our faith. Our interest in becoming prayer partners was immediate, and this became the foundation for a friendship that seemed to go from "zero to sixty" in a matter of weeks.

Caught by surprise at this unexpected and delightfully fulfilling new companionship, I didn't realize at first that I would learn a wealth of life lessons from Annie, especially regarding sustaining a meaningful relationship. Annie was the embodiment of what I believed was a perfectly harmonious partner in friendship. We were both second grade teachers, which served as an exciting jump-start commonality to get acquainted.

From the very beginning of our correspondence she pursued a deeper connection by asking questions about all that was important in my life. This communicated a desire to get to know me beneath the surface—a quality of interest and compassion that developed and nurtured a relationship secured by mutual unconditional love and support. This was the hallmark upon which our friendship thrived.

Annie taught me by her life example that seasoned faith is filled with the spice of adventure along our journey. It's sprinkled with salt to share with others a vibrant testimony of God's love and grace and sparkling with a natural sweetness that reflects the fruits of the Spirit: love, joy, peace, patience, kindness, goodness, faithfulness, gentleness, and self-control. Annie personified each of these virtues and inspired me to live out these attributes, which were characteristic of how we daily related to each other.

After just a few months of learning to know and growing to love and deeply appreciate Annie, she was diagnosed with advanced pancreatic cancer. A new and profound meaning was given to our once-in-a-lifetime friendship "for such a time as this." What began as an uncomplicated, unselfish companionship strengthened into a bond that grew at an even faster rate both vertically and horizontally, but mostly in depth. Because we knew that the length of our friendship would be limited by her death, we each invested our best. Annie and I freely and openly shared our deepest joy and most tender pain and seemingly everything in between.

We committed to spending more face time together despite the sixty-mile distance between us. Sharing intimate glimpses into each other's hearts and lives, we affirmed the importance of being our true valued selves, and simply brought out the best in each other. We had reached a maturity in our partnership to be dearest of friends for the rest of our lives. But that was not the plan, and we honored that, making our moments last forever in the memories we created.

A unique dimension to our relationship was in how we learned to comfort each other in our last months together. Her physical strength was waning, yet she remained one of the strongest encouragers I've ever known. She continued cheering me on toward deadlines in various professional projects, sharing my music CDs with others, spreading the word to promote concerts, and became an even more intentional listener concerning personal matters.

Even though it became increasingly difficult for Annie to communicate, she did not cease to share her heart with me. Our conversations turned more toward dreaming about heaven together, imagining both her heavenly and earthly fathers greeting her with open arms, being reunited with other loved ones, worshipping God in His presence, and enjoying all He has prepared for her in her new home.

As her energy level decreased, it was impossible for her to communicate the way she used to. I did the communicating for both of us, attempting in creative ways to provide a distraction from her pain and bring her peace, comfort, humor, and even joy. During this time I wrote a song as a tribute to her, and shared the words and music at her piano in her living room.

Most gifts we gave each other were the kind that could not be wrapped. We also shared some tangible "treasures" between us. My favorite gift of these from Annie was a Demdaco figurine called "Heart and Soul." Some of you Demdaco "Willow Tree" collectors may recognize or even own this figurine. It's a tender depiction of two women spending time talking and listening together. Annie and I agreed that, because of the attentive listening and responding posture of the women, either one could be either of us at any time. "They" sit near my piano. I smile and think of Annie as I play a sweet refrain reminding me of our uniquely meaningful friendship with familiar, consistent, and repeating themes of mutual unconditional love and support. Our brief but precious history was a beautiful song filled with tender melodies, rich harmony, and a very sweet refrain.

There's a warm, protected place in every heart where we hold our most cherished friends. It's a place where hope lives, peace comforts, and joy dances. It's where love and laughter keep our hopes and dreams alive.

Annie died one week ago (as of this writing). I thought it fitting to express and complete these reflections today as a loving tribute to our friendship. Blessed indeed is her memory.

There's a place inside my heart
Where a refuge holds a gem
A treasure beyond worth—
My Friend

Refrain from "A Place In Every Heart"
©Lyrics and Music by Mary Beth Carlson

WRIGHT

Share a practical example of a unique relationship-building strategy.

CARLSON

Isn't it a delight to receive a gift that's been handmade? If it was actually crafted by the gift-giver, it holds an even deeper personal meaning. As a second grade teacher, I often received letters from my students with tender messages painstakingly printed in their neatest penmanship. This unsolicited "creative writing" was a sweet blessing to me. Any handwritten letters of endearment from my children or grandchildren are precious inspirations and treasured keepsakes. They are blessings straight from their hearts.

Aspire to Inspire—The Gift of Creativity

Everyone benefits from the refreshment of "out-of-the-box," imaginative ways to renew and revive a relationship. Encouragement is especially energizing. Be creative!

We don't have to be a professional author, poet, or journalist to sincerely express our thoughts in writing to someone of significance in our life. Who doesn't enjoy the satisfying anticipation of sealing and sending an envelope concealing the gift of a thoughtfully worded letter of encouragement, knowing it will be received and appreciated when it's needed most? There is likely as much pleasure in giving creative encouragement as in receiving this gesture of kindness.

There are countless ways to creatively communicate. I'll share one idea that originated with my dad while I was away at college. This was so personally meaningful that it inspired me to carry on his legacy of encouragement with my own children as well as others in both my personal and professional life.

Although my dad may not have referred to his touching letters of encouragement as "letters of blessing," in retrospect that's what they were. Because he was a gentleman of few spoken words, I greatly looked forward to and appreciated his occasional letters.

Dad was a greatly respected man of highest integrity and was gifted with humility, wisdom, sincerity, and a sweet spirit of gentleness and sensitivity. These attributes shone through in each handwritten letter he sent, whether he was persuading me to continue my interest in piano performance, persevere in applying my study skills to reach my maximum potential, or giving me advice on how to live a God-honoring life. He planted within my heart a desire to inspire others with my own letters of blessing to family members and friends. I sincerely hope this inspiration will be further passed along.

Invited to speak on the value and process of identifying and sharing our gifts at conferences throughout the country, I engage participants in a letter-writing activity during one of the sessions. I so enjoy receiving notes about the meaningful, appreciated results. A husband of one of the women attending a conference in Arizona approached me the following morning in their church. With tears in his eyes, he thanked me for this activity. He said his wife had chosen to write a letter to *him*, and it was the most beautiful gift he'd ever received.

How often do we take the time to think of someone who may benefit from our encouragement, especially during a difficult circumstance, and then follow through by writing and sending a thoughtful, personal letter?

Consider this process:

1. Organize your thoughts; perhaps compose a rough draft to stimulate more interesting creativity.
2. Handwrite the letter, sharing your encouragement with themes in the content related to the recipient. It doesn't need to be lengthy. Even a brief, heartfelt handwritten note on a card is greatly appreciated.

Consider these suggestions:

1. Share sincere compliments specific to the inner qualities most admired and respected in the person.
2. Include inspirational quotes or scripture verses appropriate to the context of the letter.
3. An original poem would give the letter a meaningful, personal touch. This is going "the extra creative mile." When I've given a letter of encouragement along with the gift of an original song to someone dear to me, it's been graciously received.
4. An enclosed photograph is always warmly welcomed, especially a picture of each other together at a memorable gathering.
5. Something as simple as an acronym using the person's name can be a clever idea. Below is an example:

TAYLOR

T	Tender-hearted
A	Adventurous
Y	Yearns to achieve
L	Loving
O	One of a kind
R	Refreshing

6. Whether writing to someone within a personal or professional relationship, consider exactly what is needed at the particular time. Sincere words of hope and compassion? An upbeat day-brightener seasoned with some humor?

7. There are many other topics that could be the focus of your letters: gratitude for a variety of reasons, sharing thoughts about memories of a special occasion spent together, or even a message of forgiveness, the "grace note."

Imagine the letter being read. Isn't it gratifying to think someone may be heartened or even experience a fresh sense of self-confidence and renewed esteem? We all possess the creativity to implement a variety of ideas and touch a heart in a uniquely kind way.

During the past ten years, our daughter, Jody, who was born with cerebral palsy and autism, has regularly received correspondence from a dear elderly woman. Ollie attended an event during which I spoke about rising above the challenges of raising our daughter with disabilities and, over the past several years, severe mental illness. Following the presentation, Ollie asked me if Jody might like to receive a letter from her. To my surprise and delight, Jody began receiving cheery cards, letters, original poems, and even a book written by Ollie. This is a gift of a truly unconditional relationship, an offering of unconditional affection, encouragement, and support for Jody.

Everyone appreciates receiving a sincere, personal letter. I've used a similar strategy of building and enriching relationships in my business communication with customers who order CDs and DVDs. Within each package I include a handwritten note thanking them for their faithful support of my music endeavors along with a specific personal connection when appropriate. Occasionally, in turn, they send notes to me about how meaningful this was to receive. This interaction is one of the aspects I enjoy most about my career. These customers have remained loyal, and our supportive relationships continue.

Communication in any form is healthy to every relationship. However, there's something very endearing about the personal touch of a handwritten note or letter. Amid a high-tech society in which this form of communication is nearly a lost art, it is a distinctively special gift to both give and receive. This act of thoughtfulness just may be the glue needed to seal the bond in a relationship at a crucial point in time.

"The best gift is a handwritten card. I don't know where some of my awards are, but I can tell you exactly where those cards are. I treasure them most."

—Hugh Jackman

WRIGHT

Adversity is a part of each of our lives and can interfere with the process of building and sustaining a relationship. How do you prevent times of adversity from negatively affecting relationships?

CARLSON

As previously discussed, endurance in a relationship results from effectively applying attributes including resilience, patience, and perseverance. It is imperative to strive to keep the relationship alive by ensuring it thrives. Overcoming adversity in the life of either or both relationship partners or within the relationship itself depends upon utilizing these principles.

Expect the Unexpected—Improvisation Along the Journey

Apply resilience to rise above a season of adversity and preserve a relationship. In difficult times of change and challenge, we may need to reorganize and improvise.

Adversity indeed encroaches upon each of our lives, but we cannot allow it to enslave us. It can be a remarkable season of healing. Facing it with a spirit of determination and resolve to rise above will help to illuminate a direction of hope leading to victory on the other side of the pain. To fend off an attitude of defeat, it's important to engage every bit of strength and endurance we've acquired as well as to enlist the help of professional counsel and also others we trust and respect, if needed. This will empower us to come through this season with renewed vision both within ourselves and in our relationships.

We don't have to fear adversity. We can live learning to expect as well as accept the unexpected repercussions of life's turbulence. Knowing we will occasionally experience hardship, it's helpful to proactively prepare by diligently conditioning ourselves with tenacity to be strong physically, mentally, emotionally, and spiritually.

Those who have practiced resilience, patience, and perseverance have stronger coping skills and are far better equipped to manage and bounce back from change and challenge. It's easier to access these character qualities when needed if we've developed and improved upon them over time and experience.

> *"I'm not afraid of storms, for I'm learning to sail my ship."*
> —Louisa May Alcott

Shopping in a gift store recently, a sign caught my eye. *Live, Laugh, Love.* I smiled, nodded, bought it, and put it up on our bedroom wall. But something bugged me about the sequence of these three words. Just for fun, I turned the sign upside down. That's better—*Love, Laugh, Live!*

Now, the first and the greatest of these is love. When we demonstrate genuine compassion, love, and support toward each other, filling each other's emotional tanks with encouragement, we're more likely to live peacefully and contentedly.

Being able to unconditionally give and freely receive love helps us to release our inhibitions. Consequently, we laugh more easily and more often. It's no secret that humor lends a huge contribution to our health. Love and laughter are miraculously healing and flood our hearts with joy, which helps us to live a healthy life with the energy, strength, and endurance necessary to maneuver through times of adversity. We're better equipped to care for our personal well-being and to protect and preserve our relationships.

Research shows that when we love, laugh, and enjoy friendships we help to:

- boost our immune system
- lower our blood pressure and even our cholesterol
- promote relaxation and decrease our heart rate
- reduce stress
- alleviate depression
- increase the oxygen level in our blood, giving us more energy and promoting healing
- increase the endorphin activity in our brain resulting in a sense of well-being

Overall, we're better able to keep things in perspective and immeasurably increase our quality and enjoyment of life.

Gifts of love and laughter shared within meaningful, enduring relationships are like music with healing harmony and a magnificent melody. But sometimes life *isn't* very funny. Sometimes adversity can intrude in the form of significant loss, and we have to create light-hearted moments just to be able to put one foot in front of the other.

The loss that changed my life began fourteen years ago. Jody, the second of our three wonderful daughters, used to call herself the "middlest." She was happy, friendly, and delightfully engaging. After losing her grandfather to Alzheimer's disease and experiencing other subsequent losses, she regressed from being a relatively high functioning, well-adjusted young woman with cerebral palsy and autism to someone we scarcely recognized.

Within weeks of the beginning stages of a serious mental illness, Jody lost eighty pounds, her once remarkable cognitive abilities, much of her speech and processing skills, and basically, as doctors told us, her will to survive. One psychiatrist told me, "Mary Beth, this is *not* Jody's autism getting worse. She is demonstrating behaviors consistent with schizophrenia and psychosis"—really big words for a mom. These were devastating consequences, and we felt helpless. Our once peaceful home became filled with Jody's unpredictable and even bizarre behavior.

We've learned that Jody *is* predictably unpredictable and to expect the unexpected. There have been many years of reorganizing plans and improvising on life as we proceed with steps forward. We do all we can to continue searching for medical answers and providing the best possible care. Most important, we lavish her with our unconditional love and pray for peace and comfort for Jody and each of us in our family.

The experience of loss can certainly be disheartening and even crushing, but the consequences don't need to be debilitating. There are ways to prevent the effects of loss and other adverse circumstances from negatively affecting relationships when we've prepared ourselves in advance. We may well need to organize a new plan of surviving and thriving throughout this time of distress. This entails improvising, thinking wisely on our feet, making important decisions with common sense and "pulling it all together" despite a departure from the norm. Fine-tuning of the improvisation comes with a return to "taking care of business," not necessarily as usual, but as effectively as possible. In the business of life as well as our career, the show—life—must go on.

1. We must continue to maintain relationships by reaching out and seeking help from reliable sources when necessary. Keep actively networking.
2. Set realistic goals and keep the vision alive.

3. Compartmentalize when working on these goals, taking things step by step. We cannot let challenging times rule our thoughts and actions and paralyze us from moving forward.

4. Take opportunities to express our thoughts and feelings honestly with trusted, respected people within our relationships. This will help to relieve stress and the pressure of "flying solo."

5. Expect and look forward to a positive outcome.

The journey with Jody continues to be challenging, but the intensity has lessened. She has stabilized somewhat and now lives in a group home with three other young women with disabilities. She still lives in that mysterious world she created for herself, and we have not yet discovered the key to unlock the door to this private place. We will never stop trying.

My husband and I often reminisce about things we did to keep ourselves and our family healthy during the greatest crises of her mental illness. We recognize that humor was and still is essential. We enjoy laughing over stories related to the years during which Jody was healthy and happy.

Our favorite was an incident in which we eavesdropped on Jody and her younger sister planning to play school, one of their favorite "games"—not surprising, having elementary teachers for parents. They were arguing about who would be the teacher. A thoroughly amusing exchange ensued. "I'm the teacher!" "No, *I'm* the teacher!" Back and forth this continued until Jody, with her most emphatic posture, yelled, *"Fine!! You're* the teacher. But *I'm* the substitute, and you're gone today!" Not bad deductive reasoning for a child with autism! I smile even this moment as I write . . .

Among the most important lessons we're learning is to look for a significant purpose born out of adversity. There are frequent opportunities to share the peace and joy found in leaning on our faith. I continue to write and record songs with messages of hope to nurture a healing process not only within myself, but also to inspire the hearts and hopes of others along their journeys. One of the greatest benefits and blessings in rising above times of challenge is that we acquire experience and skills to help others in their time of need.

In coming through the strains of adversity, the ending can be a wonderful new beginning. The fresh focus of a new season following hardship will likely provide a keener sense of how and when to recognize an opportunity to help someone else across a bridge. And that very gift of kindness and empathy could be the start of a new and mutually rewarding partnership.

"If I could build you a bridge
It would reach over time and space
Rise above pain and fear
And lead to a kinder place . . ."

Excerpt from "A Bridge Over Time"
©Lyrics and Music by Mary Beth Carlson

WRIGHT

What are your personal goals for improving existing personal and professional relationships and achieving mutually gratifying future relationships?

CARLSON

One of the first of many lessons Mom and Dad taught me was The Golden Rule: "Do unto others as you would have them do unto you." Treat everyone else as we want to be treated. Along the growth curve of life, I'm learning that expanding this concept and readjusting a "give-and-take, 50–50" mentality to an unconditional "give-and-give" attitude gives deeper meaning to this ethical code with far greater results.

Above and Beyond—The Encore

A meaningful partnership worth preserving is worthy of the effort to sustain it. Go the distance, then go the extra mile.

My husband, Kent, is also my best friend and business and life partner. When we were newlyweds, our pastor's wife shared something I've never forgotten. The essence of her advice was: forget everything you've heard about partners in a marriage needing to give 50-50. Think 100-100, then think beyond that, and live and give accordingly. We continue to aspire to that level of maturity in our marriage and in other partnerships. Even after thirty-eight years of marriage, it remains a daily commitment.

It isn't realistic to cultivate and nurture several relationships to the extent discussed in this chapter and still enjoy a life well-balanced. Few of us would ever experience such an overwhelming opportunity. Yet it is imperative to faithfully commit to successfully sustaining existing personal and professional partnerships worth preserving and keeping a healthy life balance appropriate to each of our unique levels of energy and time commitments. Personally, it's helpful to frequently check and reset a balance within my priorities of faith, family, friends, and career. If my relationship with God is in a place of prominent priority, other relationships fall into balance more naturally.

I continue to be amazed by how the principles of successfully relating to others in both life and business relationships reflect everything I learned beginning from when I was a child. To get along with others in this world, it sure helps to share—to give generously with a spirit of partnership and a goal of extending ourselves the extra mile to sustain meaningful relationships.

"The most important single ingredient in the formula of success is knowing how to get along with people."

—Theodore Roosevelt

214

It's always a joy responding to an encore request at my concerts. This is often a solo performance fueled with the last rush of adrenaline to express my gratitude to the audience and to give them "something more" of myself, frequently an original composition or a requested favorite. Leaving a positive, lasting impression is never to be underestimated in any circumstance.

Exceeding expectations certainly paves the way toward a promising outcome. But there is no easy route or shortcut to achieving a fulfilling, meaningful, enduring partnership. The pathway to harmony is typically one of detours, U-turns, and potholes; however, the journey is a worthwhile, exhilarating adventure when we invest our heart and soul along each step of the way.

WRIGHT

Thank you, Mary Beth, for a very inspiring and interesting conversation. I appreciate the time you've taken with me here today. It's been delightful. I've learned a lot, and I'm sure your readers will, too.

CARLSON

Thank you, David. It's a pleasure to share my thoughts and contribute to this book.

WRIGHT

Today I've been talking with Mary Beth Carlson. Mary Beth is a songwriter, performing and recording artist, author, and inspirational speaker. She performs nationally as a pianist and speaker for a wide variety of special events and for organizations including the International Special Olympics and the Billy Graham Evangelistic Association. She has recorded twenty-three albums of internationally distributed piano orchestral music.

WRIGHT

Mary Beth, thank you for participating in our project, *Words of Wisdom.*

Mary Beth Carlson is a songwriter, performing and recording artist, author, and inspirational speaker, as well as a former Teacher of the Year. She has produced and recorded twenty-three albums of internationally distributed piano orchestral music. Much of her original music is inspired by her daughter Jody who was born with cerebral palsy and autism.

Blessed with opportunities to perform nationally for a variety of distinguished audiences, she was particularly honored to have been invited by the Billy Graham Evangelistic Association to present a concert of restoration to guests from forty countries at The Cove in Asheville, North Carolina.

In 2009, Mary Beth collaboratively created a comprehensive music experience program for residents in Memory Care for The Goodman Group Inc., LLC, a company that owns and manages senior living, health care, and residential communities throughout the United States and Europe. The project involved arranging, producing, and recording familiar vocal/instrumental music and co-authoring a correlating book of thematic curriculum. Due to its overwhelming success, Volume II was completed in 2012.

Married for thirty-eight years to her husband Kent, they've raised three daughters and reside in Eden Prairie, Minnesota. They immensely enjoy spending time with their six grandchildren.

Mary Beth Carlson

MBC Productions
PO Box 46063
Eden Prairie, MN 55344
marybeth@marybethcarlson.com
www.marybethcarlson.com

CHAPTER TWELVE

The Interview

By Brian Tracy

DAVID WRIGHT (WRIGHT)

Many years ago, Brian Tracy started off on a lifelong search for the secrets of success in life and business. He studied, researched, traveled, worked, and taught for more than thirty years. In 1981, he began to share his discoveries in talks and seminars, and eventually in books, audios, and video-based courses.

The greatest secret of success he learned is this: "There are no secrets of success." There are instead timeless truths and principles that have to be rediscovered, relearned, and practiced by each person. Brian's gift is synthesis—the ability to take large numbers of ideas from many sources and combine them into highly practical, enjoyable, and immediately usable forms that people can take and apply quickly to improve their life and work. Brian has brought together the best ideas, methods, and techniques from thousands of books, hundreds of courses, and experience working with individuals and organizations of every kind in the U.S., Canada, and worldwide.

Today, I have asked Brian to discuss his latest book, Victory!: Applying the Military Principals of Strategy for Success in Business and Personal Life.

Brian Tracy, welcome to *Words of Wisdom*

TRACY

Thank you, David. It's a pleasure to be here.

WRIGHT

Let's talk about your new book the *Victory!: Applying* the *Military Principals* of *Strategy* for *Success* in *Business* and *Personal Life.* (By the way, it is refreshing to hear someone say something good about the successes of the military.) Why do you think the military is so successful?

TRACY

Well, the military is based on very serious thought. The American military is the most respected institution in America. Unless you're a left liberal limp-wristed pinko, most people in America really respect the military because it keeps America free. People who join the military give up most of their lives—twenty to thirty years—in sacrifice to be prepared to guard our freedoms. And if you ask around the world what it is that America stands for, it stands for individual freedom, liberty, democracy, and opportunity that is only secured in a challenging world—a dangerous world—by your military.

Now the other thing is that the people in our military are not perfect because there is no human institution made up of human beings that is perfect—there are no perfect people. The cost of mistakes in military terms is death; therefore, people in the military are extraordinarily serious about what they do. They are constantly looking for ways to do what they do better and better and better to reduce the likelihood of losing a single person.

We in America place extraordinary value on individual human life. That is why you will see millions of dollars spent to save a life, whether for an accident victim or Siamese twins from South America, because that's part of our culture. The military has that same culture.

I was just reading today about the RQ-1 "Predator" drone planes (Unmanned Aerial Vehicles—UAVs) that have been used in reconnaissance over the no-fly zones in Iraq. These planes fly back and forth constantly gathering information from the ground. They can also carry remote-controlled weapons. According to www.globalsecurity.org, the planes cost $4.5 million each and are shot down on a regular basis. However, the military is willing to invest hundreds of millions of dollars to develop these planes and lose them to save the life of a pilot, because pilots are so precious—human life is precious. In the military, everything is calculated right down to the tinniest detail because it's the smallest details that can cost lives. That is why the military is so successful—they are so meticulous about planning.

A salesperson can go out and make a call and if it doesn't work that's fine—he or she can make another sales call. Professional soldiers can go out on an operation and if it's not successful, they're dead and maybe everybody in the squad is dead as well. There is no margin for error in the military, that's why they do it so well. This is also why the military principles of strategy that I talk about in *Victory!* are so incredibly important because a person who really understands those principals and strategies sees how to do things vastly better with far lower probability of failure than the average person does.

WRIGHT

In the promotion of *Victory!* you affirm that it is very important to set clear attainable goals and objectives. Does that theme carry out through all of your presentations and all of your books?

TRACY

Yes. Over and over again the theme states that you can't hit a target you can't see—you shouldn't get into your car unless you know where you are going. More people spend more time planning a picnic than they spend planning their careers.

I'll give you an example. A very successful woman who is in her fifties now wrote down a plan when she was attending university. Her plan was for the first ten years she would work for a Fortune 500 corporation, really learn the business, and learn how to function at high levels. For the second ten years of her career she talked about getting married and having children at the same time. For that second ten years she would also work for a medium sized company helping it grow and succeed. For the third ten years (between the ages of forty and fifty), she would start her own company based on her knowledge of both businesses. She would then build that into a successful company. Her last ten years she would be chief executive officer of a major corporation and retire financially independent at the age of sixty. At age fifty-eight, she would have hit every single target. People would say, "Boy, you sure are lucky." No, it wouldn't be luck. From the time she was seventeen she was absolutely crystal clear about what she was going to do with her career and what she was going to do with her life, and she hit all of her targets.

WRIGHT

In a time where companies, both large and small, take a look at their competition and basically try to copy everything they do, it was really interesting to read in *Victory!* that you suggest taking vigorous offensive action to get the best results. What do you mean by "vigorous offensive action"?

TRACY

Well, see, that's another thing. When you come back to talking about probabilities—and this is really important—you see successful people try more things. And if you wanted to just end the interview right now and ask, "What piece of advice would you give to our listeners?" I would say, "Try more things." The reason I would say that is because if you try more things, the probability is that you will hit your target

For example, here's an analogy I use. Imagine that you go into a room and there is a dartboard against the far wall. Now imagine that you are drunk and you have never played darts before. The room is not very bright and you can barely see the bull's-eye. You are standing along way from the board, but you have an endless supply of darts. You pick up the darts and you just keep throwing them at the target over there on the other of the room even though you are not a good dart thrower and you're not even well coordinated. If you kept throwing darts over and over again what would you eventually hit?

WRIGHT

Pretty soon, you would get a bull's-eye.

TRACY

Yes, eventually you would hit a bull's-eye. The odds are that as you keep throwing the darts even though you are not that well educated, even if you don't come from a wealthy family or you don't have a Harvard education, if you just keep throwing darts you will get a little better each time you throw. It's known as a "cybernetic self-correction mechanism" in the brain—each time you try something, you get a little bit smarter at it. So over time, if you kept throwing, you must eventually hit a bull's-eye. In other words, you must eventually find the right way to do the things you need to do to become a millionaire. That's the secret of success. That's why people come here from a 190 countries with one idea in mind—"If I come here I can try anything I want; I can go anywhere, because there are no limitations. I have so much freedom. And if I keep doing this, then by God, I will eventually hit a bull's-eye." And they do and everybody says, "Boy, you sure where lucky."

Now imagine another scenario: You are thoroughly trained at throwing darts—you have practiced, you have developed skills and expertise in your field, you are constantly upgrading your knowledge, and you practice all the time. Second, you are completely prepared; you're thoroughly cold sober, fresh, fit, and alert with high energy. Third, all of the room is very bright around the dartboard. This time, how long would it take you to hit the bull's-eye? The obvious answer is you will hit a bull's-eye far faster than if you had all those negative conditions.

What I am I saying is, you can dramatically increase the speed at which you hit your bull's-eye. The first person I described—drunk, unprepared, in a darkened room, and so on—may take twenty or twenty-five years. But if you are thoroughly prepared, constantly upgrading your skills; if you are very clear about your targets; if you have everything you need at hand and your target is clear, your chances of hitting a bull's-eye is five years rather than twenty. That's the difference in success in life.

WRIGHT

In reading your books and watching your presentations on video, one of the common threads seen through your presentations is creativity. I was glad that in the promotional material of *Victory!* you state that you need to apply innovative solutions to overcome obstacles. The word "innovative" grabbed me. I guess you are really concerned with *how* people solve problems rather than just solving problems.

TRACY

Vigorous action means you will cover more ground. What I say to people, especially in business, is the more things you do the more experience you get. The more experience you get, the smarter you get. The smarter you get, the better results you get. The better results you get, the less time it takes you to get the same results. It's such a simple concept. In my book, *Create Your Own Future* and *Victory!* you will find there is one characteristic of all successful people— they are action-oriented. They move fast and they don't waste time. They're moving ahead, trying more things, but they are always in motion. The faster you move, the more energy you have. The faster you move, the more in control you feel and the faster you are, the more positive and the more motivated you are. We are talking about a direct relationship between vigorous action and success.

WRIGHT

Well, the military certainly is a team "sport" and you talk about building peak performance teams for maximum results. My question is how do individuals in corporations build peak performance teams in this culture?

TRACY

One of the things we teach is the importance of selecting people carefully. Really successful companies spend an enormous amount of time at the front end on selection. They look for people who are really, really good in terms of what they are looking for. They interview very carefully. They interview several people and they interview them several times. They do careful background checks. They are as careful in selecting people as a person might be in getting married. Again, in the military, before a person is promoted he or she goes through a rigorous process. In large corporations, before people are promoted, their performance is very, very carefully evaluated to be sure they are the right ones to be promoted at that time.

WRIGHT

My favorite point in *Victory!* is when you say, "Amaze your competitors with surprise and speed." I have done that several times in business and it does work like a charm.

TRACY

Yes, it does. Again, one of the things we teach over and over again that there is a direct relationship between speed and perceived value. When you do things fast for people, they consider you to be better. They consider your products to be better and they consider your service to be better—they actually consider them to be of higher value. Therefore, if you do things really, really fast then you overcome an enormous amount of resistance. People wonder, "Is this a good decision? Is it worth the money? Am I going in the right direction?" When you do things fast, you blast that out of their minds.

WRIGHT

You talk about moving quickly to seize opportunities. I have found that to be difficult. When I ask people about opportunities, it's difficult to find out what they think an opportunity is. Many think opportunities are high-risk, although I've never found it that way myself. What do you mean by moving quickly to seize opportunity?

TRACY

There are many cases were people have ideas, they think they're good ideas, and they think they should do something about it. They think, "I am going to do something about that but I really can't do it this week, so I will wait until after the month ends," and so on. By the time they do move on the opportunity it's to late—somebody's already seized it.

One of the military examples I use is the battle of Gettysburg. Now the battle of Gettysburg was considered the high-water mark of the Confederacy. After the battle of Gettysburg, the Confederacy won additional battles at Chattanooga and other places but they eventually lost the war. The high-water mark of Gettysburg was a little hill at one end of the battlefield called Little Round Top. As the battle began, Little Round Top was empty. Colonel Joshua Chamberlain of the Union Army saw that this could be the pivotal point of the battlefield. He went up there and looked at it and he immediately rushed troops to fortify the hill. Meanwhile, the Confederates also saw that Little Round Top could be key to the battle as well, so they too immediately rushed the hill. An enormous battle took place. It was really the essence of the battle of Gettysburg. The victor who took that height controlled the battlefield. Eventually the union troops, who were almost lost, controlled Little Round Top and won the battle. The Civil War was over about a year and a half later, but that was the turning point.

So what would have happened if Chamberlain had said, "Wait until after lunch and then I'll move some men up to Little Round Top"? The Confederate troops would have seized Little Round Top, controlled the battlefield, and would have won the battle of Gettysburg. It was just a matter of moving very, very fast. Forty years later it was determined that there were three days at the battle of Gettysburg that cost the battle for the Confederates. The general in charge of the troops on the Confederate right flank was General James Longstreet. Lee told him to move his army forward as quickly as possible the next day, but to use his own judgment. Longstreet didn't agree with Lee's plan so he kept his troop sitting there most of the next day. It is said that it was Longstreet's failure to move forward on the second day and seize Little Round Top that cost the Confederacy the battle and eventually the war. It was just this failure to move forward and forty years later, when Longstreet appeared at a reunion of Confederate veterans in 1901 or 1904, he was booed. The veterans felt his failure to move forward that fateful day cost them the war. If you read every single account of the battle of Gettysburg, Longstreet's failure to move forward and quickly seize the opportunity is always included.

WRIGHT

In your book, you tell your readers to get the ideas and information needed to succeed. Where can individuals get these ideas?

TRACY

Well, we are living in an ocean of ideas. It's so easy. The very first thing you do is to pick a subject you want to major in and you go to someone who is good at it. You ask what you should read in this field and you go down to the bookstore and you look at the books. Any book that is published in paperback obviously sold well in hardcover. Read the table of contents. Make sure the writer has experience in the area about which you want to learn. Buy the book and read it. People ask, "How can I be sure it is the right book?" You can't be sure; stop trying to be sure.

When I go to the bookstore, I buy three or four books, bring them home, and read them. I may only find one chapter of a book that's helpful, but that chapter may save me a year of hard work.

The fact is that your life is precious. A book costs twenty or thirty dollars. How much is your life worth? How much do you earn per hour? A person who earns fifty thousand dollars a year earns twenty-five dollars an hour. A person who wants to earn a hundred thousand dollars a year earns fifty dollars an hour. Now, if a book cost you ten or twenty dollars but it can save you a year of hard work, then that's the cheapest thing you have bought in your whole life. And what if you bought fifty books and you paid twenty dollars apiece for them—a thousand dollars worth of books—and out of that you only got one idea that saved you a year of hard work? You have a fifty times payoff. So the rule is you cannot prepare too thoroughly.

WRIGHT

In the last several months, I have recommended your book, *Get Paid More and Promoted Faster,* to more people. I have had many friends in their fifties and sixties who have lost their jobs to layoffs and transfers of ownership. When I talked with you last, the current economy had a 65 percent jump in layoffs. In the last few months before I talked with you, every one of them reported that the book really did help them. They saw some things a little bit clearer; it was a great book.

How do you turn setbacks and difficulties to your advantage? I know what it means, but what's the process?

TRACY

You look into it—you look into every setback and problem and find the seed of an equal or greater advantage or benefit. It's a basic rule. You'll find that all successful people look into their problems for lessons they can learn and for things they can turn to their advantage. In fact, one of the best attitudes you can possibly have is to say that you know every problem that is sent to you is sent to help you. So your job is to just simply look into it and ask, "What can help me in this situation?" And surprise, surprise! You will find something that can help you. You will find lessons you can learn, you will find something you can do more of or less of, you can find something that will give you an insight that will set you in a different direction, and so on.

WRIGHT

I am curious. I know you have written a lot in the past and you are a terrific writer. Your cassette programs are wonderful. What do you have planned for the next few years?

TRACY

Aside from speaking and consulting with non-profits, my goal is to produce four books a year on four different subjects, all of which have practical application to help people become more successful.

WRIGHT

Well, I really want to thank you for your time here today. It's always fascinating to hear what you have to say. I know I have been a Brian Tracy fan for many, many years. I really appreciate your being with us today.

TRACY

Thank you. You have a wonderful day and I hope our listeners and readers will go out and get *Focal Point* and/or *Victory!* They are available at any bookstore or at Amazon.com. They are fabulous books, filled with good ideas that will save years of hard work.

WRIGHT

I have already figured out that those last two books are a better buy with Amazon.com, so you should go to your computer and buy these books as soon as possible.

We have been talking today with Brian Tracy, whose life and career truly makes one of the best rags-to-riches stories. Brian didn't graduate from high school and his first job was washing dishes. He lost job after job—washing cars, pumping gas, stacking lumber, you name it. He was homeless and living in his car. Finally, he got into sales, then sales management. Later, he sold investments, developed real estate, imported and distributed Japanese automobiles, and got a master's degree in Business Administration. Ultimately, he became the COO of a $265 million-dollar development company.

Brian, you are quite a person. Thank you so much for being with us today.

TRACY

You are very welcome, David. You have a great day!

One of the world's top success motivational speakers, Brian Tracy is the author of many books and audio tape seminars, including *The Psychology of Achievement, The Luck Factor, Breaking the Success Barrier, Thinking Big* and *Success Is a Journey.*

Brian Tracy

www.BrianTracy.com

CHAPTER THIRTEEN

Wisdom and Wooden: Lessons For Life

By Lynn Guerin

DAVID WRIGHT (WRIGHT)

Today I'm talking with Lynn Guerin, MA. Lynn is one of America's leading performance improvement experts and consultants. A dynamic, passionate, and inspiring speaker and trainer, Lynn serves as President of Guerin Marketing Services, his family-owned marketing services firm in Tustin, California. He is also a senior partner and co-owner of the John R. Wooden Course, LLC. He describes his mission as having a powerful effect on the businesses, organizations, and people he serves, helping them become the best they are capable of becoming in the marketplace and in life. His mission is carried out serving corporations, universities, schools, and public agencies. Lynn's clients have included many of America's top premier companies, including Infiniti, Nissan, Mercedes-Benz, Toyota, General Mills, IBM, Dial Corporation, Nationwide Insurance, Chic-fil-A, In-N-Out, Microsoft, Pacific Dental Services, and the U.S. Navy and Air Force.

Lynn, welcome to *Words of Wisdom.*

233

Lynn Guerin (Guerin)

David, it is wonderful being with you today.

Wright

So how did your relationship with John Wooden begin and develop?

Guerin

I have been in the performance improvement field for many years doing consulting, training, and team development for major corporations. I was working on a project to help launch The University of Toyota. We were developing new modules on coaching. In the business world, we have moved from the management model to the leadership model to the coaching model. We thought it was important to define how great coaches do what they do and why they do it so well.

We reached out to some of America's best coaches and obviously, when you do that, John Wooden's always going to be first on your list. I got an opportunity to develop a relationship with Coach Wooden in building these management modules for The University of Toyota. I saw and experienced his remarkable wisdom, integrity, and humility.

I began to do research to see if anyone had ever assembled Coach Wooden's teaching on the Pyramid of Success, and his ideas on values, character, leadership, and team building. I found out it had not been done. He had distributed his Pyramid of Success over the years. He gave away fifteen hundred a year as people would write and request them. He would sign them, send them, and even pay the postage.

I sat down and wrote Coach Wooden a heartfelt, five-page letter giving him a vision of what the John R. Wooden Course could be and could do. I set up an appointment with him and presented my proposal ideas.

He said he liked the ideas very much and enjoyed our meeting, but he said no to the project. My heart sank and I was disappointed. But, I immediately got a vision of The Pyramid of Success in my head. I began to think of the blocks: *Industriousness*—hard work and careful planning; *Patience*—good things take time (and they should); and *Enthusiasm*—love what you do. I told myself not to give up on this, it's a great idea, and if you get ready, perhaps your chance will come. That's exactly what happened a year later after doing a leadership event with Nissan. The family called and said they wanted to work together to build the John R. Wooden Course.

Wright

How has this relationship affected your life?

GUERIN

David, it's almost hard to describe how the relationship has affected my life. But he quickly became the coach, teacher, philosopher, mentor, father, and grandfather I never had growing up. His wisdom, grace, and humility absolutely changed the way I thought about almost everything in my life. His life represented the mission for the course. I wanted to help as many people as possible understand all that Coach had learned about achieving true success. The world would be a better place if more people followed his example.

WRIGHT

Why do you think it's so important to learn and preserve the wisdom and life lessons of Coach Wooden?

GUERIN

David, I think everybody today is looking for an authentic hero—a role model, a mentor, the kind of coach you can look to for guidance. There is an expression, "he is a self-made man." But I don't think there is any such thing as a self-made man. We are who we are because of the people we meet, the experiences we have.

Almost everything we learn, we learn from somebody else. Coach Wooden's life and wisdom represents a compass, a true north star for how life should be lived, how families ought to develop, and why character and integrity are so vital. He set an example for what it means to give your maximum effort to become all that you are capable of becoming.

Coach Wooden represents that rock solid foundation of traditional values that have made America great. Coach Wooden would say that the two most important words in the dictionary are love and balance. He said, "Do not be so busy making a living you forget to make a life."

WRIGHT

So what are some of the core elements of the Wooden Way that represent Coach Wooden's legacy?

GUERIN

His definition of success provides life-changing perspective in a world obsessed with materialism. "Success is peace of mind, which is the direct result of self-satisfaction in knowing you made the effort to do your best to become the best you are capable of becoming."

The Pyramid of Success was developed in fourteen years and identifies the twenty-five key behaviors essential for success as Coach Wooden defined it. This blueprint for true success along with hundreds of his favorite maxims that are short, powerful statements that say so much in just a few words, such as:

- Do not mistake activity for achievement.
- Be quick but don't hurry.
- Happiness begins where selfishness ends.
- Big things are accomplished only through the perfection of minor details.
- If I am through learning, I am through.

- Ability may get you to the top but it takes character to keep you there.
- Don't let what you cannot do interfere with what you can.
- It is what you learn after you know it all that really counts.

These are the core elements of The Wooden Way.

WRIGHT

So why is the wisdom of Wooden more important now than perhaps ever before?

GUERIN

We see the erosion of core values in our culture. We see so many single parents struggling to raise their children these days, particularly the challenge of young men growing up without fathers. This comes at a time when there is more information in our world but less clear direction for the way in which we could and should live. We have had an opportunity to work with and teach audiences from grade schools to college campuses to America's best corporations. We sense and understand the struggle that everybody seems to be having to try to get life anchored to things that can really be meaningful and to produce the kind of success that people are looking for, not just economically.

WRIGHT

So how can the wisdom of Coach Wooden be best applied to a person's life today?

GUERIN

I think the *Pyramid of Success* is the most powerful template for true success that exists today. The twenty-five behaviors he worked on for fourteen years to define can help any individual, any family, any company or organization be successful in a more meaningful way.

When he would talk about hard *work* and *enthusiasm* and *friendship* and *loyalty* and *cooperation*, he set an example for those behaviors every day. As he would describe the importance of *self-control* in life, he knew that he had to exercise that kind of self-control himself, in every situation in his own life. He would talk about things like *alertness* and *initiative* and *intentness* and *condition* and *skill* and *team spirit.* He ultimately knew that he needed to be the embodiment of those things every day to his players and to his family.

At the top of his *Pyramid of Success* he had a great definition of what he called *competitive greatness*—"the enjoyment of a difficult challenge and being your best when your best is needed." That's a formula for taking on some of the most difficult things in life.

I've been battling cancer for the past year and I've known Coach Wooden for twelve years. I've never understood *competitive greatness* any better than I do now. I understand what the enjoyment of a difficult challenge means. I have learned what it takes to be your best when your best is needed. These lessons are so meaningful when you are at the lowest point of your physical capability, attitude, and energy. When the student is ready, the teacher does appear. Coach Wooden's messages resonate in the best of times, but, more importantly, in the most difficult challenges of your life.

WRIGHT

This has been an interesting and a great conversation, Lynn. I do appreciate the time you've spent with me today to answer these questions. This, along with all the things you talked about that comes from Coach John Wooden's wisdom and experience, has made an exciting chapter in the book and I thank you doing it for us.

GUERIN

Thanks so much, David. There is nothing I'd rather do than share the wisdom, character, love, and life lessons of Coach John Wooden.

WRIGHT

Today I have been talking with Lynn Guerin. Lynn is one of America's leading performance improvement experts and consultants. He describes his mission as having a powerful effect on the businesses, organizations, and the people he serves, helping them become the best they are capable of becoming in the marketplace and in life. For the past twelve years, he has had the unique and life-changing privilege of partnering with an American treasure, legendary basketball coach, philosopher, and writer, Coach John R. Wooden, in the conception, development, and delivery of the John R. Wooden Course, "Timeless Wisdom For Personal and Team Success."

Lynn, thank you so much for being with me today on *Words of Wisdom*.

GUERIN

Thank you, David, for the opportunity to share Coach John Wooden with others.

Coach Wooden was as revered for the person he was as for the success his life produced. America has never known a better coach or a finer man.

The wisdom that you are about to read is taken from actual interviews conducted with Coach John Wooden at public events held between August 2005 and April 2009. Coach Wooden's answers are taken from transcriptions of the video recordings of those events.

I had the never-to-be-forgotten privilege and blessing of interviewing this remarkable man. Once you sat with the master, you just wanted to be a better person, and share what you learned from him with everyone you meet.

LYNN GUERIN (GUERIN)

Coach Wooden, tell us about the Two Sets of Three's and The Seven-Point Creed.

COACH JOHN WOODEN (WOODEN)

Growing up, my father gave me two sets of rules:

- Don't Lie
- Don't Cheat
- Don't Steal

He said if you don't lie, you don't have to remember what you said.

- Don't Whine
- Don't Complain
- Don't Make Excuses

Just do the best you can.

Then I graduated from a small country grade school and Dad gave me a little card. On one side it had a verse by Reverend Henry Van Dyke that said: Four things a man must learn to do if he is to make his life more true:

1. Think without confusion clearly.
2. Love your fellow man sincerely.
3. To act from honest motives purely.
4. To trust in God and heaven securely.

And on the other side of the card was the Seven-Point Creed. All Dad said was, "Son, try to live up to these seven things. The first of seven points on dad's creed was:

1. **Be true to yourself**. Certainly if you are true to yourself you are going to be true to all others. You may be familiar with *Hamlet*, one of Shakespeare's immortal plays when Polonius was speaking to his son, Laertes, who was leaving and going out into the world. His dad thinks he should give him some advice. He doesn't listen much,

but he says to him, "Neither a borrower nor a lender be for loan oft loses both itself and friend, and borrowing dulls the edge of husbandry. This above all else, to thine own self be true. And it must follow the night the day thou canst not then be false to any man."

2. **Help others**. If you just stop and think, your greatest joy comes when you have done something for someone else. There is no greater joy than when something that has been said or done has been meaningful to another, especially when it was done with no thought of something in return.

3. **Make each day a masterpiece**. Just do the best you can every day, no one can do more than that—they may have more ability, no one can do more than making the effort to do the best they can.

4. **Drink deeply from good books—especially the Bible.** The quality of our output is directly related to the quality of our input. Our behavior is determined by what we think, learn, and say.

5. **Make friendship a fine art**. You must work at making friends and work at making friendships flourish. The best time to make friends is before you need them.

6. **Build a shelter against a rainy day**. Consider all things, not merely material things. We have become so infatuated with material things that we have gotten away from lasting values. Refuse to place possessions out of proportion, ahead of family, faith, and friends.

7. Pray for guidance and count and give thanks for your blessings every day. We take our blessings for granted. We fail to give thanks because we are busy looking at what we don't have instead of being thankful for what we do have. And we have so much.

That was Dad's Seven-Point Creed. People ask me if I have lived up to it. I say no, but I've tried. I think that's all Dad would have expected. That's all I expect from young people under my supervision, my children, my grandchildren, and all my thirteen great-grandchildren. All I ask is do your best.

GUERIN

Many would say of course, you've been very successful, but you have a different definition of success than others do. Will you share that definition?

WOODEN

I wrote my own definition of success in 1934. I was unhappy with the way many parents judged the success of their youngsters or the teacher in my English classes. If they didn't make an A or a B, some parents would make the youngster or the teachers feel that they had failed. I didn't like that. I noticed that most parents thought that if the neighbor's children got a C, the average grade, that was all right because they were all average. For their own children, they didn't like that. I didn't like that way of judging. I wanted to come up with a definition of my own. There were two or three things from my father's teaching that I remembered: Never try to be better than someone else; you have no control over that. But never cease trying to be the best you can be. And learn from others. Then I ran across a very simple verse:

> At God's foot stool to confess,
> A poor soul knelt and bowed his head,
> "I failed," he cried.
> The Master said, "Thou didst they best,
> That is success."

I believe that is true. I also recall a class discussion of success that I had been in a number of years before. From those things, I coined my own definition of success: "Success is peace of mind, which is a direct result of self-satisfaction in knowing you made the effort to do the best of which you are capable." You are the only one to know that. I have a book for children out, *Inch and Miles*. Now, for children, I define success a little different. I define it as: happiness in your heart in knowing you tried your best. A short poem expands on that idea of success for children:

242

"Success isn't having trophies or toys,
It isn't a medal or friends of your choice.
What is success that is easy to see?
It's trying to be the best you can be.
Don't worry what others might have or might say,
When trying your best, success comes your way."

GUERIN

How did you communicate to your players about winning and about the competition? Did you talk about winning a lot?

WOODEN

I don't think you could find any player to tell you that I mentioned winning. I wanted winning to be the by-product of the preparation, and failure to prepare is preparing to fail. I always wanted them to have that satisfaction within themselves, that peace of mind within themselves, when they made the effort to execute near their own particular level of competency. Not trying to be better than someone else, but being the best that they could be.

One of my players, a very interesting person, some of you I'm sure have heard of, Bill Walton, once said, "We had to send a manager, when we were dressing for a game, to get a program, to find out who we were playing." I never mentioned the opposition, which is a little different. I wanted the emphasis placed on the improvement of ourselves, the commitment to give our very best effort, and our total dedication to the team concept.

GUERIN

Did you ever have players break the rules deliberately? How did you handle that?

WOODEN

They were denied the privilege of practicing. If they didn't practice, that meant they were not going to play. So much of their playing time would be cut. I had three rules:

1. **Be on Time**. I was a stickler for time. They had to be on time for everything—to class, to practice, to the training table. I insisted they be on time. Maybe I was too strong at times but if they didn't show up in time for practice, they didn't practice.

2. **Not one word of profanity**. I would not permit one word of profanity—you deliver one at practice, you are out of there for the day. I don't hold it against you, but you are out for the day—it's going to cost you some playing time. If it happens at a game, you are going to come out. I didn't say you're going to sit for the rest of the game, but you are going to sit.

3. **Never criticize a team mate**. I say that's my job, I was paid to do it, not you. I was paid pitifully poor in those days, not like today. The coaches today make more in one year than I made in forty years, but that's all right. At one time, I could buy six hamburgers for a quarter, too and gas for fifteen cents a gallon. Things have changed, but my rules did not.

GUERIN

How about disciplining children? What are your thoughts on that?

WOODEN

Well, I believe our children cry out for discipline. But as parents and teachers, we must remember that when you discipline, you discipline to help, to prevent, to correct, to improve. You do not discipline to punish. Punishment often times antagonizes and it is difficult to get productive results when you antagonize. Now, I do think that one of the best motivators is a pat on the back but sometimes that pat has to be a little lower and a little harder. I think denial of privileges is probably one of the best forms of discipline.

Abraham Lincoln once said, "The best thing a father can do for his children is to love their mother."

GUERIN

Tell us why you think *love and balance* are the two most important words in our language.

WOODEN

Well, if you come into the little condo where I live, you will see three bookcases that I have. Each bookcase is carved with a title. One is titled *Love.* The second bookcase is titled *Balance.* The third bookcase reads *Drink deeply from good books—especially the Bible.*

Love is obviously the most important word in our language. If we had more of it throughout our troubled world—and we had it for one another—our problems would not be as severe. We'd have problems, of course, but they would not be unmanageable, if we just had more love and consideration for other people. I like the simple verse:

> "A bell isn't a bell until you ring it,
> A song isn't a song until you sing it.
> The love we have inside, wasn't put there to stay,
> Love isn't love until you give it away."
> —*Oscar Hammerstein, II*

We must keep things in perspective. Balance is keeping things in proper perspective. Don't get carried away if things are going too well or too poorly. Just continue to make the effort to do the best you can at whatever you're doing. You must always be learning— learning from others—to improve yourself and the activities you're involved in, whatever they might be. I really believe all words are important of course, but I believe love and balance are the two most important words.

GUERIN

How did you develop The Pyramid of Success?

WOODEN

I didn't like the way many people were judging success—getting the highest grades, or scoring the most points in an athletic contest, having more material possessions than your neighbor, or a seemingly higher position with more power and prestige. Those are fine, but I think you can be successful without any of those things. I wanted to come up with something that would help me become a better teacher.

I coined my definition of success in 1934, but it was not working as well as I hoped. I tried to analyze why it wasn't, and decided to come up with something more tangible, something you could see. Here again, from the hidden recesses of my mind, I recalled something called a ladder of achievement. Someone had taken a ladder—five rungs in the ladder—and they named each rung in the ladder, a particular trait or characteristic that this individual thought was necessary to get to the top of the ladder, where we would all like to get. We might differ on what we might consider the top of the ladder to be, but we'd all like to get there. I couldn't use the ladder, but it gave me an idea. I came up with the Pyramid.

I started working on this and I began with my definition of success at the apex. I didn't know how many blocks I would have, but the first two blocks I chose were the cornerstones. If any structure is to have any strength or solidity it must have a strong foundation. Of course, the cornerstones anchor the foundation. The first cornerstone is *Industriousness.* There is no substitute for hard work. If you are looking for a shortcut the easy way or a trick, you are not developing the strengths and talents that lie within you. The other cornerstone is *Enthusiasm.* You have to enjoy what you are doing. If you don't enjoy what you are doing, you are not going to work as hard as you are capable of doing.

On the foundation, between the two cornerstones, I had three blocks: Friendship, Loyalty, and Cooperation. We must be friendly, which comes from mutual esteem, respect, and devotion. We must be loyal, to some things and someone. And we must be cooperative, which means we are more interested in finding the best way than in having our own way.

The second tier, I chose four blocks: Self-control, Alertness, Initiative, and Intentness. We must always maintain our self control, in the home, at work, in every situation. Keep emotions under control. We must always be alert and learning, eager to improve. We cannot be afraid to fail and we must be determined and persistent.

At the heart of the structure, I placed three blocks: *Condition, Skill, and Team Spirit.* Condition means mental, moral, and physical. Moderation must be practiced. Skill means being able to properly and quickly execute the fundamentals. Consideration for others, that's team spirit.

Nearing the apex are three more blocks: *Poise, Confidence, and Competitive Greatness.* Poise means just being yourself. Confidence means respect without fear and keeping all things in proper perspective, being at your best when your best is needed, and enjoying the difficult challenge. That is what it means to a great competitor.

GUERIN

At ninety-six years old, it is so apparent you have lived such a full and rich life. What comes to mind as you think about the road ahead and the road behind?

WOODEN

Well, actually the words to a poem come to mind. This was written by a former major league baseball player, who later became a major league umpire. His name was George Moriarty. When he became an umpire, some of the players used to comment on the unusual spelling of his name. They said that even though there was only one "I" in his name; that was one more than he had in his head. The poem goes something like this:

"Sometimes I think the fates must grin,
as we denounce them and insist,
the only reason we can't win
is the fate themselves have missed.
Yet there lives on the ancient claim,
we win or lose within ourselves,
the shiny trophies on our shelves
can never win tomorrow's game.
You and I know deeper down;
there is always a chance to win the crown.
But when we fail to give, our best,
we simply haven't met the test,
in giving all and saving none,
until the game is really won.
Showing what is meant by grit,
by fighting on when others quit.
Playing through not letting up,
it's bearing down that wins the cup.
Dreaming there's a goal ahead,
hoping when our dreams are dead,
praying when our hopes have fled,
yet losing, not afraid to fall,
if gamely we have given all.
For who could ask more of a man,
than giving all within his span.
Giving all it seems to me,
is not so far from victory.
So the fates are seldom wrong,
no matter how they twist and wind,
it's you and I who make our fate;
we open up or close the gate,
on the road ahead or the road behind."

And there is only one real gate that we want to be open to us.

GUERIN

As you have shared with us the importance of "making each day a masterpiece," what are your thoughts when you look back at nearly a century?

WOODEN

I had the opportunity a while back to speak to a group that had a number of elderly persons present. They asked me pretty much the same question. I responded with the words to a poem I had written for the occasion. I like to dabble. I'm not a very good poet. I'm a rhymer, as one of my grandchildren once said. Here is what I shared with them. The title happens to be "Don't Look Back."

> The years have left their imprint
> on my hands and on my face.
> Erect no longer is my walk,
> and slower is my pace.
>
> But there is no fear within my heart
> because I'm growing old,
> I only wish I had more time
> to better serve my Lord.
>
> When I've gone to Him in prayer
> He has brought me inner peace.
> And soon my cares and worries
> and other problems cease.
>
> He has helped me in so many ways,
> He has never let me down.
> Why should I fear the future?
> when soon, I could be near His crown.
>
> Though I know down here my time is short,
> there is endless time up there.

And he will forgive and keep me,
forever in His loving care.

May I not waste an hour
that's left to glorify the Name
Of the One Who died, that we might live,
and for our sins, took all the blame.

GUERIN

You have a very unique and powerful perspective on what it really means to be a great competitor. Would you explain that to us?

WOODEN

Well, that takes us to the top of my Pyramid of Success, where I define *competitive greatness* as "being at your best when your best is needed, and the enjoyment of a difficult challenge." The competitor enjoys it when it's difficult. There is no great joy in doing anything anyone else can do. Yet most of the things you and I do in our daily lives anybody else can do.

Whatever we are doing we should try to do the best of our ability. The difficult fight is valuable, regardless of the outcome. It reveals how competent you are and helps you improve toward your goal of becoming the best you can be.

Grantland Rice, the famous sports writer, captured these ideas in his poem, "How to be a Champion."

"Beyond the winning and the goal,
beyond the glory and the fame,
He feels the flame within his soul,
born of the spirit of the game.
And where the barriers may wait,
Built up by the opposing Gods,
he finds a thrill in bucking fate,
and riding down the endless odds.
Where others wither in the fire,

or fall below some raw mishap.
Where others lag behind or tire,
or break beneath the handicap.
He finds a new and deeper thrill,
to take him on the uphill spin.
Because the test is greater still,
and something he can revel in."

The competitor enjoys it when it's difficult, and revels in it. But you can't do that unless you are prepared. And failure to prepare is preparing to fail.

GUERIN

You have often stated that your father had more influence on you than any other person in your life. What did he teach you about dealing with adversity?

WOODEN

He never complained at all. I think he had reason to complain on occasion, especially, when we lost our farm. He did not blame anybody. I think somebody should have been blamed. He just accepted it. And he wouldn't tolerate his sons being critical of other people. He was a calming influence. I learned to accept things. It was a great help to me, without my realization, when I got into teaching sports, learning to accept things. I was able to do that primarily for him.

For example, my senior year we lost a state high school basketball championship game by one point in the last few seconds, on a miracle shot by the other team. I think everybody on the team cried, except me; I didn't cry. And I'm sure I felt like the others. But, I'd been taught to do the best you can and accept the consequences. I believe that came from Dad and carried over to a lot of other things later in my life.

I tried to get my basketball teams to always accept things as they were. I never wanted excessive exuberance because you outscored somebody in the game. Nor did I want excessive dejection if you were outscored in the game. Because, you know, you are the only one who would know that you did the proper things to prepare yourself for the game. And if you gave your best, there is nothing to be sorry about.

GUERIN

When you look back on your life, how would you really like to be remembered?

WOODEN

I would like to be remembered as a normal person who was considerate of others. That would be enough for me.

For the past twelve years, Mr. Guerin has had the unique and life-changing privilege of partnering with an American treasure, legendary UCLA Basketball Coach, philosopher, and writer Coach John R. Wooden and his family. The partnership produced the John R. Wooden Course, "Timeless Wisdom for Personal and Team Success." This Wooden Way performance improvement system includes a curriculum and a set of personal and team diagnostic and sustainment tools. It also includes a unique team camp delivery method. All of this is designed to develop coaching, team, and leadership knowledge and skills.

Lynn received his BA and MA from Western Michigan University. He is a frequent speaker on the Prayer Breakfast Network, a Little League baseball manager, a youth basketball coach, lay leader for a men's Christian ministry, and serves on the Board of Directors of Joni and Friends, the disability ministry of Joni Eareckson Tada

Lynn Guerin

John R. Wooden Course
14742 Plaza Dr., Suite 205
Tustin, CA, 92780
lynn.guerin@guerinmktg.com
www.woodencourse.com

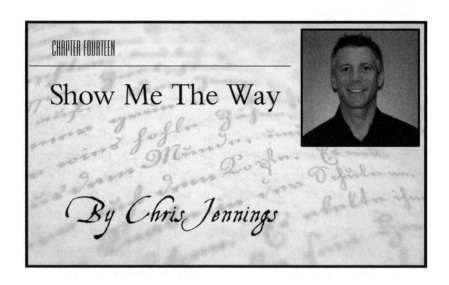

CHAPTER FOURTEEN

Show Me The Way

By Chris Jennings

DAVID WRIGHT (WRIGHT)

Today I'm talking with Chris Jennings. Chris is the owner of nationally acclaimed Sandler Training of Irvine, California. He frees his clients from wasting time and energy on unqualified prospects that cannot or will not see the benefits of their product or service and shows them how to target prospects who really do want to buy. His relaxed style and keen awareness of almost any sales situation helps pinpoint mistakes and shift to techniques that work.

Chris is a Graduate of UCLA and loves UCLA basketball.

Chris is available as a keynote speaker and offers ongoing private and group coaching that leads to increased efficiency, confidence, and control of the sales process.

Chris, welcome to *Words of Wisdom.*

CHRIS JENNINGS (JENNINGS)

Thank you, David; glad to be here.

WRIGHT

Will you give me two or three factors that help predict success in people?

JENNINGS

Sure. I'd say the key things we look for are in three different areas. Number one is behavior and activity—how clearly focused are people on their goals? Do they have a clear plan of exactly what they're supposed to do? Are they tracking what they said they would do or not? Do they have pictures of what their goals represent? Frequently we'll ask as a question, how many of us have this and people will nod their head saying that they have goals. But I challenge any one of your listeners and I guarantee we'll get fewer than 1 percent who can say, "I have clear short- or long-term written goals with a daily weekly plan of what my specific activities are each week. I also have a daily and weekly tracking system that I complete at the end of each week and show to another individual with pictures of what my goals represent." It's that clear focus on behaviors and activities that help people accomplish what they need to.

Secondly I'd say it's attitude and beliefs—whatever people believe is true is true. People have some helpful beliefs and they have some self-limiting beliefs, and those beliefs get in the way. Those are what we call head trash. The conversations that people have within themselves, include talking themselves out of calling somebody, talking themselves out of calling on the right person, and convincing themselves they're not entitled to a referral when clearly they are. Looking at the right attitudes and the right beliefs is critical for us to get where we want to go.

The third component I say is a technique—what systems do you follow? Do you have a clear playbook of plays drawn up that you're executing on a daily basis to help you accomplish your goals? If you have a system in place and you go on a sales call and the sales call doesn't go well, you can fall back to that system and ask yourself a series of questions about what you should or shouldn't have done. If you don't have a system and everything is a flying-by-the-seat-of-your-pants experience and you're going by gut instinct, then you never really quite know what changes to make along the way and how to adapt and how to grow.

A combination of those three areas will help predict success.

WRIGHT

How does one overcome childhood and early adulthood negative scripting?

JENNINGS

The truth is, while we're all adults in business I often think that many people are still seven-year-olds just in bigger clothes with more responsibility. The fact is that many of us had a lot of imprints at an early age; by the time we were seven years old, it is predicted how we act throughout the course of our lives, whether it was things we learned at home and habits. What habits did we pick up as a child? What habits did we pick up in early adulthood from that first boss. We have some good habits and some not so good habits. If our scripting tells us we shouldn't talk to strangers, well no wonder we don't want to pick up the phone and call somebody new.

If your scripting tells you that it's impolite to talk about money and you wonder why you're not calling on prospects who can afford what you offer because you haven't asked any of the right questions, then it all comes back to that scripting. Many of those early bosses probably just said, "Just go out there and get a lot of quotes and something will come through." I've watched companies put together a hundred million dollars a year in quoting only to get twelve million dollars a year in business. If you subscribe to the idea of just quote a lot of business, some of it's bound to come to the surface but you're going to miss out on so many opportunities because you're too busy quoting stuff that you don't really need.

What's necessary is to rewrite those scripts, and rewire those beliefs. You need a set of affirmations that will replace the old negative head trash. If you have written out beliefs or if you've read them into a tape recorder, play them back to yourself. Post them in front of you, journal on a daily basis. Look at what old beliefs are getting in your way and replace them with your new beliefs. That's the process we have to go through to clean them up.

WRIGHT

Everybody experiences disappointment. Can you suggest ways to deal with failure and adversity?

JENNINGS

It depends on how you look at failure and disappointments. If you embrace them and look at each experience as an opportunity to learn and grow, whether it went your way or not, then that is certainly a healthy way to approach it. I've heard it said, "Fail and fail fast, make as many mistakes as you can, as quickly as you can early in your career so you can get them out of the way so you can experience all that life has to offer." If you are focused on where you want to go, what you're trying to accomplish, and you have the vision of what that means to you, then you will relentlessly pursue that vision and overcome the challenges and obstacles that are natural in any situation.

One of our favorite strategies is to have a goal board. Create a goal board or a dream board or a vision board; call it what you want. Place pictures that represent where you're trying to get to in life with certain phrases that have a meaning for you. Post it in your home, in your home office, in your office at work, perhaps in your car, or the binder you carry with you. If you're very focused on those goals and what you're trying to accomplish and you have pictures of what that would represent to you, then you will work through the struggles, the natural disappointments, the natural failures that are going to come up. You'll learn the lessons and the changes you need to make, and what responsibility you have in what happened and why it didn't go forward, and you'll keep moving toward those goals.

WRIGHT

So how do we fit it all in? What do most people leave out?

JENNINGS

This is such a great question. I think the older we get and the more experience we get and the more activities we have in our life, our schedules get crowded and we lose sight of the priorities. If you're trying to grow a business, you're in sales, you own a business, you're a professional trying to develop a business, or someone who works in a professional services firm, there is a key concept we refer to as "pay time versus no pay time." Pay time for us is on the phone or in front of prospects and clients. Unfortunately most people are just not getting enough pay time in their day.

Typically the national average for a full-time salesperson is only forty-five minutes to an hour actually spent each day in pay time. We recommend four hours a day of pay time. What we have found is that people who can get four hours a day, day in and day out, of time on the phone and in front of prospects and clients will 100 percent hit their goals. They will not only hit them but blow those goals away.

Unfortunately people aren't getting that because they're distracted by several no pay time activities. Some of the no pay time activities are legitimate, such as putting together a proposal, internal staff meetings, and so on. However, a lot of no pay time activities are significantly detrimental. Most salespeople and business owners spend more time deleting e-mails from their inbox than they spend time talking to prospects and clients. Facebooking friends, fantasy football leagues, Angry Birds, the computers and screens and iPhones and other devices that were designed to be great communication tools have unfortunately cluttered our lives with inordinate amounts of no pay time. We are no longer having nearly the quantity of live conversations with prospects and clients that we need to have.

What we need to do is schedule out an ideal week—from the time we get up Monday morning to the time we go to bed each day, Monday through Sunday. Write in your quality downtime and no pay time activities. What are the things that you want to do at night? Do you want to be at the gym? Is there a softball league you're involved in? Are you involved in a church group. Do you need to help your kids do their homework? Schedule the things that are important to you in your life in your downtime hours, right through the weekends. Then schedule the time you're in pay time hours. Whenever your hours are, be very clear what your pay time blocks are so that if somebody wants to bring an article to read at three o'clock and you have the time reserved strictly for prospects and clients tell the person you will either meet or speak to him or her live at a certain time. Or take the article and thank the person and say, "I'll take a look at this at four-thirty when I'm done with my block of pay time."

When you schedule an ideal week, it won't be a perfect week—it's something you're working toward and is a critical exercise. You must have a picture of how you should spend your time.

WRIGHT

Why do you think people have such a hard time asking for help?

JENNINGS

Another great question. I would say it comes back to a lack of confidence. People don't like to look weak, they don't like to be perceived as somebody who doesn't know what they're doing when the reality is that all great people ask tons of clarifying questions. They ask for help from those around them, they seek out role models. Look at all the great athletes—Michael Jordan, Kobe Bryant, and every Olympic athlete you could ever think of. All have a team of coaches who helps them study, helps them improve. They are not bad athletes, but great athletes who are relentlessly pursuing greater heights. They have faster, stronger, and better accomplishments. They have more accuracy.

The same thing applies in business and in personal life. We all need help from others—people who have already been through that. We need a third party who is objective and a credible resource who can give us some real feedback about what we're doing that's helpful and what we're doing that's not.

I've seen many times where confident sales managers will hire people and bring them to work with sales teams, because they know that the answers that the sales managers bring to the equation aren't the only answers that exist out there. The sales managers who are not confident, who are second-guessing themselves are afraid to have somebody else looking over their shoulder, fearing that they might be seen as not doing everything right. We're human beings—we are all built with imperfections. None of us have all of the answers. When we seek outside help and outside answers, we grow stronger.

I find it so interesting that we spend so many years in school from the ages of five to twenty-one to twenty-two, but then at twenty-two, most people stop going to school—they stop learning. Why wouldn't we continue to grow as adults? We now have real-world experience. We should seek out more answers and ask more questions from those who have been there. It comes back to confidence—we must keep building our confidence to be able to ask the questions.

WRIGHT

If there were only one strategy you could offer a sales team to improve performance, what would it be?

JENNINGS

There are so many things you can do to improve sales; however, if I could only give somebody one specific answer I'd say that it includes obvious choices to me—referrals and introductions. It's the most efficient, shortest sales cycle, with the highest closing percentage. It's the best way to go. If every client you work with today only introduced you to one more client, how much more business would you be doing? The answer is double, right? At least. If each client just introduced you to one more client you could double your business.

The interesting observation I've had having done this for many years with many organizations, is that very few people, less than 1 percent of the people I ever survey, are not actually asking for referrals on a regular basis. The number one reason people don't get referrals is they don't ask.

However, the number two reason is the fear associated with asking—they don't want to look stupid, they don't want to appear needy, or they feel like they're not entitled to it. Again, this stems from a lack of confidence. If you truly had confidence and you recognize the real nature of the partnership between you and your customer, of course you would ask for referrals and introductions. But people aren't sure how to bring it up and they're not sure when to bring it up. They wait too long and they ask in a sheepish way as opposed to being assertive. Unfortunately, most people don't have the systems installed in their business to remind them to do it.

I speak all the time on referrals and introductions. It is my absolute favorite and the most time-efficient way to go about it. If you don't have a process and if you don't have the confidence to ask, it won't happen; unfortunately you'll be doing it the hard way. Keep struggling along with web leads who don't know who you are, they sought you out as well as five of your competitors. They ask you to quote on something and they choose the vendor with the lowest price, as opposed to having your good clients refer you to somebody new. If you became focused on it, anything is possible.

WRIGHT

Aside from personal role models, who are the people who have served as your role models for success?

JENNINGS

I'd say the primary figure I've always looked to is somebody I would strive to model my business after. In my personal life I have always looked up to John Wooden. John Wooden was the head coach of the UCLA men's basketball team that won an unprecedented ten national championships. He retired in the mid '70s to spend more time with his family. He lived to be ninety-nine years old and was a coach and a mentor to many. He had some very clear principles he followed in his life. Even though his job as a basketball coach was to help win championships, every one of his players ever interviewed would certainly agree that he cared much more about the players as people than he did the basketball performance. While he expected nothing less than everybody's best efforts, he was a caring humanitarian.

Interestingly enough, in business people get so squeezed for time they have too many things to do, they're overburdened, managers appear as uncaring and insensitive, and people leave organizations all the time.

The intention that many have is to be a caring manager but their actions speak differently. John Wooden was a person who held himself to a high standard. He reminded us that the hard thing to do and the right thing to do are usually the same; he was willing to make the hard choices. He reminded us that it's what you learn after you know it all that counts, to inspire us to keep growing even when we feel like we've become very good. The concept of the good being the enemy of the great is a well-known concept. He encouraged us to give our best effort, and he held us to disciplines about practicing our craft.

Very few people in their busy lives take the time out to practice their craft. By the time Coach and his team got to a basketball game, every drill, every play that they ran on the court had been drilled and practiced time and time again. They weren't having success in the way they were in undefeated seasons by accident—it was because of the practices they'd had. He instilled in me a commitment to helping the people I work with to invest time into practicing. If you want to be a better salesperson, put two or three hours a week into practicing at being a better salesperson. If you want to be a more efficient business owner, put two or three hours a week at least into being a more proficient business owner. Have a coach that gives you feedback, have somebody who pushes you and makes you run faster than you would on your own.

Those are some of the many beliefs that Coach Wooden helped me develop, as well as balancing out, time between business success and family success. He spent time with me, personally and gave me good advice about how to raise my three daughters and be actively involved as a coach. He was the one who told me to let my business grow at the rate that it's going to grow but make sure I give those kids the time. I'm proud to say I've been able to do that.

WRIGHT

So what do you think are the biggest obstacles people face in trying to become successful?

JENNINGS

It's a recurring theme that people often ask me, "Chris, what's the most important characteristic for anybody to achieve self-success?" I always tell them, and it's always consistently the same, confidence. The very best salespeople I've ever worked with had the highest degree of confidence and are most interested in performing and doing well. If you're not confident, then you just won't accomplish what you need to accomplish. Unfortunately society has raised a lot of people who second-guess themselves and they haven't done the work to take care of themselves to make sure that they're accomplishing what they want to accomplish.

When I say "take care of themselves," I mean physically, mentally, and spiritually. There are a lot of broken souls out there who are not in good physical condition and who are not doing what they said they would do. Unfortunately when we break promises and commitments to ourselves and we break those promises, we don't feel entitled to the success because we know we're not doing the work required to get there. So what I do is say to myself, "I'm going to call twenty new prospects this week" and I don't do it, then I undermine my own confidence because again I've broken another promise to myself.

So we often ask people, let's step back and figure out if you want to become more confident. On a scale of one to ten, in a ten meaning your self-confidence rating, what is the plan you're going to need to create, what will you need to do? Do you need to be at the gym four times a week and if you need to spend time with friends, go to that remote place on a mountain to spend time with a spiritual advisor, nourish your confidence, take care of yourself, follow through on the commitments that you made and you'll find you grow to become a more confident person.

WRIGHT

Would you tell our readers a little bit about what drives you to be successful?

JENNINGS

I think I've always been a very goal-oriented person, I'm fortunate to have three daughters who depend on me. My third daughter will start college, so I've always had reasons to be successful. The truth is what that drives me the most; I'm passionate about what I do. Anybody who has ever seen me speak in front of a group would agree that I care for my audience. I challenge the salespeople. I will get on their case for not doing what they're supposed to be doing; however, nobody is rooting for them harder than I am.

When I made a decision to get into this business, I worked for Mobile Oil and I eventually was promoted to the training department. We did a lot of training in sales and marketing but we also covered topics other than sales. One day, after covering a topic that some would have considered to be a boring or mundane, at the end of the program somebody said, "Chris, you have a real gift and you did a great job with the program." It occurred to me that this was a sign of the direction I needed to be moving into.

Later I owned a different business. I was at a weekend seminar with a gentleman in the front of the room giving us great ideas, and one suggestion after the other about how to make our business more profitable. I had an epiphany at that moment. I said I was in the wrong chair—I was sitting in the audience when I felt like I should be at the front of the room. I made a decision at that point to go on and become a sales and marketing coach and trainer and I started to create a business plan for Chris Jennings. While developing my best ideas for sales and marketing, I was introduced to the Sandler

Training Method and instantly decided it was the right thing to do. I opened up my business and I never looked back.

I'm pushing a twenty-year career now, where I feel eager to go to work each day. I never regret getting up and going to work, I always look forward because I get to go to work. I know there are more people out there who need my help and I'm rooting for them as hard as anybody. I'm their biggest fan, and I know the challenges they face and I'm passionate about it. I always tell the people I work with that if you're not passionate and you don't have conviction about what you do, find somebody who can help you find that conviction and passion or go do something else. If you're passionate about what you do, it will come across and people will follow you. People need that help and you've got to be passionate about it. I think that's what drives me.

WRIGHT

What is the message that you want people to hear so they can learn from your success?

JENNINGS

I think the primary message is that anything is possible, don't hold yourself back. If you believe it can happen, it can. If you believe it can't happen, it won't happen. Don't try and do it on your own, remain teachable. Find a good teacher, there are several out there. Find somebody who is committed to helping you and find somebody who will show you what he or she has done; let that person inspire you to reach new heights. Anything is truly possible if you think it is but do the work that's required to get there. Create the plan, have the right beliefs, and get the help from a coach or trainer or someone who will lead you there. Stay disciplined, expect it to be hard; you don't want it to be easy. When things aren't going your way, expect that and know that those are opportunities. If it were easy, everybody could do it—everybody would be successful at what you're doing. You want challenges that you worked hard to overcome. Anything is possible—you just have to stay focused on the goal.

WRIGHT

How did you begin speaking and why did you choose sales as a main topic?

JENNINGS

I talked a little bit before about my first ah-ha moments and how I got into speaking. I'm passionate around sales being a topic because there is no formal education for sales, there is no four-year degree, there is no master's degree in sales and there is no PhD.

If I look at a business as a sport's team and you say you've got half offense and half defense, offense in the business is sales. Defense in the business is operations, accounting, supply chain, HR systems and so on. In sales there is no formal education whatsoever and there is a desperate need for help. My goal is to help people figure out how to fill that gap. It's been a joy of mine, as I'm entering my third decade, and hope to do this for at least three more decades.

WRIGHT

So how did you conclude that speaking was your passion?

JENNINGS

I realized that speaking was a passion of mine many years ago after delivering a program, and frankly, after every program I deliver, there is the feedback that I get from that audience. I know how challenging it is for people out there, I know that people need help, I know that many of them are lost or misguided, they're confused, they don't know who to talk to, and speaking to large audiences whether that large audience is a dozen people at a local sales meeting or a thousand people at a conference, I've felt like that's a way for me to reach as many people as I can. As I said I'm their biggest fan, I root the hardest for every salesperson out there. I know the challenges that they face and I know they need help.

Life isn't easy, life is filled with challenges, life is filled with obstacles, and we need some guides and teachers out there. I feel that I have some clear answers filled with common sense that are fairly easy to follow. I look to reach people in a real way. I'm a very real and authentic person and I'm alongside of them trying to help them. I feel like speaking is a way I can do that. The more people I can reach, the more people I can help, the more lives I can change.

When a salespeople grow their income from $50,000 to $100,000, that's a life changing event for them. That will change their lives and the lives of their children, and their children's children for many years. The more people I can reach, the more people I can help, the more satisfaction I get.

WRIGHT

What a great conversation, Chris. I appreciate your time here today and for answering all these questions. I certainly learned a lot and I'm sure our readers will.

JENNINGS

Thank you David, I appreciate your comments and feedback.

WRIGHT

Today I have been talking with Chris Jennings, the owner of nationally acclaimed Sandler Training in Irvine, California. Chris will free you from wasting time and energy on unqualified prospects that cannot or will not see the benefits of your product or service. He shows you how to target clients who do want to buy. Chris, thank you so much for being with us today on *Words of Wisdom*.

JENNINGS

David it's been my pleasure.

Chris Jennings is the owner of nationally-acclaimed Sandler Training, in Irvine, California. Chris frees his clients from wasting time and energy on unqualified prospects that cannot or will not see the benefits of their products or services and shows them how to target clients who really do want to buy. His relaxed style and keen awareness of almost any sales situation helps his clients pinpoint mistakes they are making and shift to techniques that work.

Chris is a graduate of UCLA and loves UCLA basketball. He is available as a keynote speaker and offers ongoing private and group coaching to companies that leads to increased efficiency, confidence, and control of the sales process.

Chris Jennings

Sandler Training
Irvine, CA
949-450-1425 (office)
949-463.5755 (cell)
949-261-1336 (fax)
chris@lrn2sell.com
www.lrn2sell.com
www.jenningschris.com

CHAPTER FIFTEEN

Work Life Wisdom

By Helen Harkness

DAVID WRIGHT (WRIGHT)

Today I'm talking with Helen Harkness, PhD, CMF, pioneer in career management, who founded Career Design Associates Inc. in 1978. She is a resourceful, strategic catalyst who spurs others to act while providing resources and direction for changing careers. She is a teacher, futurist, consultant, researcher, speaker, and published author of *Best Jobs for the Future* (1995), *The Career Chase* (1997), *Don't Stop the Career Clock* (1999), and *Capitalizing on Career Chaos* (2005).

She is regularly quoted in *USA Today, Financial Times, Los Angeles Times, International Herald Tribune, Chicago Tribune, Good Housekeeping, Fast Company* and *The Dallas Morning News.* She received the first Professional of the Year Award from the Dallas/Fort Worth Chapter of the Association of Career Professionals International, and the award is now permanently named for her.

Dr. Harkness, welcome to *Words of Wisdom.*

HELEN HARKNESS (HARKNESS)

Thank you, David. A century ago, someone asked Freud, "What should a normal person be able to do?" Freud simply replied: "He should be able to love and work." I connect with the work part—I am strongly committed to helping my clients develop the wisdom necessary to know the purpose they can pursue with passion, and a plan of action for gaining meaning and money.

Of course, David, this must be based on their internal needs and talents, coupled with the needs, demands, necessities and the reality of our rapidly changing world. As a result, they can manage their career and work life more effectively, resulting in a happier and more successful personal, family, and community life. I trust that helps explain the "love part" Freud mentioned. I provide my career clients with the information, techniques, and insight for gaining this external and internal insight for a successful career—as they define it.

Why am I taking the time to write on wisdom in the midst of all our current workforce problems? According to Mark Twain, "You can't no more teach what you don't know than come back from where you ain't been!" When it comes to developing and achieving a plan for career success, despite all the detours, road blocks and closed highways, and countless other unexpected problems, I have probably learned more from the School of Hard Knocks than all the universities I've attended. I responded positively to this because frankly, I've had several clients recently say: "Dr. Harkness, tell us what you base all your insight on. Why are you into the career field with such determination? What's going on with you? Tell us all how you learned this!" I hear: "We want to be like you—give us a class in being like you!" This request absolutely floors me since I can vividly recall my own earlier countless "dark nights of the soul" as I moved to where I am today.

Also, I didn't jump on this project because of the title, *Words of Wisdom*—I never thought of myself as wise. I have no problem labeling myself as a futurist, a pioneer, a teacher (I've taught every level from seventh grade through PhDs), and I am a catalyst, consultant, coach, entrepreneur, and whatever—but nowhere have I ever used the word "wise" in any description of myself, present or past. However, David, perhaps my appropriate response to creating words of wisdom is to define my current career work commitment as an expression of my "wisdom." I take responsibility for being the best at providing the resources for helping clients identify and achieve their career success—as they define it.

As background, Karen Sands (a professional friend) interviewed me and included it in a book, *Visionaries Have Wrinkles: Conversations with Wise Women Who are Reshaping the Future*. It has just been released on Amazon's Kindle. This was totally unexpected! I told my clients, "Yes, I have strong foresight and visions of the future, built on my more than twenty years with the World Future Society. I certainly have the wrinkles (even after a facelift at age fifty), but I am not putting big claims on wisdom!"

So, writing this chapter was my chance to research and think on wisdom from a contemporary focus. However, instead of my usual style of in-depth research into the past, I sent out an e-mail to a random list of clients and friends, asking them to give me their definition of wisdom. I wanted to learn from them. Does that make sense?

WRIGHT

Absolutely.

So how did your clients respond and define wisdom in the e-mails they sent you?

HARKNESS

David, the response was overwhelming! I received ninety-eight replies within three days. Some were very in-depth and others were only two or three words—all very interesting! I can't get their definitions in this chapter, but I plan to blog them on the CDA Web site (www.Career-Design.com) exactly as they were sent to me.

In summary, however, there seems to be an agreement that formal education has little connection with wisdom. Also, gaining wisdom

273

involves effectively utilizing lessons learned, and many stated that they wish they had known wisdom when they were younger! This has caught my attention! I wondered if the generally accepted concept that "wisdom is reserved only for elders" needs to be rethought.

Words and phrases repeated in these wisdom e-mails include: thoughtful, reflective, insightful, hopeful, compassionate, empathetic, self-acceptance, serenity, understanding, self-trust, lessons learned, courage to speak the truth, practicing the art of listening (this element grants wisdom), and seeking and learning lessons that change you in a positive way. Knowing when, where, and how to strategically use all collective wisdom is a challenge. I thought this, from a client, was interesting: "Wisdom without use is no more valuable than a closed book." These definitions go on for page and pages, David.

The replies were mostly from typical Baby Boomers. A lawyer client, who is in a particularly difficult situation, wrote, "Dr. Harkness, to me, power without wisdom is tyranny!" This directly reflects what countless numbers of my clients are experiencing currently and unrelentingly in the workplace. They hate their jobs because somebody over them is using tyranny instead of wisdom in managing them. This is a big issue! I found this definition absolutely on track!

WRIGHT

So have you ever researched and written on wisdom before this time?

HARKNESS

Yes. Yes, I have. When I wrote the book, *Don't Stop the Career Clock: Rejecting the Myths of Aging for a New Way to Work in the 21st Century*, there was a chapter titled "Cultivating Wisdom." In my usual style (because I am a researcher), I dug deep into defining and researching wisdom for elders. What I found—and didn't find— shocked me! In researching the psychological material in 1999, there was an almost total neglect of the concept of wisdom and aging! I was genuinely surprised! The one thing that elderly people are supposed to have is wisdom, so I thought, "Oh, there'll be a lot written about that!" but it was obvious almost immediately that there was practically nothing! The 1996 edition of *The Handbook of the Psychology of Aging* had a total of 416 double-columned pages, but David, out of all that there was only *one* paragraph on wisdom.

This is weird—the author labeled wisdom as an ancient topic that traditionally includes formal knowledge, moral behavior, and awareness of what one doesn't know. An earlier (1973) handbook, which was supposed to summarize everything on psychology, does not even index the subject! You cannot even find the word "wisdom" in its forty-five chapters.

Now, David, this remarkably small amount of research and writing on wisdom may indicate that "wisdom" is of little concern, since it is a major strength supposedly connected with aging. Perhaps this silence indicates a reluctance to attribute any positive attribute to older adults; this is what we might think about. Perhaps the late nineteenth and early twentieth centuries placed wisdom off-limits since the psychologists of those times were more behaviorists.

However, according to research initiated by *The Harvard Business Review* in 1997, the need and respect for wisdom in the workplace is highly critical. Five of the most important business leaders of this time, including Peter Drucker, Esther Dyson, Charles Handy, Paul Saffo, and Peter Senge were asked to select the most important business issues of this age. These five came up with what they believed were its current and upcoming challenges.

Surprisingly, these did not include the traditional technical and rational issues of business, but concentrated on cultural and philosophical ones, stressing the need for wisdom. These were: 1) Lead organizations that create and nurture knowledge, 2) Know when to set machines aside and rely on our human instincts and judgments, 3) Live in a world where companies have increasing visibility, 4) Maintain, as individuals in organizations, our ability to learn, 5) Meet the continuing challenge, not of technology, but the art of human and humane management. These five experts said that these were the five challenges identified for leading business success today and in the future.

In 1997, Peter Senge said that their research and our responses may lead us, ironically, to a future based on more ancient and more natural ways of organizing communities of diverse and effective leaders who empower their organizations to lead with head, heart, and hand. This is a return to an older model of community.

Senge continues by saying that traditional societies gave equal respect to the elders for their wisdom, to teachers for their ability to help people grow, and to warriors, weavers, and growers for their life skills. He further states that our new world of technology requires an abundance of and proficiency in wisdom, human relation skills, and sound judgment.

So, David, this is what the very top leaders are saying. However, when people come to me with major career issues, they are not associated with organizations that do this. These researchers concluded that the notion of wisdom as wealth and power has been around since Plato, but has been overlooked in our more recent modern times by the notion of wealth as the more tangible source of personal consumption and possession. I contend strongly that all of us need to pick up more on wisdom and focus on it regardless of chronological age.

WRIGHT

So why do you say wisdom is not just for the aging?

HARKNESS

David, the rule "Wisdom is only for the aged"—that wisdom is only for the aging is an outdated myth—a *former* truism! It's a concept we automatically accept and we don't even question it. There are so many of those myths that, once we look at them, they simply don't hold up!

I say that we should be focusing more on wisdom at an earlier time—perhaps introducing it into the school systems! I'm not saying that we should have kids passing wisdom tests, and so on, but I have found two contemporary thinkers who have some very important things to say about integrating wisdom into our educational system.

They are: Nicholas Maxwell, author of *From Knowledge to Wisdom*, (1984), and Copthorne MacDonald, author of *Toward Wisdom: Finding Our Way to Inner Peace Love & Happiness* (1995). Incidentally, MacDonald also has a Web page that is strictly devoted to wisdom. (URL is http://www.wisdompage.com/)

The intense research of both of these writers advocates that wisdom become more integrated into our educational system. The idea of separating wisdom—keeping it like it's something to be accumulated only down the road or in the distant future—is dysfunctional thinking.

I hesitate saying this, David, but one of the traits that I have developed with a bit of my wisdom gained from experience is that I have a sharp *crap detector!* And maybe this is what my clients are asking me about. I seem to have a knack for detecting and questioning these rules and absolutes that we're automatically supposed to accept. And when we examine them closely, we realize that they might have been true at one time in the past, but they're not true at all now! I've collected lists of them.

So, I think we need to think about getting wisdom integrated into our current lives regardless of age. Actually, MacDonald emphasized, in talking to a university group, that we absolutely should have courses that would teach wisdom in order to integrate what he calls the Philosophy of Information with the Philosophy of Wisdom.

Another sweep that is coming this way and altering our current thinking is "positive psychology." David, have you connected with the positive psychology movement at all?

WRIGHT

Well, I am familiar with it, but I don't know how connected I am to it.

HARKNESS

I've gone to their two international meetings in Philadelphia, and can certainly say that this is a growing world-wide movement. Now they're offering degrees in positive psychology, which moves traditional psychology to a higher level. Martin E. P. Seligman, who initiated this movement, says that psychology in the past has taken people from minus (-10 to 0), and then dropped them. He maintains we should continue on, and take people from zero to +10!

In connecting this with wisdom, Seligman and Christopher Peterson researched and created a book in 2004 called *Character Strengths and Virtues.* Their thinking was that we already have a book, the *Diagnostic and Statistical Manual for Mental Disorders (DSM),* for all of the mental problems, but we don't have anything that lists all the positive character strengths and virtues! So they came up with twenty-four specific traits, and wisdom is the first strength they focus on defining—breaking it down into five parts:

1. Creativity (Originality, Ingenuity)
2. Curiosity (Interest, Novelty-Seeking)
3. Open-Mindedness (Judgment, Critical Thinking)
4. Love of Learning
5. Perspective (Wisdom)

Go to their Web site http://VIACharacter.org and take either the free or paid assessment of 240 questions.

Seligman and Peterson say that without a doubt we must get more attention focused on wisdom in our society instead of thinking that it's something that should be ignored or delayed. *Therefore, my purpose is to help my clients connect with their career wisdom as early as possible.* David, does this make sense to you?

WRIGHT

Oh, yes.

Who are you connecting with their career wisdom? Who are your clients? What is their education and career background?

HARKNESS

All who come to me are very dissatisfied in their work life. They're all ages, though originally most clients were primarily somewhere in midlife. Currently, I'm getting many more young people looking for career direction, since the jobs that used to be out there automatically, if you had a college degree, are simply not there now. David, the reality is that between 60 and 70 percent are going home to live with their parents because they can't find a job to pay their living expenses and tuition bills. Many didn't know what they were preparing for anyway, and countless more can't find jobs in their career focus. Now we have a new group of workers called the *gray collar workers*—those with degrees who are definitely underemployed.

Most of my clients may have worked in a job for ten, fifteen, or twenty years and they don't want to do it anymore, but they have no idea how to reinvent their work life. My client base is about 25 percent lawyers, numerous PhDs, psychiatrists, psychologists, and housewives who are entering or reentering the workforce. My clients are those who are seriously seeking a career change. They cannot continue doing what they're doing, and they have no idea what to do next. Also, David, our current economy, plus the expectations of the current work environment are creating a very difficult time for about 70 percent of those in the workplace. They will move out when they see the opportunity.

WRIGHT

What is the recareering process you take clients through, and how do they learn about you and your work?

HARKNESS

When people with a career problem hear about me, they can contact me and come in, or call to discuss their issues. There is no charge for this first meeting because I want to make a judgment on whether they need my services. If they are looking for a job and they know the job they're searching for, there are countless others in the community (including churches and other organizations), who can help them. My focus is to help them to carefully determine their best career focus, and then help them get a job in it.

When we meet, I have them fill out a form to identify their career unrest and dissatisfaction on five levels. We want to determine if the problem is the culture of the company they're working for, our current workplace chaos, the skills they're using daily, or is it the lack of connection and commitment they feel for what they are doing in their work? Do they see it as a waste of time and talent? I also identify whether they have any negative personal issues, such as divorce, illness, or addictions. I discuss and show them a Chaos of Change Model, stressing that when one is making a major change, it creates "a dark night of the soul." People relate very well to this image, and this understanding helps them make the best decisions to be able to move successfully through it.

I then explain the CDA 4-Step Process that I take clients through, and tell them very explicitly that changing careers is not an easy or automatic one, two, three passage.

I *do* know exactly how to help them, but I stress that it's not quick or easy. I also explain that when we do anything creative (including creating one's future), there can well be a "miserable middle" for some. This may occur just before they decide to turn loose of the old and to cut loose and move forward. There can be doubts and thoughts such as, *"Oh, I can't do this!"* My value is that I can recognize when my clients are in the "miserable middle" and I keep them moving through it. It takes work and confidence to move beyond it, but it is very doable! I also describe the different levels of service at CDA, which will depend on how much time they need. I'm very up-front with program costs.

WRIGHT

So what is Career Design's 4-Step Process?

HARKNESS

The Career Design 4-Step Process is:

1. **Looking Inward:** Who am I? What can I do?
2. **Looking Outward:** Where can I do it? What's out there?
3. **Looking Forward:** What do I want? What is my future image?
4. **Action Steps:** How do I get there? What are my options, and what do I do to get there?

In *Looking Inward*, the first step, they spend hours on assessments and a notebook answering questions about themselves. As part of this self-assessment, they go through thirty-five to forty-five hours of Skills Workshop with eight to ten other clients. They are focusing on their strengths and what's important to them from a thorough and deeper level.

During this first step *they're getting to know themselves*. I have each client keep a *Success Criteria Sheet*, which is a list of their important "glass balls" (elements they *must* have to feel successful) versus the "rubber balls" that can clutter up their life (but don't really matter, and can be safely dropped). Again, identifying and cultivating their glass balls are essential steps for them to feel successful.

At the bottom of this Success Criteria Sheet, clients come up with what we call their *Meaning Magnet*. This is their *taproot*, essentially their *personal brand*—the magnet that absolutely holds them together. This brand or meaning magnet is a representation of who we are. It's the sum of all of our parts, and we must keep it very simple. I always show clients my own list of Success Criteria and my brand, which is very clear to me. I am a grower—I want to grow people and their potential, and I excel at sensing the growth potential in others! I also grow trees. I have my ten-acre Future Tree Farm that was originally a burned-out cotton field with one lone tree. Now it has about seven hundred trees of all kinds and sizes! I am not a frustrated horticulturist, I just want to see the trees grow. I also want to grow ideas, so I'm a researcher and a synthesizer who gains ideas from all directions. I want all my clients to understand their Meaning Magnet, and let it be a basic guide through their current Career Chaos.

If you have studied physics and the complexity theory, which I have (since that's what my last book is about), anytime you have chaos, there is an attractor that holds the system together. I want my clients to understand their attractor—this is their *Meaning Magnet.* When chaos is going on, they need to know what to hold onto. Knowing your *Meaning Magnet,* taproot, brand, or attractor (whatever we wish to call it) is currently critical because chaos abounds in our work world!

So, first of all we *Look Inward* to Who Am I and What Can I Do? I create a Career Profile for each client by pulling together the results of all their written assessments and the skills identified from their accomplishments in the workshop series. Then, based on this information, I have my clients pick three careers that they want to research. I provide much help to them in researching those careers.

For example, CDA has what we call the Pathfinders Meetings for the Future. I bring in consultants or former clients to talk about careers and we video everything. Because I've done this for more than thirty years, we have nine hundred career tapes! They're not all up-to-date, but whenever anyone is interested in a particular career we can go to the library of career DVDs and select related ones. They're for research and loaning out (not for sale). When clients need specific career information and we don't have it, I find someone who knows about the field and who can tell them the reality of it, and I bring them in to talk. I teach clients that it is critical to find out the reality of a career before they make the decision to go into it.

One critical thing: we do not automatically jump back into an additional educational degree. I emphasize this to my clients because many think that if only they have a PhD or an MBA, then their career problems will be over! I tell them that they must know specifically and absolutely how they're going to use that degree before they pursue it. This means that they need to do research so they'll know all the possibilities and details about it, because countless people come out with degrees and tuition debt, but without a career fit!

For instance, I had one client who was a surgeon. She didn't like that, so she went back to law school, and when practicing law didn't work out, then she came to see me. I do stress that you cannot rely on the power of a degree to do it for you, as degrees are less and less important today.

So, after my clients research these possible matching careers carefully, they decide on their *Future Image*. This is the answer to what you can and want to do in the future. As a last step in the career change process, we help the client determine the *Action Steps* to move into their *Future Image Career*. Maybe it's a radical career change, a new job, more training, or starting a business! So, David, these are the different steps that clients take to change careers.

WRIGHT

So are there negative traits that hold clients back?

HARKNESS

Yes, David. Unnamed fear, or fear of the unknown, is a powerful negative. Clients tell me: "I'm afraid of failing." Perfectionism—the need to do everything absolutely right—is the biggest fear and obstacle. When I identify someone who's a perfectionist, they are often the most difficult person to work with, because it's never good enough or it's never right enough. They lack the confidence to start and learn along the way; they're never confident.

Also, David, there's a group of those who fear success—and this is somewhat complex—but the thinking of those who fear success is: "If I succeed, what will they expect of me next?" And so they don't want to move forward. There are people who are afraid of looking silly for doing something different. And there is the threat to security. In addition, sometimes my clients have what I label the "double-bind syndrome." They say, *"Yes, that's good! I need to do this,* but—" and then they give negative reasons for not moving on. So no matter what comes up, they never can get around the "but" of it.

David, going through major change, is extremely fear-inducing to most people. I remember in my early forties I was afraid to embrace change (and, of course, that was quite some time ago), but we have to understand ourselves and our possible options and get on with it. Jung stresses that we only begin to really know ourselves at forty.

WRIGHT

So how is wisdom related to what you do at CDA?

HARKNESS

I see myself as a catalyst. I can recognize talent and potential in others, and I can activate it. I had a client who sent me a message recently that I highly value. She said, "This is what you do, Dr. H. You plant seeds of greatness in us."

I do have a knack for recognizing the major strengths of others. I'm not a psychologist that says, "We're going to fix this negative thing." I look for what's positive and what's strong, and has the potential to grow and develop to a higher degree. We find a career where a client can utilize that. There are so many things that I personally do not do well, but the one thing I have learned is that I do have very strong (what is called) emotional or social intelligence. I can read people, and I have the foresight and the drive to help them see what's coming and then use their strengths to succeed. Also, David, I have learned to question many "set rules" and assumed absolutes, which is my sharp "crap detector" in action.

I'll conclude with this summary of what I identify as career wisdom to determine your purpose to pursue with passion for both meaning and money.

Ten Tips for Achieving Career Wisdom

1. Determine your career options: advance in your current work, find a new job in your field, make a career change, or start a business. All are achievable, though certainly not a quick, easy, or painless process. Follow the CDA 4-Step Career Model.

2. Accept the possibility that an uncertain workplace forcing job and career changes is a current reality, even for the most experienced. The *Yo-Yo—You're On Your Own!* career model has replaced the previous forty-year, secure, Womb-to-Tomb Career.

3. Determine your satisfaction in your current job. How much do you really like and value your current job/career? If you question this, *carefully explore alternative options.* Career changes are currently a reality but are not easy or quick!

4. Explore possible career options and opportunities in your organization and your career field. Using reality-based but innovative thinking, ask yourself the following:
    a. What needs to be done for improvement in my work area?
    b. Do I have the talents and skills, or can I get them, to accomplish this?
    c. Would I value and feel successful doing this?
    d. How can it work financially for me and the organization?

5. Stay on a strong innovative learning curve for perceived future changes that can impact your organization, job, and career. Determine the specific talent needed for you to move forward. *Continual learning is absolutely essential, but don't confuse learning with the acquisition of degrees.*

6. Since our work is a central organizing principle of our lives (the primary way most of us identify ourselves),

when a job is lost unexpectedly, we may initially have no sense of self—of who we are. Unexpected job loss can create a "dark night" of anger, powerlessness, frustration, and denial that ultimately can be *initiators* into new ways of being and thinking. *We can come out stronger and wiser, with more personal power.*

7. Identify your strengths—your skills, values, personality, lifestyle needs and communication style. Be able to clearly verbalize, tell a brief story of what you value based on your specific accomplishments. Also, a lot of people think: "I'll be successful if I just shore up my weaknesses." But no way—we focus on your major strengths. Drucker said, "If you want to know what your weakness is, look at your strengths, because your weaknesses are going to be your strengths carried too far. So, we are all going to have weaknesses, no matter how strong we are."

8. Carefully determine and list your Success Criteria. These will be the "glass balls" necessary for your success, as opposed to the "rubber balls" that merely clutter up life. On a scale of one to ten, with ten being the highest, determine how much of each glass ball you have currently.

9. Begin to practice "six degrees of separation" by keeping a list of everyone you know who might have knowledge or connections in your field of interest. For this read the *Power of Who* by Bob Beaudine.

10. Move from mindless myths to mission, meaning, and money at midlife. Forget chronological age (deduct twenty years), and *focus on your functional age! Replace calendars and clocks with a compass.* Mark Twain said it best, *"Age is an issue of mind over matter. If you don't mind, it doesn't matter!"* Read my third book, *Don't Stop the Career Clock.*

Summary of Career Wisdom: Know your career destination, feel the fear of change, but move forward after thoughtful internal and external research. Get comfortable traveling with an incomplete map and unexpected detours to achieve success in our age of uncertainty and complexity. We must have a purpose to pursue with passion, and a plan! Also, recognize that the dark night of the soul, which is created by major change, is really the first major step in renewal and moving forward; we learn lessons from the dark night.

WRIGHT

Well, this has been a great conversation. I appreciate your taking this time with me to answer all these questions. This is going to be an important part of our book, and I appreciate it so much.

HARKNESS

Thank you.

WRIGHT

Today I have been talking with Helen Harkness, PhD. As a career consultant, researcher, writer, speaker, and entrepreneur, she founded Career Design Associates, Inc., thirty-four years ago with the motto: *Freedom Is Knowing Your Options.* She has helped ten thousand clients move from mindless myths to meaning and money at midlife by providing resources for identifying their purpose to pursue with passion.

Dr. Harkness, thank you so much for being with us today on *Words of Wisdom.*

HARKNESS

Thank you, David.

ABOUT THE AUTHOR

"Think of Helen Harkness of the Fairy Godmother of Career Reincarnation-for Finding Your Labor of Love" (Headliner, p. 1, July 11, 2004, *Dallas Morning News).*

As a career consultant, researcher, writer, speaker, and entrepreneur, Dr. Harkness founded Career Design Associates, Inc. thirty four years ago with the motto of *Freedom is Knowing your Options.* She has helped ten thousand clients move from mindless myths to their purpose to pursue with passion.

She is author of: *Best Jobs for the Future, The Career Chase, Don't Stop the Career Clock, Capitalizing on Career Chaos,* and pending *Moving from Mindless Myths to Meaning and Money at Midlife.*

Her speaking presentations include:
- Shattering the Mindless Myths of Aging
- Re-Career: Redefining and Rethinking Retirement
- Creating Career Options
- Turn the Page on Age
- Entrepreneurship: Search for Meaning, Money, Creativity, and Control

Dallas/Fort Worth ACP International created a "Helen Harkness Professional of the Year Award" permanently named for her. She is a member of the World Future Society, International Positive Psychology Association, Association of Professional Futurists, National Speakers Association, International Association of Career Professionals, and Collaborative Law Institute of Texas.

Helen Harkness, PhD, CMF

Career Design Associates, Inc.
2818 South Country Club Road
Garland, Texas 75043
972-278-4701
options@career-design.com
http://www.Career-Design.com

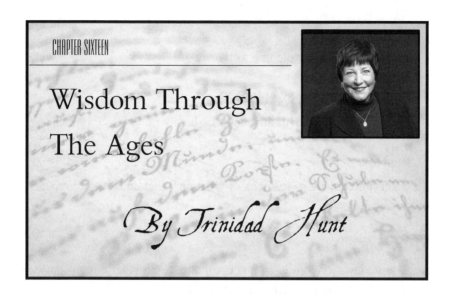

CHAPTER SIXTEEN

Wisdom Through The Ages

By Trinidad Hunt

DAVID WRIGHT (WRIGHT)

Today I'm talking with D. Trinidad Hunt. Trinidad has won the prestigious 2010 VIP Woman of the Year Award from The National Association of Professional Women located in New Jersey. She captured the honor for her expertise as a motivational speaker, corporate coach, consultant, and trainer. Known as a woman of vision, versatility, and insight by her clients, she has a captivating personality with a compelling message. She also hosted her own radio talk show on America's East Coast called *Drawing Outside the Lines: Becoming a 21st Century Change-maker.*

Disturbed by what Trinidad recognized as vacuums in education, she and Lynne Truair established a world youth network internationally in 1998. This nonprofit offers character education to students in grades kindergarten through twelfth grade. Included is an anti-bullying program called "Breaking Out of the World Game: An Intervention and Prevention Program."

Trinidad has been invited to join "Heroes for Humanity," a prestigious body of men and women who have made a contribution to the lives of others.

WRIGHT

D. Trinidad Hunt, welcome to *Words of Wisdom.*

D. TRINIDAD HUNT (HUNT)

Thank you, David. I'm thrilled to be here with you.

WRIGHT

So, Trinidad, when we speak of wisdom, what does wisdom mean to you?

HUNT

In my view, wisdom is an inner response to an outer circumstance. It's not an inner reaction, it's an inner response and it's based on the mind and the heart being in total coherence. I come from Hawaii where the wisdom of the ages is handed down to every generation by the generation that came before. It is clearly defined as wisdom of the heart, for in the ancient Hawaiian tradition, it is the heart that gives guidance to the mind.

From my perspective, what's really exciting about all this is that at this time in human history we are experiencing an explosion in neuroscience, as well as the science of the heart. The research is showing that the human heart does not just pump blood through our bodies. The human heart—our hearts—have a system of neural networks within it. The heart communicates a vast amount of information to the brain. In fact, more communication flows from the heart to the brain than vice versa. In other words, the human heart seems to send more feelings, thoughts, and ideas to the brain than the brain sends to the heart.

So when we talk about wisdom, we're talking about going beyond the use of pure intellect. Instead it is brain-mind working together with, or even guided by, the human heart. The heart communicates feelings, thoughts, ideas, and a sense of values to the mind.

Let me say that in another way, David. From my perspective, wisdom is a way of operating in the world that is inclusive of both the inclinations of the heart as well as the mind working together. It is a concert of heart and mind working in unison to respond to events that occur, situations and challenges we face, and people with whom we engage in our lives.

WRIGHT

Will you expand on that a bit?

HUNT

It seems to me that wisdom means the ability to act in a way that is conscious and cognizant of the larger ramifications of one's actions. Wisdom is then expressed and experienced in the living of our lives. When we live by the intuitive wisdom of our hearts, wisdom guides all our intentions and directs our actions. Wisdom of the heart tenders our words and guides our behavior.

WRIGHT

I have heard you say that wisdom is more important today than ever before. What do you mean by that?

HUNT

We're living in a very different time in history today, David. Maybe wisdom is just as important as it's always been. However, I would like to discuss the idea that wisdom is critically important today in the light of two main areas.

The first of these is that our society today is challenged by *access to excess*. I believe that self-reflection and the wisdom that it brings can help counterbalance this. Wisdom is knowing who you are in the midst of all this.

Wisdom is extremely important because with access to excess we have to make choices that align us with the highest good for self and others. We also owe it to our children to help them make choices that are positive, that are good for all, that are meaningful for society.

We have the power to damage ourselves or even destroy ourselves today. And because of this I think it's more important than ever that we bring wisdom to bear on how we operate, how we think, how we work, and how we interact with others. As human beings we have the ability to choose how we behave, and because of this, we owe it to ourselves and our children to act in a judicious and wise manner.

In recent times, we have made tremendous advancements in science and neuroscience. I was amazed to hear a neuroscientist speak of our "inner knowing." He said that within the heart of hearts of each and every one of us there is sense, or a knowing, of who we are, what our gifts and talents are, and why we are here. Now, that's a pretty powerful statement coming from a neuroscientist. I was delighted to hear these words coming from a man of science. But even more than that, I felt that he was expressing the very tip of the iceberg of a breakthrough in thinking that might be occurring on the leading edge of science. I felt that I was touching the edge of a paradigm shift where science and wisdom were no longer polarized but were merged along a continuum or spectrum of understanding.

WRIGHT

That is quite an amazing idea coming, as you say, from a neuro-scientist. But you said that there were two areas you wanted to discuss in the light of the importance of wisdom today, Trin. The first was that we have access to excess. What's the second?

HUNT

Honestly, David, there are so many areas that require wisdom. We could speak of politics, international relations, climate control, and so many other areas. But I wanted to focus specifically on the sphere of my direct experience.

This is the area of business. As you know, I'm a corporate consultant and trainer. I have had an opportunity to coach executives and managers throughout the years. And it is here that I feel we need to develop and enhance the wisdom of our business leaders.

The economic environment or climate in business today has been one of broken trust and massive breaches of integrity. We have definitely experienced what access to excess has done in the financial domain. And it is here that I believe we need to apply wisdom in order to make judicious decisions and act in accordance with a higher wisdom.

Organizations speak of values. Executive teams write their corporate values and vision for all to see. There is much espousing of wisdom. Yet the real question is one of congruency. "Are our actions (as the leaders of the organization) aligned with our words?" Or are our words just hypothetical conjectures based on what we think is politically correct?

In January of 1993, I had the opportunity to spend four days with Dr. W. Edwards Deming who is best known for Total Quality Management or TQM. Dr. Deming said something that shifted my world: "It is impossible to lead, without a philosophy of leadership." And then he added, "The first step is writing it. The second step is living it." This statement by Dr. Deming personally transformed my life and altered the course of my professional work from that day on.

I went home and worked diligently on my philosophy of leadership. The first question I asked was, "What is the purpose of leadership?"

And then I asked, "What are the principles and practices and values that I am committed to living by?" It took me weeks to come up with a document that reflected my vision, values, and intentions.

The self-reflection and inner review that it took transformed me in a number of ways. It made me rethink and reinvent myself and then rewrite my own life script. Further, my philosophy became my mentor and my guide. I was inspired to reflect daily on my words, behavior, and actions and to measure them by the standards I had set for myself.

As years went by, I discovered that my philosophy of leadership was a living document. It has grown with me as I have grown. Yet as it morphed and transformed, it also transformed me by guiding my thoughts and actions, and molding my character into the me that I want and intend to be.

One of the programs I deliver today is a three-day leadership course. The graduate thesis that each person must deliver for this program is his or her philosophy of leadership. The program is done over a two-month period allowing time for reflection and revision. The result for most students is stunning! I continue to be inspired by the breadth and depth of wisdom that I hear from our graduates.

It has been said that that there are two ways to be: You can do your best and let others decide how you've done, or *you can decide how you would like to be and then act that way*. This second way is the high road, the proactive path, and the path I inspire leaders and aspiring leaders to choose.

WRIGHT

So it seems that you feel that wisdom can be enhanced or even developed.

HUNT

Absolutely, David. There is no doubt in my mind that wisdom, like any quality we aspire to, can be enhanced, enriched, and developed. Each of us has the power to change our life.

Neuro-scientists tell us that there is more neural real estate allocated to looking for the negative than looking for the positive. Obviously this was a survival mechanism. Our brain had to be attuned and alert to danger when we were tribal wanderers. So if you want to be a better person, you have to choose to change. You have to choose to override the negative and literally recreate yourself.

The first step then, is deciding to change. The second step is deciding *how* you want to change and *who* you want to become. That is where the philosophy of leadership comes in. I have experienced its transforming effect in my life and in the lives of others.

To live is to change. We never remain the same. And with the discovery of neuroplasticity we know that our brains are changing all the time. Our brains are always creating new mental maps, connecting these maps to other maps, and pruning old unused maps. Our brains are creating new neural pathways every moment in response to our thoughts, feelings, and life experiences.

In order to develop wisdom, we only need to understand the power of the *quantum Zeno effect*. The quantum Zeno effect says that the act of focusing our attention alters the brain by holding neural circuits in place.

WRIGHT

I've never heard of the quantum Zeno effect, Trin. Where did you discover this concept?

HUNT

I happen to have a passion for brain research, David. I love the study of how the latest neuroscientific discoveries can help us change behavior in a positive way. I have been following the breakthroughs occurring in neuroscience for many years now. The quantum Zeno effect was first theorized in the early 1980s and has received a lot of attention since then. Yet today it is coming to be understood in a whole new light through the lense of neuroscience.

The quantum Zeno effect says that focused attention or *attention density* over time changes the brain. Simply put, where we put our attention is where we get the result. Another way of saying this is that the act of focusing our attention consistently on the same thing eventually lays new neural pathways in our brains.

By applying this idea of the quantum Zeno effect, or attention density over time, we will begin to change how we see and how we "are" or how we interact with others in our world. Although it is said differently, the same concept can be found in the ancient Hawaiian training. It was stated simply as this: *"Where our attention goes, our life energy flows."*

Time is life and it is our most precious resource. In order to develop wisdom, we need only practice a form of intentional self-directed mental focus for a few minutes every day. Using the concept of attention density and by the power of neuroplasticity, we can systematically alter our brains in the manner we choose.

So, by writing your philosophy of leadership, you begin the process of change. Then by reading it and reflecting on it daily, you activate the quantum Zeno effect. In this way, you begin by moving in the direction of your intention.

WRIGHT

That's remarkable. But it sounds as if it takes a lot of work to change the brain and to develop wisdom.

HUNT

I really believe in making it easy for people, David. I have been a long time practitioner of meditation and mindfulness training myself. I had the time to take the time when I was younger.

However, I realize that most people are really busy today. So rather than teach a thirty- or even twenty-minute meditation, I now teach something called the *One Minute Meditation* or *One Minute Med* for short. This is a short and simple way to begin the process of developing wisdom.

I start people on a minute of focused attention on compassion. The purpose is to engage the heart with the head. There are five steps to the process.

> **Step 1:** Put your attention on your heart.
>
> **Step 2:** Imagine a channel opening from your heart to your head.
>
> **Step 3:** Feel the energy of compassion flowing from the heart through the channel to your head.
>
> **Step 4:** Imagine (and feel the positive emotions) that all your words and actions during the day will be guided by your compassionate heart in alignment with your head.
>
> **Step 5:** Express your gratitude for the achievement of your intention as if it were already done.

298

Notice that these steps can be done very quickly. However, it's important not to rush the steps. Give yourself a full minute to move through them. Remember to be still, be present, and feel the flow of energy within as you complete the five-step process. This will set the tone for your day.

This doesn't mean that you give up discernment, clear thinking, coaching, or any other of the vital leadership practices. Compassion is not a path for the weak of heart. It is the path for the courageous. Compassion is an aspect of wisdom and it works in the following way:

Wisdom guides what *you do*
while compassion guides how *you do it.*

You might imagine that by doing the One Minute Med in the morning, you are opening a loop that will need to be closed at the end of the day. To close the loop, I ask those with whom I work to reflect on their words, behavior, and actions during the course of that day.

Below are three questions that I always invite executives and managers to ask themselves to wrap up their day. These are questions that will help guide and align their actions with their highest intention to act with wisdom in any and all situations. Naturally, by the time I initiate this process with the executives and managers, they have already written their core values and their leadership philosophy.

- What have I done today that expresses and demonstrates my philosophy of leadership and my core values?
- What have I done inadvertently that might have expressed or demonstrated something different from my leadership philosophy and core values?
- What do I need to do differently tomorrow to more fully express my leadership philosophy and core values?

By doing the One Minute Med in the morning, and closing the loop with these three questions at the end of the day, leaders start to pay attention to what they say and do. And what's more, they begin to pay attention to their attention. In this way they begin to modify their brains in a practical, consistent and dynamic manner. I call this intentional praxis ARC:

A – Attention
R – Reflection
C – Change

WRIGHT

One thing I notice, Trin, is that your practice, or praxis as you call it, is simple but not simplistic. In fact, it's simple yet profound.

HUNT

I spent most of my life reading every book and studying under every teacher I could. Most of them had complicated, time-consuming systems—systems that took thirty to forty minutes a day to practice.

I don't regret the work I did under my coaches and teachers. I'm thankful that I did "the hard yard." But today I work with people who truly cannot find, or even make, the extra time to do what I did. So I spent many years developing a simple, attainable system. This is a method that anyone can use to become a better person.

And while we're on the subject of becoming a better human being, I'd like to share my paradigm or my mental model with you.

WRIGHT

I'd love to hear it.

HUNT

In my mind, I see a distinction between the education that takes place in our classrooms and the education that takes place during our life on the Earth. We usually think of education as what happens when we go to school. This includes elementary grades, middle and high school, college or university, and even grad school.

All of this education is wonderful and necessary. Yet there is another learning that takes place for our entire lifetime on Earth. I call this our *planetary education*. This education has a definite and well-developed curriculum. We might call it the *planetary curriculum*. It is this curriculum that all the great teachers came to teach. Christ, Buddha, Mother Teresa, Mohammed, Lao Tzu and Gandhi were of the few who came to teach the curriculum for this planet. Each of them taught it in their own way and their own style, yet each proposed a greater curriculum or a curriculum that includes all other curriculums. Their teachings contextualize and permeate all other teaching and learning on the planet.

For myself, this curriculum is the profound curriculum that leads to wisdom, compassion, and kindness. Plato said, "Be kind because everyone you meet is on a hard journey." I think that's a central theme in the curriculum for planet Earth. If there is a wisdom and if there is a wisdom path, it begins and ends with relationships. It begins with our relationship with ourselves and ripples out to how we deal with other people.

WRIGHT

Can you give me an example?

HUNT

Absolutely! Let's look at executives, leaders, and managers who manage teams of people. If wisdom guides *what* these leaders do and compassion guides *how* they do it the result will, more likely than not, be a high performing team.

In fact, Dr. Deming, said, and I paraphrase, *Treat people well and you will experience a statistically significant increase in productivity.* Of Deming's famous fourteen points, number thirteen says this, "Institute a vigorous program of education and self-improvement."

Leaders influence others. It is their actions, behaviors, and words that set the tone in their departments and organizations. In other words, leaders and managers influence those around them by who they are. Self-development, therefore, is not an option; rather, it is a *responsibility* of leadership.

I've worked with everything from toxic organizations to high-performing organizations and it is leadership that makes the difference. Every leader influences others. The only decision that they have to make is what kind of influencer they want to be.

WRIGHT

So what are your guiding principles, Trin?

HUNT

Let me start by saying that there is a difference between a product and a process. And I am truly a work in progress. Every day is a new day and every moment a new opportunity to grow. Because life is a process, questions seem to be more powerful than answers. The quality of my life is in direct correlation to the quality of the questions that I can ask myself.

There is one main guiding question that I live by. This question, for me, is like the stars might have been for the ancient navigators. This question guides and inspires me to always reach for higher levels of service and contribution. The question I always ask myself is, *What does it mean to be truly human in this situation?* Or *What does it mean to be truly human in this conversation?* Or, *What does it mean to be truly human as I work with this person who is on my professional team?*

For me, this question is a living question. It's a question I constantly ask myself as I'm working with others and going through my daily experiences in life.

I think this question is probably one of the most important questions ever asked by any human being down through time. It's an eternal question and yet at the same time it is a profoundly personal question. It is a question that lives at the center of a person's search for meaning, a person's search to understand him or herself in relationship to his or her world, family, community, country, and even the universe. I believe that this question is at the heart of the course curriculum for all human beings on planet Earth. You see, down through the ages great teachers and thinkers have wrestled with this question or similar questions. And it was by reflecting on these questions that each of their personal truths and life paths were revealed.

Let's take Gandhi as an example. Gandhi was living in India at a time when India was ruled by the British Empire. When Gandhi sought to answer this question for himself, it clarified his purpose and guided his actions. For Gandhi, to be a human being was to be a free man or woman. Thus Gandhi set out on his historic 250-mile march to the sea. Seventeen years later, India was freed from British rule. But even more than that, the legacy that Gandhi left was a model of how to resist tyranny through non-violent civil disobedience.

But the power of the question is that it has no singular answer. The question is a living question and must be answered in the living of each of our lives.

By asking what it means to be truly human, Gandhi lived a simple life in a profound way. But there were many other great individuals who answered the question through the living of their lives.

By Michelangelo's hand and eye, his sculpture titled "David" became the perfect man. In René Descartes' estimation, man's greatest ability was his ability to think. "I think, therefore I am," he said.

Marcus Aurelius believed that the arrow of one's life should be always focused on the attainment of virtue. While Plato felt that the goals of life were truth, beauty, and goodness.

Again, Leonardo da Vinci's drawing, titled "Vitruvian Man," was born out of the same question. Da Vinci answered it in his perfectly proportioned human being who served as a symbol of perfect spiritual, mental, emotional, and physical balance.

And there were thousands of other people, both known and unknown, who contributed to the lives of those around them. When you think about it, it doesn't matter if the question was conscious or unconscious. Wherever we see a simple life lived in a extraordinary way, somehow that question served as a context for the content of their lives and actions.

So I live by the question, I ask the question of myself daily. When confronted with a challenge or a situation where I'm not sure which way to turn, I will internally ask myself what does it mean to be truly human, the highest possibility of my humanity in this moment, in this situation? It has guided me by clarifying my values. It has inspired my goals, raised my vision, and directed my actions. It has transformed my life, my brain, my thinking, and how I operate in my relationships.

WRIGHT

I admire the depth of your thinking, Trin. But can you give a practical example that everyone can utilize?

HUNT

I understand what you're saying, David. First, please know that I invite leaders to live with this question. They tell me it serves as a guide for their actions and behavior on a daily basis. And I invite everyone to use it. The power of the question lies in its ability to help us think and act in alignment with our highest intentions.

So now let's see if we can connect the dots to come up with a practical path of action that everyone can use. If you don't mind, I'd like do this through a clear and simple list. We've already shared the theory. So this will be a plan of action.

WRIGHT

Great! That will make it easy for everyone.

HUNT

All right. Here is an explicit, step-by-step, simple yet strategic path to constant never-ending higher levels of personal performance. It will work for people who choose to grow themselves so that they can support others in growing around them.

1. Decide first who you want to be, not what you want to do. (What you want to do will naturally arise out of who you decide to be.)
2. Write your leadership or life philosophy. (Be patient with the process. It may take you a few weeks or even a few months to come up with something you are satisfied with. But just do it! Just thinking about your philosophy and writing it will transform your brain by creating new, more positive neural pathways.)
3. Do the *One Minute Med* every morning. And close the loop at the end of the day with the three questions.
4. Live your life as a question and not an answer. (You can use the question I use, *What does it mean to be a human being?* Or you can use any guiding question that inspires you to act in an honorable, integrous, and kind manner.)

WRIGHT

That seems easy enough except for one thing, Trin. It seems as if it's a long-term process.

HUNT

That's right, David. It's very much like life—life is a long-term process. So I invite people to be patient with the process. Remember that one year from now each of us will be a year older. And at that time, we can look back at having done something to transform ourselves in a positive manner or not.

Maybe understanding the Levels of Competence Model attributed to Abraham Maslow will help. The Levels of Competence model works for all types of learning or any type of mastery that one wants to attain. Let me review the model with you.

In stage 1 of the of the model, a person realizes that he or she has been clueless. The individual is unconscious and incompetent in the new proficiency. The awakening or "A-ha" starts at this point. And the question that will move the person forward is, "Are you teachable?" This really means, do you want to learn?" Do you want to improve?

In stage 2, people are now conscious that they are incompetent. If a person wants to learn, he or she will go through much AFL (After the Fact Learning). This means there will be lots of try and fail, assess what the person has done and get up and try again. And the question that will move a person forward is, "Are you willing to keep working at it?" Actually, lots of people give up here because it looks too hard.

In stage 3, the person is now consciously working to improve his or her level of competence. In this stage the person is consciously and intentionally working to improve. Here people begin to experience more and more success. And the question that will move a person forward is, "Are you truly and totally committed to mastery?" There may be a tendency to rest on our laurels at this stage because the biggest barrier to being really great is that we are already good. But if a person is committed, he or she moves to stage 4.

In stage 4, the person attains mastery. And many of the leaders I coach arrive at this level. The question here is whether or not they are willing to be patient with those who have not yet attained mastery. At this level, they become the coaches and mentors of their people.

WRIGHT

That's great, Trin. It's clear every person has a choice. And if one chooses to change and grow, there are clearly defined stages he or she will go through in the process.

HUNT

Exactly, so be patient with the process. At every stage in the process, choose to keep going. Then choose again and you will keep growing.

WRIGHT

Those are definitely words of wisdom, Trin. So in closing, what is the one thing you would like to leave our readers with?

HUNT

Not to make a cliché of this, but it is really important that each of us realize that our lives truly do make a difference. Remember that relationships are everything. If we realize that they give us our greatest challenges but also our greatest joy, we can intend to make a positive difference with everyone we meet.

We are connected, no one is an island, no one can stand alone, no human being can make it without others. As we transform ourselves, we impact other human beings in a positive way.

I would like to leave with something that comes from one of my mentor teachers. This particular man was one of the greatest hidden geniuses of the last century. His name is Walter Russell. Walter Russell said this, and I paraphrase: *success is often measured by the achievements in money or finances or our achievements in the world.* But the real achievement is something he called the life triumphant. He said that *the life triumphant is measured by how much we give to others rather than how much we take from the world.*

WRIGHT

Thank you for that, Trin. I had not heard of Walter Russell. But his words offer a perfect close to an incredible conversation.

HUNT

Thank you, David, I thoroughly enjoyed being with you.

WRIGHT

And I really appreciate you taking all this time to answer these questions. I have learned a lot and I can just imagine how much our readers will gain when they read this chapter in our book. They're going to learn so much about how they can tap their inner wisdom. I appreciate your doing this.

HUNT

Well, David, I so value the opportunity to bring together some wisdom of great thinkers and teachers on the planet. It is through shared wisdom that all of us can become better human beings. I so appreciate being with you in this conversation. And I also appreciate being able to work with you throughout the last few years. I just want to take this opportunity to thank you for the contribution you're making in the world.

WRIGHT

Today we have been talking to D. Trinidad Hunt, winner of the prestigious 2010 VIP Woman of the Year Award from The National Association of Professional Women. She is also an invited member of the Hero's for Humanity. Trinidad is known as a woman of vision, versatility, and insight by her clients. She is a captivating personality and, as we have found out here today, she has a compelling message.

Ms. Hunt, thank you so much for being with us today on *Words of Wisdom.*

HUNT

Thank you, David, it's been an honor and a joy to be with you.

ABOUT THE AUTHOR

D. Trinidad Hunt, an international author, consultant/trainer, and keynote speaker, has more than thirty years of experience in program development and training. As cofounder of Elan Enterprises LLC, Trinidad has delivered organizational training programs for business leaders and staff nationally and internationally for such companies as Pepsi Cola, Frito Lay, and Sprint. As cofounder of World Youth Network International (WYN) in the United States, Australia, Malaysia, Philippines, and Canada, she designed, developed, and delivered curricula for leaders, students, parents, and teachers. The resultant effect has been education for the entire community.

Whether they benefit from Hunt's *IQ-EQ-SQ Model for Leadership in the 21st Century*, or change management, Hunt has trained thousands of people. She also hosted her own radio talk show on America's East Coast called, *Drawing outside the Lines: Becoming a 21st Century Change-Maker*. Hunt's *Leadership Dimensions Program has been presented* in both corporate and education sectors, and is an integral part of her *Women in Leadership Course, The Art of Facilitation* and she has led retreats on *The Power of Personal Purpose* that provides a powerful structure for creating and supporting change.

Trinidad has authored and co-authored twenty-one books in total. She has co-authored eight books: four in *Chicken Soup for the Soul* series and four for businesses. She has authored thirteen curriculum books for the educational system.

A few of Hunt's honors include:

- The prestigious 2010 VIP Woman of the Year Award from the National Association of Professional Women (NAPW)
- Who's Who American Women in Business
- Heroes for Humanity

- Award for a national best seller for Learning to Learn—
  Maximizing Your Performance Potential—published in four
  countries

TrinidadHunt

Elan Enterprises LLC
World Youth Network Int'l
Contact: CEO/Cofounder Lynne Truair
Toll Free: U.S. & Canada 800-707-3526
Phone: 808-239-4431
Fax: 808-356-0622
elantrin@aol.com
TrinidadHunt.com
www.elanlearninginstitute.com
www.worldyouthnetwork.com
www.quest4character.com
www.end2bullying.com

CHAPTER SEVENTEEN

Real Life Relationship Strategies

By Janice Bastani

DAVID WRIGHT (WRIGHT)

Today I'm talking with Janice Bastani. Janice is an author, speaker, mentor, and credentialed coach with The International Coach Federation. She holds multiple credentials in the coaching arena. She is a credentialed John Maxwell Leadership Coach, Emotional Intelligence Coach, Energy Leadership Coach, Brain-Based Neuro-Leadership Coach, and she holds an additional credential in Group Coaching. She holds a BA in Journalism from the University of Arkansas.

Janice began her coaching business in 2004 and has facilitated more than thirty-five hundred successful coaching sessions. She is a published author on the topics of women in business, emotional intelligence, and energy leadership. Janice is a platinum author with *E-Zine* articles and she is also a popular keynote speaker.

Janice, welcome to *Words of Wisdom.*

JANICE BASTANI (BASTANI)

Thank you so very much; I'm happy to be here.

WRIGHT

So let's start with the obvious—what is your definition of a relationship?

BASTANI

A relationship is a connection with another human being in its simplest form. We derive all kinds of things from our relationships. We derive such things as emotional connection, physical connection, mental connections, and social connections. We also get things such as significance, dependence, fame, wealth, friendship, professional connections, and many, many more.

The important thing in a relationship is its worth. What do we get out of any relationship is the question we often ask ourselves. We know we must give something to get something in return in the connection and we must keep up the give-and-take in order to maintain the relationship.

WRIGHT

So what is the difference between a life relationship and a business relationship? Do you have specific insights into this in addition to the obvious?

BASTANI

I've done a lot of study in this area and my experience tells me that life relationships have different components to them than do professional ones. Life relationships have intimate bonds that are very personal, with, say a spouse, a lover, or significant other.

Another type of personal relationship in the life relationship area is social ones. These might be, for example, with your neighbor, another member of the PTA, a golf buddy, and then you might have another type of personal relationship that I classify as a friendship. A friendship is with a person you call a friend—someone you have coffee with, you do things together, you share secrets with. So life relationships are personal relationships made up of intimate relationships, social relationships, and friendships.

On the other side of the coin, the professional business type of relationships, are those you have with peers, colleagues at work, customers, suppliers, your boss. This is what I quantify as professional or business relationships.

It's my experience that all relationships feed off each other. Let me give you an example. Let's say you take your kids to school and one of your children forgets his or her lunch or something he or she needs for class. You go back home, pick it up, and deliver it to your child. Now you're late for work.

When you drop off that forgotten item, do you disconnect entirely from the energy from that relational personal experience? No, you bring it right through the front door of the office with you. The same thing is true in reverse. Let's say you got news this afternoon that your position was going to be cut in half—your hours will be half of what they were yesterday. You absolutely bring that right on home with you into your family or personal life.

That's the difference between the life and business relationship.

WRIGHT

Who has shaped how you view relationships in your life?

BASTANI

That's an interesting question. I think that most of us first have an impression of this when we're kids so my parents, of course, shaped my view of relationships.

Later on in my life, my outlook on relationships was honed by influencers and role models who came into my life. As I matured, I looked for successful people ahead of me on the road of life, those I looked up to or whom I wanted to be in that season of life. Some of the people in my early years—in my later twenties and thirties—who influenced my view of relationships were people such as Florence Littauer, Emily Barnes, *Focus on the Family,* because I was raising children, Gary Chapman, and John Maxwell.

As I launched our children, my focus changed and a continuing new set of mentors shaped the way I viewed my relationships and my life today such as Charles Stanley, Chip Ingram, and, again, John Maxwell. There are a host of others who shaped who I am today in my personal and business life.

I am a lifelong learner and I am constantly reading, studying, and reaching out to others who are successful and from whom I can learn in many different genres.

WRIGHT

What determines a person's depth of relationship in these two areas?

BASTANI

Now the coach is going to come out of me. One determining factor is what you see your role is in the relationship. For instance, do you do all the talking and giving of advice or do you do most of the listening?

Another determining factor is what the relationship is built around. Is it built around your professional life and is that its contents or is it personal? Is it a friendship? Perhaps it's intimate or maybe it's a mentor relationship. Elements like those are determining factors. Some questions you can ask yourself about the depth of your relationship include what value you bring to the relationship. You might ask yourself why you are in the relationship in the first place. Another great question is what is your ultimate purpose or outcome by being in this relationship. We all have reasons for forming any relationship whether it is professional or personal; most of those reasons come from our own inner core foundation.

Not all of these are audible answers that we give ourselves; most of the time they are self-talk loops that are stuck up in our head.

WRIGHT

Where does a firm foundation originate in order to form a relationship?

BASTANI

Throughout the many years of my coaching experience, what I came to find out is that regardless of whom it was—a CEO, a stay-at-home mom, or a small business owner—each had a personal foundation he or she was building their lives upon. Here's what I discerned: at our core, in the deepest part of each of us is a burning desire to be of *worth*—"Am I worthy?" is the question people are always asking themselves. It doesn't matter what position you hold in life, worth is determined through the answer to two fundamental questions. Those questions are: What do I believe? It's not a religious question, that's a question about your belief regarding anything that's tripping you up at the moment. The second question is: Why do I hold this belief?

Wrapped around worth and belief are some very important life areas and when we ask these questions about our life areas we start to uncover what our foundation is, in our life. Outside of the life areas I have found there are about sixteen different foundational blocks that we are constantly building and changing and moving around in our lives.

Finally, one of the firm foundations for forming relationships has to do with our four cornerstones: mental, physical, social, and spiritual.

WRIGHT

So how does a person form strategies for life and business relationships?

BASTANI

I doubt that many of us sit around and say, "I'm going to strategize about life and business relationships." That's not the way

315

we necessarily think about this segment of our life. I doubt that many of us wake up and go out into our world and ponder these things. What we normally do is roll out of bed in the morning and immediately jump into what I call default behavior and that's what drives our relationships. In my experience, life is just one great big wonderful opportunity. You can be mindlessly fed and walk through your life day in and day out and just accept what comes to you and do the things you've always done, or you can be highly engaged in life.

WRIGHT

So, how would you go about forming a strategy around your relationships?

BASTANI

That's a great question. When I do this exercise with my clients, I ask them questions. In order to form a strategy for life and/or business relationships, I ask, "Who values you? Who cares for you? Who helps you?" In other words, who lifts me up and makes me feel good about myself? Who can I trust, who adds value to my life, who adds value to my business relationships? Then the most important question is: who drains the very life out of me?

One strategy is to be only in relationships with people who energize you and encourage you and life you up. Another might be a mastermind group where others are of like mind and value with you are and they are a couple of years ahead of you. That's another way relationships can lift you up.

The bottom line with all of this is we are products of our relationships—who you associate with determines who you are; what you read during the next five years is who you will become; what you watch, what you hear, what you think all determine who you are becoming. Who's feeding you, who's associating with you, and what is your strategy after all?

WRIGHT

What stops a relationship from growing?

BASTANI

I'll bet there are as many answers to that as there are people who will ask the question. We don't normally sit around and think about this one either. We don't do it in an audible way, but we think about it all the time. My experience is that if we don't have a firm core foundation and we don't know where we want to go, it doesn't matter what road we actually take, because the relationship will stop growing. If you don't know what you want from the relationship it's a 100 percent certainty that's exactly what you're going to get from it.

You have to ask yourself: What does my relationship with_____ look like? You then fill in the blank: What does _____do for me? How is this relationship with_____? Is _____getting me where I want to be in my life? You can qualify it in your personal life as well as in business.

The reverse is also true, if you aren't adding value and benefit to someone else in the relationship that person will just gradually fade out of your life. We all have people like this whom we can think of right away. We wonder whatever happened to so and so. What happened was that the relationship was not maintained so it stopped growing. Relationships are a two-way street, you give and you get and when the relationship is one-sided, when one person takes more from the relationship than the other, it stops growing.

WRIGHT

Janice, your tagline is adding value to lives and businesses. How do you do that?

BASTANI

In my coaching business, when I speak or write, or in my daily interaction with people, I'm always asking questions in order to lift up the other person. That's what I'm all about—adding value. I'm not there to blame or suck the life out of others. I have a very distinct process and it's called *Awareness> Growth >Freedom*. It's three steps. In the *Awareness* phase we take a 360 degree view around the person and a 36,000-foot view from where the person is during this given moment in his or her life. We then assess and make make ourselves aware of where he or she is at this moment.

In the *Growth* phase of the three-step process, I come along beside my clients and together we develop a plan to get them to their desired goal. I coach them through the roadblocks or the stumbling blocks along the way and I hold them accountable for what they say they want to accomplish.

In the *Freedom* phase, together we celebrate every learning point and success along the way. I actually believe that this is the most important step because it deposits into that core I talked about earlier of the individual's self-worth. So often when we give a compliment to people, they brush it off with comments like, "It was nothing" or "This old thing?" They immediately change the subject. I know you've heard people do this and you may have even done this yourself. I don't let my client's get away with that because taking in the *freedom* of the compliment, is actually depositing and growing the individual's self-worth.

At the end of any of my interactions with people, I always ask, "What is your takeaway today? What value or benefit have I been able to provide for you?" I ask this because often, we don't see the connection.

WRIGHT

How would you coach a twenty-something today and how would it be different or the same for a Baby Boomer on this topic of relationships?

BASTANI

That's a very funny question because I deal with twenty-somethings up through to late Baby Boomers in my coaching

318

business and a strong core foundation is a key starting point in any of our client coach conversations.

I'd ask the Gen Y—the twenty-somethings—where are your most fulfilling relationships? Often, they don't have an answer to that. In our high-tech, media-driven, nanosecond society of rapid life changes, Gen Ys don't have time to process the vast quantity of images, sounds, the massive amounts of information that they are bombarded with every single day. They are holding an extension of all their relationships in their handheld communication devices.

The next thing I usually ask twenty-somethings is, "How are you guarding your *gateways*?" "Gateways" is a word that's not in the vernacular of a Gen Y, so most of the time Gen Ys don't actually know what I'm talking about. *Gateways* are those parts of our bodies where influencers can invade us. I use those terms very deliberately because we don't automatically have a filter or a blocking mechanism. We get everything through our senses—we look and read and watch with our eyes, we listen with our ears, we touch with our skin, feet, hands, lips, we speak with our mouth, we taste, we think, we reason with our brain, we feel and react in our hearts and in our souls. We must put up defenses to filter each of these things thoroughly before we allow them in. What I find in relationships is that Gen Ys don't do this—this step is missing.

When you're in your twenties, your whole life is in front of you. In contrast, when I speak with Baby Boomers their perspective and their season of life is so very different than people in their twenties who is a Gen Y. Both Gen Ys and Baby Boomers are products of their decisions. Baby Boomers are further down the road than a Gen Ys. For these individuals I ask questions such as: What relationships do you cherish and value today? What or who shaped those relationships? When did you know a relationship was toxic and what did you do about it?

One of the very most revealing things that I do with Boomers is to ask them to have a picture of themselves at each decade in their lives and define the relationships they had as a twenty-something up through a sixty-something. When you're in your sixties, the bulk of your relationships and your life is behind you—they're in the past. You're trying to hold on to something and build on those things that are cherished in your relational past.

WRIGHT

Where does this passion come from to add value to the lives of others?

BASTANI

You know, "passion" is an interesting word. If I don't jump out of bed every day and want to get started or when I finish talking to a client and I hang up the phone and I say, *"Yes!"* that's what I'm talking about. I am just as impassioned and jazzed as the person I've just been working with. That's what passion is.

People I interact with who don't take 100 percent responsibility for their roles, their actions, their thoughts, their feelings, their decisions, just drive me nuts. I'm of the opinion that you have to catch that passion and you catch it from those people who are your earliest role models in life. I'm sad to say that my experience is that people are usually looking for someone else to blame. You hear a story, the tale of woe, the inevitable "but" or "because." We all tell a story about how we are, the way we are, or how we got into the mess we're in.

In my area of expertise, I call that story your *agreement* with yourself. We have devised them to make us feel okay for the unexpected and/or unmet expectations of something that has happened to us.

I just wrote a chapter in another book today that tells all about these stories, these agreements, that we tell ourselves. We tell them all the time. We're trying to save face, we're trying to look good. I come along and lift a person up with an awakening of his or her awareness of this agreement in a nonjudgmental fashion. It uncovers a burden the person is dragging along behind him or her like a ball and chain or like pulling a huge heavy trunk through an airport. It's a heavy task lifting that sucker every single morning and it really wears us out.

Think about it, we all have *agreements* in all parts of our lives. We have agreements with every area of our life. We have an agreement about every single one of our foundational blocks that form who we are as people. I have the distinct honor and the ability to lift another person up through coaching or mentoring, mastermind groups, programs, articles, blogs, books, or whatever I am doing. It fuels my passion to add value and benefit to people.

I'm reminded of a verse in a book written by Hosea in the Old Testament. He put it so perfectly when he wrote, "My people are destroyed for lack of knowledge" (Hosea 4:6 KJV). My passion comes from discerning this lack of knowledge in others; somewhere on their life road they were not equipped and I'm here to help equip them.

WRIGHT

You mentioned relationships by way of handheld devices. Why are relationships important to our lives today?

BASTANI

The bottom line here is that we were created as relational beings and yet, to this point, all of our trouble and dissatisfaction comes with and from our relationship with people, our relationship with money, our relationship with life, our careers, our emotions, food, drugs, everything that we come into contact with we have a relationship with. Think about it. People tend to think that relationships are just with people but that really isn't so. Relationships are very multifaceted—we are in relationships that are good, that are bad or passive, that are in that default place I was talking about before. We leave our gateways wide open and absorb everything coming toward us. Our society today is consumed with labels, possessions, and positions. The question is: what is the purpose of a relationship?

WRIGHT

So what does it take to be a master of life in business relationships?

BASTANI

What does it take to be a master? I think that in order to relate masterfully in all relationships we must lock in discernment by knowing what we believe, where that belief came from, why holding on to that belief propels us upward and forward? Or does holding on to that belief keep us stuck in the agreement of our past? We have agreements and they are like a wall—they're a protection mechanism for us. The truth is lying right in front of us and we cannot discern it due to the noise, drama, and distractions in our lives.

I once wrote a really wonderful lesson on this. When we get tripped or pushed over the edge of our limit of our being, in mastering our life, these are the three things that actually drive us right over the edge: the noise that surrounds us all day long, the continually whipped up drama where there is no drama, and the distraction of so many things coming at us all at the same time; we cannot filter them out.

It's like being in a race, in a track-and-field race, you've got to realize what lane you're in. If you're in the wrong lane you've got to take a moment and pause. Gain awareness of where you are, ask those key questions in every aspect of your life. Once you have decided to keep, reject, or create a new belief you can create a growth plan out of the mud and thorny bush mess where you seem to be stuck and get in your right lane. It gives you a clear path to freedom and to healthy relationships whether they are in life or in business.

In order to do this a person must commit to the introspection of work, which is what this is all about. It's about looking inside and sorting out that internal yammering mental roommate—we all have one. That little voice yammering away inside our heads causes us to fear things. One of the things you probably know about fear is that it's an acronym for False Evidence Appearing Real; it's a well-known concept. We need to ask ourselves: "Is this life your dream or someone else's?" That's all about mastering your life. If you're not motivated to act, then I would suggest to you that it's not your dream.

The same is true for relationships. When we are congruent on the inside and the outside we flourish. When we are not congruent we are running around in circles and feeling despair and unfulfilled. We are constantly bombarded by unmet expectations repeatedly. Ask yourself, "Does this relationship, this belief, this decision, this struggle I'm having, fit my image of who I am?" That's part of the mastery. "How do I reflect on the world?" If your answer is "Yes" to the question, this image fits who I am, then I keep it. If it doesn't, then it is time to eject it.

I once heard Darren Hardy of *Success* magazine talk about having your own board of advisors, a mastermind group, a mentor, a coach to keep you in your lane and continually moving forward. These people lift you up, they keep you accountable, they keep you focused, they support you, they give you encouragement, they have confidence in your so that you can rise up and be the master of your relationships. The most important thing these kinds of individuals do is they keep depositing value into that heart of who you are—your self-worth. These are the ways we master all our relationships. I think it is a brilliant idea.

WRIGHT

What an interesting conversation we've had here today, Janice. I have learned a lot about relationships.

BASTANI

Thank you; it's been my pleasure.

WRIGHT

Throughout my life I have been very fortunate to have made some great life relationships that first started with business relationships. So that was good. They're not mixed either, they're still separated, but they're valid just the same.

I really enjoyed talking with you, Janice. I've learned a lot today and I know that our readers will, too.

BASTANI

I hope this chapter opens a new category of questions for them.

WRIGHT

I really appreciate the time you've spent with me today answering these questions. I think this will be a great chapter for our book.

BASTANI

Wonderful!

WRIGHT

Today I have been talking with Janice Bastani. Janice is an author, a speaker, a mentor, and she is also a coach with The International Coach Federation. She holds multiple credentials in the coaching arena including the John Maxwell Leadership Coach, Emotional Intelligence Coach, Energy Leadership Coach, Brain-Based NeuroLeadership, and a credential in Group Coaching.

Janice, thank you so much for being with us today on *Words of Wisdom.*

BASTANI

Thank you.

Janice Bastani is an author, speaker, mentor, and credentialed coach with the International Coach Federation. She holds multiple credentials in the coaching arena.

Janice is a credentialed John Maxwell Leadership Coach, Emotional Intelligence Coach, Energy Leadership Coach, Brain-Based Neuroleadership, and she is credentialed in Group Coaching. She holds a BA in Journalism from the University of Arkansas.

Janice began her coaching business in 2004 and has facilitated more than thirty-five hundred successful coaching sessions.

Janice Bastani is a published author on the topics of: Women in Business, Emotional Intelligence, and Energy Leadership. Janice is a Platinum author with *e-Zine* articles. Janice is also a popular keynote speaker.

Janice Bastani

Janice Bastani Coaching
1976 Armondo Court, Suite 2B
Pleasanton, CA 94566
866-534-6755
Janice@janicebastanicoaching.com
www.janicebastani.com
www.janicebastanicoaching.com
http://www.johncmaxwellgroup.com/janicebastani